Contents

Part II: Home Entertainment

Preface

Introduction

Difficult as it may be to believe, there was actually a time when only a handful of people had computers in their homes. For those of us who got on the bandwagon early, finding a use for such an expensive appliance was a challenge. Some people used their computers to run spreadsheet applications like Lotus 1 2 3. Others, like us, found that just playing around and exploring how they functioned was justification enough. And no one wanted to admit they played games on their computers; it was nearly shameful.

How times have changed. Today, personal computers are considerably more affordable, and nearly one in every four homes has at least one. More than a third of those homes have broadband Internet access. In the old days—when computing resources were enormously expensive—an idle CPU was money wasted. Today, processing power is cheap, and we've got cycles to burn.

Personal computers can enhance your life at home in ways you may not have thought of. For example, your PC can be the nerve center of an advanced environmental control system, monitoring occupancy and adjusting lighting and temperature according to your preferences. Improved multimedia capabilities allow personal computers to play a central role in home entertainment. Combining data acquisition with the general-purpose nature of computers enables your home and computer to work together to keep you comfortable and safe. "Home computing" takes on a new meaning.

The "home of the future" is here today, and the computer plays a pivotal role in making it a reality. With a few off-the-shelf devices, some homemade hardware, and a little imagination, you can be living in your own high-tech habitat. And you can say you did it yourself!

Why Your Home Will Love This Book

This book is a hands-on training kit disguised as a how-to book. Unlike a typical training kit, there are no theoretical scenarios or lab environments—each project presents a workable, practical way to improve your home. When you finish a project, you will have built something unique that you can customize to your family's individual needs.

No matter what your current skill level is, you can learn from the projects in this book. Neither of the authors is a Linux guru by any means, and you don't need to be one either. Working through the Linux-oriented projects is an excellent introduction to the Linux operating system and to both well-known and underutilized Linux tools. There are Windows-based projects as well, and wherever practical, solutions are presented for both platforms. Above all, this is a practical book. If you're reading it, you're probably a geek, but chances are not everyone you live with would wear that moniker with pride. The end product of these projects should not intimidate even the most technophobic person—your family will never have to touch a command line, or even a keyboard. The whole point of these projects is not just to enhance your home life but to make things *easier*. We've relied on the user interfaces everyone is already comfortable with: wall switches, remote controls, and occasionally a web browser. In fact, many of the projects are designed to not require *any* interaction from your family—for example, you'll learn to completely automate your lighting so that it turns on and off based on movement, time, or other factors. (Of course, you'll still be able to flip the light switch when you need to.)

This book isn't about hacking just for the sake of hacking. Each project creates something that either is not available commercially or is too costly for the average person to justify. For instance, there are many security companies who would be happy to install a security system in your home with a closed-circuit camera system, but it will cost you thousands of dollars. We'll show you how to do it for a few hundred (and a few hours of your time).

Many of these projects were developed by the authors themselves, but in some cases, open source projects were used. In such instances the original authors are given full credit. We even name those in the community who are strong advocates for the projects. Hopefully, this book will help to bring new blood into those communities.

Audience for This Book

We've tried to make this book accessible to anyone who can read. Some projects might be a bit out of range for inexperienced hackers, but there's plenty for everyone. If you fit even one of the descriptions below, then this book is for you. Jump in!

- You've always wanted to solder something but never had a good reason. Many geeks have a strong background in software but have never created anything in hardware.

- You're comfortable enough with your computer to install software. You won't be asked to do anything without easy-to-follow steps.

- You're a geek of some kind but not another. Maybe you've built your own microwave oven but you have no idea how to configure a web server.

- You want to live in the Jetsons' house. Who doesn't?

- You're not afraid to learn something new.

Organization of This Book

You should be able to understand the bulk of each project with very little reading. The pictures alone tell a story. At the beginning of each chapter we include a conceptual diagram, a "What You Need" list, and a small "Project Stats" section that describes the relative difficulty, time involved, and cost of the project. We assume that you've already got a PC, so we typically don't take that expense into account in the overall cost of the project.

The 13 projects in Home Hacking Projects for Geeks are divided into three categories: Home Automation, Home Entertainment, and Home Security.

Part I, Home Automation

Chapter 1, Automate a Light (written by Tony Northrup), introduces you to lighting that responds to your needs without request. We'll show you how to automate a light using a motion sensor, and you'll never need to walk across a dark basement again.

Chapter 2, Automate Your Porch Light (written by Tony Northrup), expands upon the concepts in the first chapter. This chapter introduces a component, the light sensor, but more importantly, it offers a simple solution to a complex problem by integrating your lighting control system with your computer. You'll learn a little bit of Perl by using scripts that should be simple to read if you're familiar with any programming language.

Chapter 3, Remotely Monitor a Pet (written by Tony Northrup), shows you how to extend the reach of your home using the Internet. This chapter covers the basics of configuring a web server using either Windows or Red Hat Linux. You'll see some new hardware here, too, and use some concepts from the previous projects to rig up a system that takes snapshots of your pet when it passes in front of a motion sensor. When you're done, you'll be able to check in on your pet from any web browser in the world!

Chapter 4, Make Your House Talk (written by Tony Northrup), allows your house to reach out to you. You'll implement a whole-house audio system using cheap computer speakers and a wireless audio transmitter. You'll then configure your PC to find information for you and present it via synthesized speech. This project uses no-cost software, but you can spend a little money on good speech synthesis software to make it really cool.

Part II, Home Entertainment

Chapter 5, Remotely Control Your Computer (written by Eric Faulkner), introduces you to soldering. You'll build a simple circuit from easy-to-obtain parts that allows you to control your PC using any infrared remote. You'll teach your PC how to access your digital media library while you kick back on the couch. There's a Linux version and a Windows version of this project. If you want to continue on to the next project (recommended), you should complete the Windows version.

Chapter 6, Control Your Home Theater (written by Eric Faulkner), is another hardware project that's slightly more difficult than the previous one but still fairly easy to complete. In this project you'll be scripting the control of any devices that respond to infrared remote controls. If you have too many remote controls on your coffee table, this allows you to do everything with one remote, without having to switch modes.

Chapter 7, Build a Windows-Based Home Theater PC (written by Eric Faulkner), is a more complex software integration project with unique PC hardware requirements. This chapter gives step-by-step instructions on how to assemble a PC for use in this and the next project. You'll be creating a computer that integrates into your home theater and features time shifting, digital video recording with a built-in programming guide, video games, and more.

Chapter 8, Build a Linux-Based Home Theater PC (written by Eric Faulkner), takes a Red Hat Linux approach to the home theater PC. You'll be interacting with Linux at the kernel level in this chapter, but thanks to some special tools, it will be safe and easy. The resulting PC will have the same features as the Windows version, but you won't have to buy Windows.

Chapter 9, Create Time-Shifted FM Radio (written by Tony Northrup), brings time shifting to your Howard Stern fix. You'll take advantage of the whole-house audio system from Chapter 4 to have your favorite radio talk show at your command.

Chapter 10, Access Your Entire Media Collection Over the Internet (written by Eric Faulkner), takes your digital audio library and exposes it to the Internet with a web server application using Microsoft IIS. You'll be introduced to Active Server Pages and VBScript; you can do your own scripting if you're interested, or simply cut and paste.

Part III, Home Security

Chapter 11, Keyless Entry Welcome Home (written by Eric Faulkner), extends the functionality of an off-the-shelf keyless remote entry system.

You'll build a small control mechanism to enable the lock to trigger events for a "welcome home" sequence. A little imagination can tie this project into every other project in the book.

Chapter 12, Watch Your House Across the Network (written by Tony Northrup), is an evolution of the pet monitoring project in Chapter 3. This time, however, you'll stream full motion video across your home network or the Internet to peek in on your home's multiple, inexpensive video cameras from any web browser.

Chapter 13, Build a Security System (written by Tony Northrup), brings physical intrusion detection, event processing, and alerting capabilities to your home. While it's possible to buy an affordable security system for your home, it will usually require a monthly maintenance fee, and it won't allow you much control over the system's behavior. After completing this project, you'll be able to configure your alarm system's behavior to your family's tastes using a simple Perl script. You can even build an off-site video storage system to securely store video evidence of a crime, even if your computer is stolen in the process.

Project Downloads

Many of the projects in this book include code. You can type it all in if that's how you prefer to learn; otherwise, you can download it from *http://www. homehacking.com*. We'll include updated and improved versions, too; after all, that's what open source is all about.

Using Code Examples

This book is here to help you get your job done. In general, you may use the code in this book in your programs and documentation. You do not need to contact us for permission unless you're reproducing a significant portion of the code. For example, writing a program that uses several chunks of code from this book does not require permission. Selling or distributing a CD-ROM of examples from O'Reilly books *does* require permission. Answering a question by citing this book and quoting example code does not require permission. Incorporating a significant amount of example code from this book into your product's documentation *does* require permission.

We appreciate, but do not require, attribution. An attribution usually includes the title, author, publisher, and ISBN. For example: "*Home Hacking Projects for Geeks* by Tony Northrup and Eric Faulkner. Copyright 2005 O'Reilly Media, Inc., 0-596-00405-2."

If you feel your use of code examples falls outside fair use or the permission given above, feel free to contact O'Reilly at *permissions@oreilly.com*.

Conventions Used in This Book

The following typographical conventions are used in this book:

Bold

Indicates menu titles, menu options, and menu buttons.

Italic

Indicates new terms, URLs, email addresses, filenames, file extensions, pathnames, directories, and Unix utilities.

`Constant width`

Indicates commands, options, switches, variables, attributes, keys, functions, types, classes, namespaces, methods, modules, properties, parameters, values, objects, events, event handlers, XML tags, HTML tags, macros, the contents of files, or the output from commands.

`Constant width bold`

Shows commands or other text that should be typed literally by the user.

`Constant width italic`

Shows text that should be replaced with user-supplied values.

How to Contact O'Reilly

Please address comments and questions concerning this book to the publisher:

O'Reilly Media, Inc.
1005 Gravenstein Highway North
Sebastopol, CA 95472
(800) 998-9938 (in the United States or Canada)
(707) 829-0515 (international or local)
(707) 829-0104 (fax)

There is a web page for this book, where you can find code files, errata, and additional information. You can access this page at:

http://www.oreilly.com/homehacking

To comment or ask technical questions about this book, send email to:

bookquestions@oreilly.com

For more information about books, conferences, Resource Centers, and the O'Reilly Network, go to:

http://www.oreilly.com

How to Contact the Authors

Let us know how you've improved our projects. We have a web page for this book, where we host a community of geeks, list errata, examples, and any additional information. Perhaps most importantly, you can download each project's source code (with updates). You can access this page at:

http://www.homehacking.com/

Acknowledgments

We got a lot of help from some great people to make this book. Special thanks to open source developers Robin Smidsrød, Robbie Harris, Shaun Faulds, and Isaac Richards for creating software that enables this technology and making it freely available. Special thanks to Axel Thimm and Jarod Wilson for helping the world by creating a Linux-based home theater PC, and to Jon Simmons for his help designing the keyless entry system.

We had a great crew of tech reviewers: Casey Ajalat, Jon Simmons, Tom Keegan, Chris Geggis, and Dale Dougherty. The time they dedicated to the early draft of this book greatly improved the quality, and we are indebted to each of them.

We'd also like to thank Mark Frauenfelder for his "geek" illustrations, used throughout the book to illustrate how the projects work.

Eric would like to thank Tony for bringing him into the world of book writing by asking for assistance with this book. It happened just days after Eric said, "I want to be more like you." He'd also like to express his gratitude to the people at O'Reilly, especially Dale Dougherty, for trusting him to complete this project without having a proven track record. He thanks his many geeks friends, Chris Russo, Tom Keegan, Bob Hogan, Chris Geggis, and Casey Ajalat, for inspiring him to learn and grow professionally. He's grateful for the folks at the Southeast Asian Restaurant whose authentic open-air market cuisine gave him a reason to go out into the sunlight every Saturday. He also wants to thank Will and Jean Winslow for picking up his slack around the house and for their feedback on projects. More than anyone else, Eric is indebted to his wife, Alyssa, for her unwavering patience and support while he toiled away in the basement. And, of course, he thanks his beautiful daughters, Amanda and Lily, for making it fun to be a dad.

Tony wants to thank his friends and family for helping him relax between projects and being patient while he worked too many long nights. Thank you, Tara Banks, Kristin Cavour, Kurt Dillard, Chris and Diane Geggis, Bob Hogan, Samuel Jackson, Khristina Jones, Tom Keegan, and Eric John Parucki (who, if he does nothing else with this book, should read Chapter 4). I'm thankful to the host, bartenders, and waitstaff at Rudy's Café in

Somerville (the best Tex-Mex experience a displaced Texan can have), who know me as "Tony for two," "Two prickly-pear margaritas no salt," and "Number four with chips and salsa," respectively. I have to thank Howard Stern, Robin Quivers, Artie Lange, and the rest of the crew for getting me up in the morning and for inspiring Chapter 9. Leo, Patrick, Jessica, Kevin, Dan, Jessica, Sarah, Yoshi, and Jessica at the Screensavers (TechTV) reminded me that 7 p.m. is time to stop work—although, because of the PVR, I often kept working. More than anyone, I have to thank my wife, Erica, for being so patient during many long days of writing. Erica's family, Mike, Michelle, Sandi, and Raymond Edson, as always, kept me in good spirits during the holidays (and by "spirits," I mean booze).

Disclaimer

Much of the information contained in this book is based on personal knowledge and experience. While we believe that the information contained herein is correct, we accept no responsibility for its validity. The hardware designs, software, and descriptive text contained herein are provided for educational purposes only. It is the responsibility of the reader to independently verify all information. Original manufacturer's data should be used at all times when implementing a design.

The authors, Tony Northrup and Eric Faulkner, and O'Reilly Media, Inc., make no warranty, representation, or guarantee regarding the suitability of any hardware or software described herein for any particular purpose, nor do they assume any liability arising out of the application or use of any product, system, circuit, or software, and specifically disclaim any and all liability, including, without limitation, consequential or incidental damages. The hardware and software described herein are not designed, intended, nor authorized for use in any application intended to support or sustain life or any of the application in which the failure of a system could create a situation in which personal injury, death, loss of data or information, or damages to property may occur. Should the reader implement any design described herein for any application, the reader shall indemnify and hold the authors, O'Reilly Media, Inc., and their respective shareholders, officers, employees, and distributors harmless against all claims, costs, damages and expenses, and reasonable solicitor fees arising out of, directly or indirectly, any claim of personal injury, death, loss of data or information, or damages to property associated with such unintended or unauthorized use.

Home Automation

Part 1 of this book eases you into home modding. In Chapter 1, you'll learn how to add a motion detector to a light inside your house. It's an easy mod that introduces you to X10 and shows you how to go about replacing light switches in your home. In Chapter 2, you'll take it a step further by automating your porch light. You'll use your experience from Chapter 1 and learn how to control your lights from your Linux or Windows computer. Chapter 3 will be your favorite project when traveling, because you'll use inexpensive wireless cameras to monitor your pet across the Internet. In Chapter 4, you'll connect your computer to inexpensive wireless speakers, and have it read you the current outdoor temperature before you even get out of bed in the morning.

Automate a Light

Cost

$55

Time

an hour or less

Difficulty

2 out of 5

- An X10 wall switch
- An X10 motion detector
- Two AAA batteries
- An X10 controller (optional)
- Replacement faceplate (optional)
- Circuit tester
- Screwdriver
- Wire nuts

For a list of specific parts used in this project, refer to Exhibit A at the end of this chapter.

If you live in a home that's more than 20 years old, there's a very good chance that you have light switches in odd places, or that you need to cross a room in order to turn on a light. In my case, I have to walk across a dark and frighteningly cluttered basement, so I often end up leaving the light on and wasting energy. If I could automate this light switch so that it turns on when I enter the room and turns off when I leave it, I would save myself both money and frustration.

> The best way to ease your household into home automation is to start small. This will build your confidence, and make the other people in your household more comfortable with the idea of you replacing switches, cutting holes in walls, and otherwise performing tasks normally done by someone who charges $150 an hour.

Figure 1-1 illustrates the project's simple design, which includes a motion detector and a control mechanism. The motion detector is triggered simply by someone entering the room, and will then send a signal telling the control mechanism (an intelligent light switch) to turn on. Just as when you manually flip a light switch, the intelligent light switch will close a circuit and provide electricity to the light.

(1) Person enters area covered by motion detector

(2) Motion detector sends signal to control mechanism

(3) Control mechanism flips power switch

Figure 1-1. The conceptual design for an automated light.

Project Overview

This simple project will introduce you to basic concepts of electricity, wiring, and the X10 home automation communications protocol by replacing a wall switch to allow for remote control using X10. While the new switch could be controlled from anywhere in the house using a computer, remote control, or other device, you'll be automating it using a motion detector in the same room.

You will start by replacing the existing wall switch with an X10 wall switch. This is a fairly easy change, but the wiring can be complex, and you must follow safety precautions. You will then install an X10 wireless transceiver, which receives wireless signals from the X10 motion detector and sends commands across your home's power lines to the X10 wall switch. Finally, you will configure and position the wireless X10 motion detector. When you're done, the motion detector will trigger the light when you enter a room by relaying both wireless and wired X10 signals, as illustrated in Figure 1-2.

This project does not require a computer. However, later projects will connect your computer to both the switch and the module and allow you to integrate both into complex applications.

Shortcut: If you don't have future plans to remotely control this switch, buy a light switch with a built-in motion detector. These are available at hardware stores for less than $30.

X10 overview

X10 is a communications protocol, similar to network protocols such as TCP/IP. However, X10 works across home power lines and is *extremely* low-bandwidth. X10 devices send about one command per second, and the commands are as simple as "Device A1: Turn on". These commands require less than 1/1000 the bandwidth of a dial-up connection. Like a broadcast network, every command is sent through every wire in your house; it's up to each

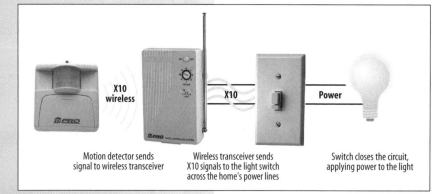

Motion detector sends signal to wireless transceiver

Wireless transceiver sends X10 signals to the light switch across the home's power lines

Switch closes the circuit, applying power to the light

Figure 1-2. Both wireless and wired X10 signals are used to turn a light on when motion is detected.

individual device to decide whether it needs to respond to a particular command.

> Perhaps we should rephrase. *Ideally*, every command is sent through every wire in your house. *Realistically*, your house may have multiple, separate circuits that X10 signals cannot cross. Furthermore, interference may cause signals to be lost unpredictably. You may even receive signals from your neighbors' homes!
>
> Happily, there are ways to fix this. For more information, visit *http://www.smart-home.com/solution04.html*.

With X10, devices that can be plugged into the wall can communicate with each other and with your computer. There are hundreds of X10 devices available, and most are fairly inexpensive—less than $40. Figure 1-3 shows some of the most common types of X10 devices: a two-way hard-wired X10 wall switch, a wireless transceiver, and a battery-operated wireless wall switch.

The simplest way to use X10 is to turn a lamp on and off from an X10 remote. To do this, configure an X10 transmitter (such as an X10 remote or wall switch) and an X10 receiver (such as a lamp module) to the same X10 address. Plug a lamp into the X10 receiver, as shown in Figure 1-4, and then turn the lamp on. Voila! You can now use the X10 remote to turn the lamp on and off.

Figure 1-3. A hard-wired X10 wall switch, an X10 wireless transceiver, and a wireless X10 wall switch.

Large hardware stores usually carry a handful of common X10 parts; in fact, you should be able to buy all the parts you need for this project at the Home Depot or Lowe's. However, I prefer to buy the parts on the Internet because prices tend to be lower and there are many more parts to choose from. I do most of my shopping at *http://www.smarthome.com*.

X10 addressing

To identify individual devices and groups of devices, X10 uses an addressing scheme that provides up to 256 unique addresses. House codes are written as a single letter in the range A–P. Unit codes are a decimal number between 1 and 16. Examples of valid house codes are A1, J13, and P16.

> If you're a network geek, think of the house code as the network portion of an IP address, and the unit code as the host portion.

Figure 1-4. An X10 lamp module turns a lamp on and off when an X10 signal is sent from an X10 transmitter.

Unlike the IP addresses used on the Internet, X10 addresses do not have to be unique. You should use a single address to configure each group of X10 devices that will respond to the same commands. For example, if you want to turn on two lamps with a single switch, connect an X10 lamp module to each lamp and configure both modules with a single address. If you want all the lamps in a room to be controlled by a single command, they should all be assigned a single address.

While most X10 devices are one-way because they are only capable of either sending or receiving, some devices are two-way. For example, one-way X10 light switches can receive X10 commands to enable them to be turned on and off remotely. You can also use the one-way light switch to control the light locally, just as you control a conventional light switch. However, when you flip the switch, a one-way X10 light switch does not transmit a signal. Therefore, while flipping the switch can turn the light on and off, it cannot turn on other X10 switches.

Two-way X10 light switches can receive X10 commands, and can also transmit an X10 command when you flip the switch. This allows you to use the switch to control both the light and another X10 device simultaneously. For example, if I replace the switch that controls my kitchen's under-cabinet lighting with a one-way X10 switch, and then replace the switch that controls my kitchen's overhead lighting with a two-way X10 switch, I could turn on both the overhead light and the under-cabinet light by using the overhead light switch.

Light Switch

In the first phase of this project, you will replace the existing conventional wall switch with a one-way X10 switch. The new switch is capable of receiving, but not sending, X10 commands. One-way X10 switches that can receive X10 commands may be turned on, turned off, or dimmed by an X10 transmitter. In this project, the X10 light switch will receive signals from a wireless X10 motion detector. Later projects will show you how X10 can be used to control almost any system in your house. For example, flipping a two-way X10 switch could dim the lights and play your favorite MP3s.

The light switch is the only piece of hardware required for the control mechanism component of this project. It will receive signals from the motion detector and apply power to the light.

1. Disconnect power

First things first: you need to use care every time you interact with your home's electrical systems. Even though replacing a wall switch is much simpler than adding a new electrical circuit, there are still risks. You will be exposing high-voltage wires, so be sure that power is disconnected before you remove the existing switch. You must also take care when wiring to ensure that all connections are solid and there are no exposed wires.

> You don't have to get your hands dirty to work with X10. X10 can be used to control lights and appliances by plugging the device into an X10 module, then plugging the module into an electrical outlet. This project covers one of the more complex ways to use X10 hardware because it requires you to disconnect power and replace an existing switch. However, if you are not yet comfortable working with your home's wiring, try one of the other projects in this book to introduce yourself to X10.

In this step, you will disconnect power to the switch that you will be replacing. First, you should test the switch or outlet to verify that it is working properly. That way, if it's not working later, you know that it's because of a recent change you made. Turn the switch on and make sure that the light or outlet it controls works properly. If the switch controls an outlet, plug a radio into it and turn the volume up loud enough so you can hear it shut off when you've found the right circuit breaker. Warn the other people in your household that you're about to turn off the power at the circuit breaker—you don't want someone discovering that the lights are out, and then reconnecting the power while you're in the process of wiring—and place a piece of tape over the circuit breaker so that everyone knows the switch was intentionally flipped.

> If you live in an older home, you may have a fuse box instead of a circuit breaker, so you'll be removing and replacing fuses rather than flipping a switch. However, I'll continue to use the term circuit breaker for simplicity.

Find your circuit breaker. This will be an easy task if the breakers are clearly labeled; however, for the rest of us, there will be some guesswork involved. My circuit breaker, shown in Figure 1-5, resembles every Perl script I've ever written: lots of poorly documented switches that can only be understood by experimentation. Flip the breaker that you think is the most likely candidate, and then see if the light has gone out or if the radio is quiet. If so, you've found the correct circuit breaker and you can skip to Step 2. If not, flip the breaker back on and keep trying until you find the right one.

Figure 1-5. A typical circuit breaker.

There's a better way to find the right circuit: use a *circuit finder*. Circuit finders cost around $30–$50, and are absolutely worth the money if you do electrical work frequently. To use it, connect one part to the electrical outlet and wave the other part over the breakers. It'll beep or light up when you wave it over the breaker that controls the electrical outlet.

2. Test the switch

After you've disconnected the power from the switch you are replacing, remove the faceplate by unscrewing any visible screws. Generally, there are two screws that hold the faceplate in place. Set the faceplate and the screws aside.

Beneath the faceplate you will see the switch recessed into a box in the wall. The box is usually made of metal or plastic, and fastened on one side to a stud that supports the wall. The box will have one or more holes in it to allow the electrical wiring to enter the box.

Before unscrewing the switch from the wall, use a *circuit tester* (also known as a voltage detector or voltage probe) to verify that it is not receiving power. This is *not* an optional step—if the circuit is live, it's dangerous, and you could receive a potentially deadly jolt of electricity if you were to touch the wires on the circuit. Circuit testers are available at any hardware store, and cost from $5 to $40.

Circuit testers come in one of two varieties: wired (or *contact*) and wireless (or *non-contact*). A wired circuit tester requires you to attach its terminals to the wires on your switch. I prefer wireless circuit testers, which only require you to hold the circuit tester near the circuit. A light or audible alarm will indicate that the circuit is live.

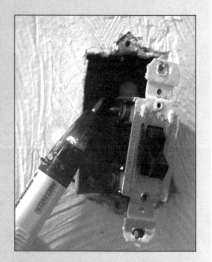

Figure 1-6. Don't touch this switch yet: the yellow light on the circuit tester shows that it's still hot.

Start by testing a known live circuit to verify that the circuit tester works properly and that you're using it the right way. If your tester has terminals, touch the red terminal to one of the screws connected to the switch, and the black terminal to the grounding wire. If you have a wireless circuit tester, hold it against one of the screws. Circuit testers vary, so follow the instructions provided with your tester. The wireless circuit tester in Figure 1-6 is alerting us that the circuit is live and dangerous.

3. Replace the switch

Before you replace the switch, read the instructions included with your new X10 switch. These should include a description of the different wires that must be connected to the switch. For this project, you do not need to connect all the wires, just the positive wire, the neutral wire, and the grounding wire.

After you've verified that power is disconnected from the switch, examine the switch and the wires connected to it. Identify the positive wire (or wires), the neutral wire, and the grounding wire (if it exists). The color of the wire usually indicates what type of wire it is, as shown in Table 1-1.

WARNING

Just as some programmers write sloppy code that still works, some electricians (or wannabe electricians) do a sloppy job of in-wall wiring. If in doubt, use a circuit tester to determine how each wire is used.

Table 1-1. Color codes for electrical wires

Color	Meaning	Description
Black	Positive	A hot wire that carries current from the power source
White	Neutral	A wire that completes the circuit from the switch
Uninsulated or green	Ground	An alternate neutral path that reduces the risk of shock
Red	Positive, or a traveler wire	A wire that carries positive current either to the device being controlled by the switch, or to another switch in a three-way switch

Most wall switches, including the one in Figure 1-6, are connected with two black (positive) wires. If the switch is at the end of the circuit, the switch will be connected to one black wire and one white (neutral) wire. For grounding purposes, the switch may be connected by an uninsulated wire to the electrical box. Three-way switches use a red (traveler) wire that directly connects the two switches.

WARNING

Just a little belt-and-suspenders protection: even though the power is disconnected, take care to not touch two wires simultaneously, or to allow two wires to touch each other.

Disconnect the switch from the electrical wires. Exactly how this is done varies depending on the type of switch you have—there may be as few as two wires or as many as five (including an uninsulated grounding wire). The wires usually connect directly to the switch using a screw, as shown in Figure 1-6.

If your new X10 switch has two dials on the back, you'll need to skip ahead to Step 5 and configure the address of the switch to C1 before connecting it.

Now, connect the X10 switch according to the manufacturer's instructions. To connect wires using wire nuts, hold the ends of both wires together so that they are parallel to each other. Then, insert the ends of both wires into a wire nut, and twist the wire nut until it holds the wires firmly together. Table 1-2 provides guidelines for how to connect the wires in the switch to the wires in your electrical box, based on color. Of course, you should rely on the instructions provided with the switch.

Table 1-2. Common ways to connect X10 switch wires

X10 switch wire	Electrical box connection	Description
Black	Black	Positive
Blue	Black or white	Positive or neutral
Uninsulated	Connect directly to the electrical box by wrapping the wire around a screw. If you have a plastic electrical box, connect it to the junction's ground wire.	Ground
Green	Connect directly to the electrical box by wrapping the wire around a screw. If you have a plastic electrical box, connect it to the junction's ground wire.	Ground
Red	Red if available. Otherwise, black or white if not already connected.	Positive, or a traveler wire
Yellow	Red if available. Otherwise, cover the exposed wire with a wire nut.	Positive, or a traveler wire

If the new switch has two black wires, simply connect each of them to one of the black wires in the electrical box. If the new switch has one black wire and one blue wire, connect the switch's black wire to a black wire in the electrical box, and connect the switch's blue wire to the electrical box's other (white or black) wire. If it exists, connect the switch's grounding wire (green or uninsulated) to the electrical box. Figure 1-7 shows a typical connected X10 switch.

If the new switch requires a neutral connection, connect the switch's white and red wires to the electrical box's matching wires using wire nuts. It's okay if three white wires go into a single wire nut. Be sure that no wire (other than the grounding wire) is left exposed. If the switch has a yellow (traveler) wire that is not being used, cover the uninsulated portion of the wire with a wire nut.

Make sure you connect the switch right side up!

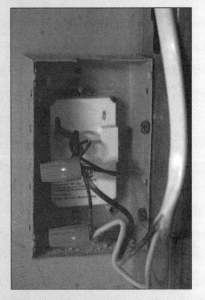

Figure 1-7. The view from behind the electrical box, showing wire nuts connecting the new switch to the old wiring.

4. Reconnect power and test the switch

Before you screw the switch into the wall, verify that it works correctly. Return to your circuit breaker and reset the switch to the original position. If you have a fuse box, replace the fuse. Attempt to turn on your X10 light; if it doesn't work, disconnect the power and verify all connections.

> X10 switches usually do not operate like conventional switches. X10 toggle switches return to a centered position after being pushed up or down. Other switches turn the light on or off each time the button is pressed.

5. Configure the switch

You must now select house and unit codes for your switch. For this project, we'll use the address C1. While you're free to choose any house code in the A–P range, you should not leave it at the default "A" setting, as this increases the likelihood that you will have conflicts with your neighbors' X10 equipment. X10 signals do not usually jump between houses or apartments, but it has been known to happen.

Consult the manufacturer's instructions for specific directions on configuring your house and unit codes. Usually, you'll use a screwdriver to twist the dials for both the house and unit code. Twist the house code dial to C and leave the unit code dial at 1. If your switch does not have dials to physically configure the X10 address, you will need to put the switch into setup mode. To do this, you generally hold down a button for several seconds until a light blinks. Then, you send an X10 command using the house and unit codes that you want the switch to respond to using an X10 controller. Alternatively, you may need to repeatedly press a button on the switch a specific number of times to define the code.

Return once again to the circuit breaker to disconnect the power from the switch. Then, attach the switch to the electrical box and reattach the faceplate to the wall, as shown in Figure 1-8. Turn on the breaker one last time. The new switch should now function just like the old one did, which clearly doesn't provide the benefit you're looking for. On to the second phase.

> If your new switch isn't the same shape as your old switch, you'll need a new faceplate. They are very inexpensive and can be purchased from any hardware store.

Figure 1-8. The X10 switch in place, with the faceplate.

Motion Detection

In this second phase of the project, you will configure a motion detector to send signals to the light switch you installed in the first phase. However, the motion detector you're using can't communicate directly to the switch because it's wireless. Therefore, you now need to install a wireless transceiver to receive the signals from the motion detector and place them onto the power line where the switch can process them. This component of the project is the interface between the human and the light switch.

1. Connect the wireless transceiver

In this step you will configure an X10 wireless transceiver (also known as an *RF receiver*) and connect it to an outlet, as shown in Figure 1-9. The wireless transceiver receives X10 wireless commands from the X10 motion detector and transmits those commands over the power lines.

First, configure the house code of the wireless transceiver. Use a screwdriver to twist the dial to set the house code to C. The transceiver will respond to wireless signals only from other devices using the same house code. For example, if you later configure other devices using the E house code, the wireless transceiver will not respond to them.

If the transceiver allows another device to be plugged into it, it probably has a dial, a switch, and a button. These allow you to control the lamp or other device plugged directly into the transceiver, and do not affect how the transceiver passes on wireless communications.

Figure 1-9. An X10 wireless transceiver is required to transfer signals from the motion detector to the light switch.

X10 wireless devices operate in the 433.92MHz radio frequency range, and will not interfere with your wireless 802.11*x* network or cordless phones.

Connect the wireless transceiver to an electrical outlet in a central location within your house. If it seems unreliable, try moving it closer to the motion detector. For best results, plug the transceiver directly into an outlet, not into a power strip, surge protector, or UPS.

2. Set up the motion detector

In this step you will configure the X10 motion detector (also known as an *occupancy sensor*) to turn on the new light switch when someone enters the room, and turn it off after a period of inactivity. You don't need to use the exact model of motion detector used here; you can use any motion detector that is X10 compatible. Alternatively, many hardware stores carry non-X10 light switches with motion detectors that turn lights on and off when someone enters the room.

There are two main types of motion detectors: passive and active. Active motion detectors transmit radio, microwave, infrared, or laser signals, and then monitor the signal for changes that indicate movement. Active motion detectors are more reliable and more expensive than passive motion detectors.

Most inexpensive X10 motion detectors are passive. They detect fluctuations in the visible light or infrared spectrum. Passive infrared (PIR) motion detectors are particularly good at detecting humans because human skin radiates a small amount of infrared energy. Passive motion detectors don't use as much electricity as active motion detectors and can therefore be battery-powered, which allows you to use them without adding electrical wiring to your home.

For this project, I elected to use an inexpensive wireless X10 passive motion detector. Though I couldn't find a technical description of how this model of motion detector works, a bit of experimentation seems to indicate that it works by detecting changes in the visible light spectrum and not the infrared spectrum, since the motion detector responds to motion from inanimate objects that do not radiate infrared energy. It also seems to have only a single sensor. A dual-sensor motion detector is not triggered when the detector itself is moved because it looks for changes that occur in only one of its sensors. However, shaking the inexpensive X10 motion detector will set it off.

Figure 1-10 shows the outside and inside of the model I am using. A dark gray model is also available with the same guts and functionality, but slightly better weather sealing.

To configure the address of the motion detector, remove the front panel. Depending on the model, you may need to remove a screw. If necessary, insert batteries into the motion detector at this time.

Figure 1-10. The most common X10 motion detector is simple and inexpensive.

I have used two different models of motion detectors, and on both of them the X10 address was configured using the House and Unit buttons. To configure a house code of C:

1. Hold the House button until the red light blinks (about five seconds). This puts the motion detector into a special mode that allows you to reset the house code.

2. Press the House button multiple times to specify the house code. To specify C you'll press it three times and hold it on the final press until the red light blinks. It will blink to indicate the new setting, so if you have successfully set it to house code C, it will blink three times.

3. The unit code is set to 1 by default, so there is no need to adjust it.

Place the motion detector in a location where it can sense motion at every entrance in the room, as illustrated in Figure 1-11. You should not have to wave your arms to trigger the motion detector. If you want to reduce the likelihood of a pet triggering the motion detector, place the motion detector high in the room or angle it toward the ceiling. If the motion detector goes off too frequently, consider covering part of the sensor with tape to reduce the field of view.

You'll eventually want to permanently install the motion detector, but don't screw it into anything until you've been using it for at least a week. I guarantee that you'll end up moving, tilting, or otherwise adjusting it, and the fewer screw holes in the wall, the better.

Generally, motion detectors have a great deal of intelligence built-in, including the ability to send signals at dawn or dusk, and to ignore motion when the room is already well lit. If you're a control freak, however, this won't be enough. Fortunately, you can use your computer to receive the signals from the motion detector and perform more intelligent processing—for example, factoring in the time of day or not turning on lights while you are watching a movie. Check out Chapter 2, Automate Your Porch Light.

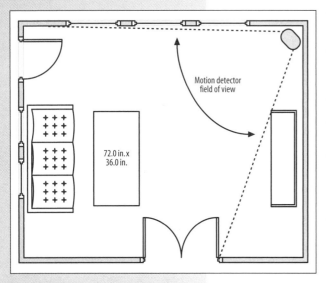

Figure 1-11. Your motion detector should be able to "view" all entrances to a room.

Wrapping Up

Congratulations on taking the first step towards an automated home! Now, before you spend hundreds of dollars automating every device in your house, live with the motion detector for a few days. Think about how you use it, and what annoys you about it. What do the other people in your household have to say about the new switch? If it bugs you at times, chances are good you can fix it by connecting your computer to the X10 network and writing a simple script.

To determine if the project was worthwhile, disable the motion detector after about a week. Does anyone miss it?

Extensions

The most basic and common use of X10 controllers is to turn lights on and off. However, X10 is extremely flexible, and the wide variety of X10 devices allows you to remotely control everything from dryers to window blinds to your home's thermostat. Here are some other common uses for X10:

- If you have a switch in an illogical place, replace it with an X10-controlled switch and add a wireless controller to the wall where the switch should be.

- If want a switch to control multiple electrical outlets, replace it with a two-way X10 controller and add lamp modules to allow it to control remote lamps.

- If you hate getting up in the middle of the night to turn off a light somewhere in the house, replace all your light switches with X10 switches and use the All Lights Off switch on your controller.

Exhibit A: Bill of Materials

The following list shows the parts that I purchased specifically for this project, though you can choose to substitute parts from other manufacturers. All parts are available from large hardware stores or home-automation web sites. The part numbers listed can be referenced at *http://www.smarthome. com*.

Item	Quantity	Approximate cost	Part number
X10 wireless transceiver	1	$20 and up	4005X or 400s
X10 motion detector	1	$20 and up	MS14A-C or MS13A
X10 switch	1	$13 and up	2031 or similar

Automate Your Porch Light

2

Cost
$90

Time
three hours

Difficulty
3 out of 5

I hate unlocking my front door in the dark. I'm never sure if I have the right key in my hand, if it's turned the right way, or where the keyhole is. The worst part is that I have a porch light *right above the door*. I can't unlock the door without the light, but I can't get to the light without unlocking the door. So, the light switch waits for me on the other side of the door, quietly mocking me. I'll teach that light to laugh at me.

From now on, porch light, I'm the boss, and these are the rules. You will:

- Turn on at dusk.

- Turn off at midnight.

- Turn on the entryway lights inside the house when someone approaches the door after dusk but before midnight.

- Turn on both the porch light and the floodlights when someone approaches the door between midnight and 6 A.M.

For the project to accomplish all this, we'll need a logic mechanism that can determine when to turn the lights on and off, and keep track of their state. The logic mechanism will control the light switch and receive input from a timer, motion detectors, and conventional light switches. You can buy or build standalone logic mechanisms, but a computer is the simplest and least expensive way to control everything. We'll also need a light switch that can be remotely controlled by the computer, and a motion detector that can

What You Need

- A load-bearing X10 wall switch
- An X10 motion detector (preferably an outdoor model)
- X10 Powerlinc Serial Controller
- Four AAA batteries
- An X10 controller (optional)
- Replacement faceplate (optional)
- Circuit tester
- Screwdriver
- Wire nuts

For a list of specific parts used in this project, refer to Exhibit A at the end of this chapter.

tell our computer when someone approaches the door. Figure 2-1 shows the components of this project.

Project Overview

This project builds on Chapter 1, Automate a Light, by connecting a Microsoft Windows or Linux computer to your X10 network. This project includes simple scripts for controlling lights based on feedback from the X10 motion detector and the computer's clock. The computer's role is fairly simple; however, once the computer is connected to X10 and you understand how to control it using scripts, you can do much more exciting things than simply turning lights on and off.

> Shortcut: Home-automation software packages that provide X10 control without requiring scripting are available for both Windows and Linux. However, these applications provide much less control and flexibility, and are not nearly as much fun.

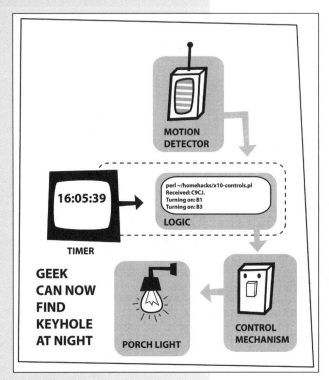

Figure 2-1. The conceptual design for the intelligent porch light.

Light Switch

The software you write in this project will turn lights on and off based partially on information provided by motion detectors and the current time of day. To enable your computer to control the lights, you must first install X10-capable light switches on all relevant lights (in this case, the porch light, the floodlights, and the entry light). You must then install one or more motion detectors. These will send a wireless X10 signal that will be forwarded to your computer when someone approaches, allowing your computer to make an intelligent decision about turning lights on. Finally, you must connect your computer to your X10 network using an X10 computer interface.

I should mention at this point that X10 isn't terribly reliable, and if you implement it extensively, it can get quite expensive. I would love to provide an alternative to using it, but I couldn't find another affordable way to enable a computer to control lights all around the house that didn't require running wires through the walls. With that said, the first step in implementing X10 control over your lighting for this project is to replace the existing switches for the porch light, floodlights, and interior light that will be computer-controlled. Each light will be independently controlled, and will therefore require a unique X10 address. For this project, we'll use the addresses in Table 2-1. Naturally, you may use different addresses, but you will need to adjust the addresses in the X10 script provided in Exhibit B.

Table 2-1. Suggested X10 addresses for the lights

Device	Address
Porch light	B1
Floodlights	B2
Inside entry light	B3

WARNING

You must use X10 switches designed for the type of light they will be controlling. High-wattage lights and florescent lights require nonstandard switches.

For detailed instructions on installing X10 light switches, refer to Chapter 1.

Motion Detection

The light switch is an admirable user interface. It's simple, requiring only the flick of a finger, and everyone knows how to use it. But motion detectors are even simpler, because they provide an entirely passive user interface. To control something via a motion detector, all you have to do is be present. In this phase of the project, you'll install a motion detector that connects to your X10 power network.

1. Install and configure the motion detector

As described in Chapter 1, X10 wireless motion detectors will be used for this phase. The difference in this case is that the motion detector will be positioned to detect motion outside of the house.

We'll use C9 as the motion detector's primary address. This is the address the motion detector will transmit an ON signal to when motion is detected, and an OFF signal to when no motion has been detected for the time-out period. The motion detectors in this project can communicate when several different events occur, including dawn and dusk; for example, we need to detect dusk to turn the porch light on in the first place. By default, the X10 motion detectors I am using transmit a code *one unit higher* than its primary address, so in this case it will transmit an ON signal to the address C10.

Table 2-2 lists all the X10 addresses the motion detector will use when the primary address is set to C9. Again, you're free to use different addresses, but you will need to adjust them in the X10 script in Exhibit B. Note that although it's not used in this project, the motion detector transmits an OFF signal at dawn to the address one unit higher than its primary.

Table 2-2. Suggested X10 addresses for the motion detector

Event	Signal
Motion detected	C9-ON
No motion detected for configured time-out period	C9-OFF
Dusk	C10-ON
Dawn	C10-OFF

To configure the address of the motion detector, remove the front panel, as shown in Figure 2-2. Depending on the model, you may need to remove a screw. If necessary, insert two AAA batteries into the motion detector.

The X10 address is configured on the motion detector by holding and pressing the House and Unit buttons. To configure a house code of C:

1. Hold the House button until the red light blinks (about five seconds). This puts the motion detector into a special mode that allows you to reset the house code.

2. Press the House button multiple times to specify the house code. To specify a code of C, press the button three times and hold it on the final press until the red light blinks. It will blink to indicate the new setting, so if you have successfully set it to house code C, it will blink three times.

The unit code is set similarly. To configure a unit code of 9:

1. Hold the Unit button until the red light blinks (about five seconds).

2. Press and the Unit button nine times, holding it down on the final press until the red light blinks. It should blink nine times to indicate the new setting.

Finally, we need to configure the motion detector to not transmit signals when motion is detected before dusk.

1. Press the Unit button once. The red light will flash.

2. Press and hold the House button. The green light will turn on. After about three seconds, the motion detector will report its dusk/dawn setting as follows:

   - The red light will blink once if it is set to detect motion during both day and night.

   - The red light will blink twice if it is set to detect motion only when it's dark.

3. Release the House button. If the red light blinks only once, change the setting by pressing and releasing the House button, and then holding it for three seconds until the red light blinks again. The red light should then report the setting with two blinks.

Figure 2-2. Configuring an X10 motion detector.

Motion detectors are available in both interior and exterior models. Whenever possible, use an interior motion detector placed inside a window that faces the area around your door. While exterior switches are designed to be weather-resistant, they can still be damaged by extreme weather. If nothing else, they may get covered with snow or ice and lose their ability to detect motion.

WARNING

Not to mention that if you stick your motion detector outside, someone may steal it. It's unlikely, but you don't want to tempt an aspiring thief.

Mounting your motion detector inside a window presents challenges, too. First, a motion detectors is meant to be mounted with its back to a flat surface, so if you want it to face out a window, there probably won't be anything to mount it to. While resting it precariously on a window shelf may get you through the proof-of-concept stage, it won't be long before your cat or kid knocks it over.

Determining the perfect placement for your motion detector can be tricky as well. Regardless of whether the motion detector is inside or outside, you need to place it so that it is out-of-view of the porch light; you don't want the porch light being on to fool the motion detector into thinking it's daylight. At the same time, the motion detector needs to be able to see incoming natural light so that it can detect dusk accurately.

If you live someplace where snow accumulates, position the motion detector as high in the window as possible. We once had a snowstorm with heavy winds, and my motion detector stopped working because snow was drifted three feet up on the window screen. Positioning it higher up makes it less likely to be disturbed, too.

Once again, you'll want to wait a little while before you permanently mount your motion detector. No one will be impressed with all the holes you left in the wall while you were attempting to find the perfect location.

2. Install the wireless transceiver

The motion detectors used in this project are wireless, so you don't have to deal with power outlets when determining where to place your detector. It's also nice to be able to place the motion detector where it won't be disturbed or noticed, such as outside under a windowsill. For detailed instructions on configuring a motion detector, refer to Chapter 1.

Logic and Timer

The intelligence for this project will be provided by a script you create and run on your computer, such as the one in Exhibit B. This script (the logic component) will receive input from the computer's internal clock and motion detectors. It will then issue commands to the control mechanism to turn the porch light on or off.

For the script described in this section to work properly, you should have a serial port on your computer and you should leave your computer running at all times.

> Some people prefer to turn their computers off when not in use because they think it will extend the life of the computer and lower their electric bills. However, it's usually better to leave them on, even if you don't have anything running. Computers today include power management capabilities that turn off unused components so the computer draws very little power when not in use. Additionally, starting and shutting down your computer can cause more wear and tear than simply leaving it on.

Don't worry if you're not much of a programmer—setting up this script requires minimal understanding of scripting. The script has a few dependencies that need to be set up first: the X10 computer interface, the Perl scripting language, and some modules that add home automation functionality to Perl. After you configure these dependencies, you will type or download the provided home automation script, test it, and then schedule it to run automatically when your computer starts.

> Shortcut: Many graphical applications that control X10 devices are available. These applications don't provide the same level of flexibility as creating your own script, but they may get you started faster if you're not comfortable with scripting. Some of the free applications include:
>
> - MisterHouse, a very complete and complex set of Perl scripts for home automation (*http://www.misterhouse.net*)
> - Java Home Automation (*http://jhome.sourceforge.net*)
> - Home Control Assistant; free, limited version available (*http://www.smarthome.com/1268.html*)
> - X10Controller (*http://x10controller.sourceforge.net*)

Your X10 computer interface probably came with software to allow you to control X10 home automation devices. It's a good idea to play with this software to make sure that the interface works, and to familiarize yourself with what home automation software can do out of the box. If you're like me, you'll be quickly frustrated with the user interface and the limitations of the free software, and will find yourself with a hankering to customize.

The simplest way to create custom logic to control your X10 devices from your computer is with Perl, a scripting language that is commonly used for parsing files and managing networks. Perl's key advantages are that it's free, it's available for just about every commonly used operating system, it's extremely flexible, and it has a wide array of available libraries.

If you've had any exposure to programming (even a high school computer science class), you should be able to quickly learn how to understand and customize Perl scripts. This book provides complete home automation Perl scripts, as well as a thorough description of how they work and how to update them. If you can understand what the following line of a Perl script does, you shouldn't have any problem customizing these scripts:

```
light_off ($porch_light);
```

The open source MisterHouse home automation project (*http://www. misterhouse.net*) uses Perl, and the massive amount of open source development put into the project is the biggest reason that Perl is an excellent language for controlling X10 devices.

Perl is particularly useful for controlling X10 devices because of the availability of the ControlX10 package, a Perl module that adds home automation capabilities to Perl. ControlX10 enables you to control your X10 devices with a single line of code. Additionally, the code you write to control your X10 devices can run on both Windows and Linux with minimal, if any, adjustments.

Instructions for Windows

This section applies to Windows operating systems such as Windows 95, 98, XP, and so on.

1. Connect the X10 computer interface

X10 devices communicate over your home's power lines. Even though you plug your computer into a power

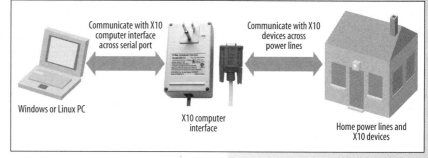

outlet, your computer cannot send or receive X10 signals without an additional interface. As shown in Figure 2-3, you must connect an X10 computer interface to your computer's USB or serial port, and then plug it into a power outlet to enable it to send and receive X10 signals.

Figure 2-3. An X10 computer interface is required to connect your computer to the X10 network that uses your home's power lines.

Nowadays, most new computers come with modems and network interfaces built-in. So why don't they add an X10 interface to the power cable? You could have a computer that enables home automation out of the box, without any additional wires!

The CM11A X10 computer interface, as shown in Figure 2-4, translates signals from applications into X10 commands and sends them over the power line. The CM11A can also receive X10 signals from other X10 devices so that your computer can respond to these messages.

Make sure to purchase the serial version of the CM11A X10 computer interface; there is a USB version, but it is more difficult to program. As a result, there are no Perl interfaces to communicate with the USB version; you can use the software included with the CM11A to control it, but you will not be able to use the script in Exhibit B.

Figure 2-4. The CM11A X10 computer interface enables your computer to send and receive X10 signals.

Another X10 computer interface, the Firecracker (CM17), is a small device that uses X10 wireless signals to communicate and is capable only of transmitting X10 signals from your computer to your home's power lines. In other words, the CM17 only enables your computer to initiate events at your home, such as turning a light on or off, but does not enable it to respond to events, such as a light switch being flipped or motion being detected.

As a result, the CM17 is a bit less expensive, but immensely less useful. Still, there are times when it is appropriate: for example, the project in Chapter 12, Watch Your House Across the Network, uses the CM17 interface for the very reason that the CM17 only transmits, and does not receive, X10 signals.

USB controllers also exist, but the complexity of programming to USB ports has kept most open source developers away from building tools to control them.

You may have more than one serial port on your computer. For the purposes of this project, we'll assume that you've connected the X10 controller to the first one. Of course, you're free to connect it to whichever serial port you like, but then need to modify the script in Exhibit B.

Plug the power cable of the computer interface directly into a wall socket. Do not plug it into a power strip or surge protector, and definitely don't plug it into a UPS. The more devices between your X10 computer interface and the power lines in your house, the more likely it is that the signals will be obscured.

2. Install Perl

Perl is not installed by default on Windows, so you will need to download and install it yourself. Fortunately, it's free. To install Perl:

1. Visit *http://www.activestate.com* and download the latest version of ActivePerl. The script in this project is based on ActivePerl 5.8.0, build 806, but will almost certainly run on other versions.

2. Install ActivePerl and the Perl Package Manager (PPM). You do not need to install the Perl ISAPI, PerlScript, or Examples components. Otherwise, accept the default selections and complete the setup procedure.

3. Restart your system to ensure that changes made to your user profile take effect.

3. Install Perl modules

Perl doesn't include modules for communicating with the serial port or X10 devices, so before you can create the script, you need to download and install modules for those two tasks.

1. Download the Win32::SerialPort module to any directory on your local computer. This module is available at *http://www.cpan.org/authors/id/ B/BB/BBIRTH/*, and is named *Win32-SerialPort-*.tar.gz*.

You can find newer versions of these modules by digging through *http://www. misterhouse.net*; however, the versions at the given URL work fine.

---

2. Download the ControlX10::CM11 module from the same location. The module is named *ControlX10-CM11-*.tar.gz*.

3. Both the serial port and X10 modules have a *.tar.gz* file extension, and must be extracted before they can be installed. Use WinZip or WinRAR to extract these files.

4. Install the Win32::API module. This module can be installed using the PPM. From a command prompt, issue the following command while connected to the Internet:

   ```
   ppm install win32-api
   ```

5. Install the Win32::SerialPort module. From the command prompt switch to the directory to which you extracted the Win32::SerialPort module and execute the following commands.

If you have more than one serial port and have connected your X10 controller to a port other than COM1, change the first line to `perl makefile.pl <port_number>`.

```
perl makefile.pl 1
perl install.pl
```

6. Install the Win32::ControlX10 module. From the command prompt, switch to the directory to which you extracted the module and execute the following commands:

```
perl makefile.pl
perl install.pl
```

4. Establish communication

Now that everything you need is installed, it's time to test the connectivity. The ControlX10 modules include the *eg_cm11.plx* script to test connectivity by turning the light with the address A1 on and off twice. If you have a switch set to a different X10 address, you can either change the X10 address to A1 or edit the *eg_cm11.plx* script to change all references to A1 to your X10 address. Using the command prompt you used to install the ControlX10 module, execute the test script with the following commands:

```
cd eg
perl eg_cm11.plx
```

If everything is working properly, you will see output that resembles the following:

```
-------

Sending A1 On OFF
-------


CM11 power fail detected.  Resetting the CM11 clock with:
 Mon Feb  9 11:12:17 2004
Sending A1 On OFF
Bad checksum in cm11 send: cs1=106 cs2=85.  Will retry
```

That doesn't look good, but it's the response I've always gotten the first time I connect the CM11A unit. If the output doesn't mention a power failure, that's okay—it just means that your controller previously had its time set by another application. Execute the command `perl eg_cm11.plx` again, and you will see a more sensible reply:

```
-------
Sending A1 On OFF
-------
Sending A1 On OFF
```

If you have a light configured with the A1 address, it will flash on and off, pause for two seconds, and then flash on and off again.

5. Create the script

You now have completely flexible and extensible control over your home's lighting. Unless you want to simply flash your lights on and off, though, your computer doesn't yet have the logic it needs to accomplish the original goal of controlling the porch light based on events triggered by the motion detector and the time of day.

To accomplish this, you'll now create a script to listen for signals from the motion detector, and send commands based on the time of day. This script must be running continuously.

You'll use the *eg_cm11.plx* script as the foundation for a script to turn off the porch light. Save the script from Exhibit B as *C:\homehacks\x10-controls.pl*. You can also download the script, along with any updates I've made, from *http://www.homehacking.com*. For you hackers, the later section "Understanding the Script" describes how the script works.

> Many applications out there make it easy to edit Perl scripts. Notepad works fine, too.

6. Run the script

To run the script, open a command prompt and switch to the directory you saved it in (*C:\homehacks*, as suggested above). Then, simply type the name of the script:

```
x10-controls.pl
```

Assuming that you've installed Perl and the required modules correctly, the script will start running and continue until you press Ctrl+C. You won't see anything happen until a signal is received from a motion detector or the system time changes to midnight. So, to make sure everything is working correctly, grab your motion detector and press the "House/On" button. You should see output that resembles the following:

```
Porch motion detected.   Received: C9CJ.
Turning on: B1
Turning on: B3
```

Of course, your output will vary depending on the time of day. Also, now that you've triggered the motion detector, the script thinks that it's dusk because you configured your motion detector to send signals only when it's dark.

> If things don't work as expected, try moving your X10 computer interface and the wireless transceiver to different electrical outlets. You could even try connecting them to outlets right next to each other.

Take a look and see if the porch light turned on. If it did, congrats! Press Ctrl+C to stop the script running so you can schedule it to run automatically in the background.

WARNING

Note that you can run only one such script at a time, because only one script can control the serial port on your computer.

---

7. Schedule the script

For your script to run, your computer must be running. At some point, however, you're going to need to turn off or at least reboot your system. You don't want to have to restart the script each time the computer restarts, so you should configure your script to run automatically at startup.

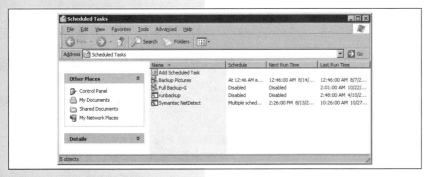

Figure 2-5. Use Scheduled Tasks to have your script run each time your computer starts.

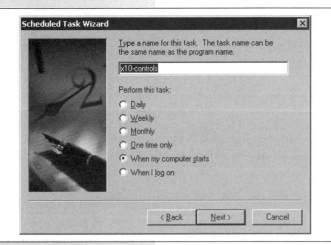

Figure 2-6. Scheduling your script to start automatically is much easier than making your script run as a service.

1. Go to Start → All Programs → Accessories → System Tools → Scheduled Tasks. The Scheduled Tasks window will appear (see Figure 2-5).

2. Double-click Add Scheduled Task and click Next.

3. Click Browse, select your Perl script, and click Next.

4. Click "When my computer starts" as shown in Figure 2-6, and then click Next.

5. Enter the username and password you use to log into the system. Alternatively, if you're concerned about security or don't want the window open when you're logged in, you can create a new user account with limited privileges and specify that account. Click Next.

6. Click Finish.

Get the script running immediately by right-clicking the script in the Scheduled Tasks window and clicking Run. It should pop into the foreground. You're done!

Instructions for Linux

This section applies to the Linux operating systems such as Red Hat, Mandrake, Debian, Lindows, or any other Linux distribution.

1. Connect the X10 computer interface

If you have more than one serial port on your computer, connect the X10 controller to the first serial port on your computer. Of course, you can connect it to whichever serial port you want, but you'll be responsible for modifying the scripts in this project.

Plug the power cable of the computer interface directly into a wall socket, not into a power strip, surge protector, or UPS. The more devices between your X10 computer interface and the power lines in your house, the more likely the signals will be obscured. For more detailed directions, refer to the "Instructions for Windows" section earlier in this chapter.

2. Install Perl

Perl probably came installed with your Linux distribution; if it wasn't, you'll need to install it now. In Mandrake 9.1, open a terminal and execute the command `urpmi perl`. If you don't have urpmi installed, follow these steps to install the development packages from the default installation media:

1. Run `rpmdrake`.

2. Expand Development, and then select Development. You'll need the development tools to compile and/or install some of the tools needed for this project.

3. Click Install and respond to any other prompts that appear.

In Red Hat 9.2, follow these steps to install the development packages needed by this project:

1. Run `redhat-config-packages` and respond to any prompts that appear.

2. Within Development, select Development Tools.

3. Click Update. When prompted, click Continue, and respond to any other prompts that appear.

For more information on Perl, visit *http://www.perl.org*.

3. Install Perl modules

Perl doesn't include modules for communicating with the serial port or X10 devices, so you need to download and install modules for those two tasks before you can create the script. If you have the CPAN.pm module installed and configured (Mandrake has it by default, Red Hat does not), you can simply execute the following commands:

```
perl -MCPAN -e 'install Device::SerialPort'
perl -MCPAN -e 'ControlX10::CM11'
```

1. If you do not have CPAN.pm installed and configured, you'll need to manually install it. Download the Device::SerialPort module to any directory on your local computer. The module is available at *http://www.cpan.org/authors/id/B/BB/BBIRTH* and is named *Device-SerialPort-*.tar.gz*.

> You can find newer versions of these modules by digging through *http://www. misterhouse.net*; however, the versions at the given URL work fine.

2. Download the ControlX10::CM11 module from the same location. The module is named *ControlX10-CM11-*.tar.gz*.

3. Both the serial port and X10 modules have a *.tar.gz* file extension, and must be extracted before they can be installed. Open a terminal, change to the directory you saved the files in, and execute the following commands:

```
tar -xvzf Device-SerialPort*
tar -xvzf ControlX10*
```

4. Install the Device::SerialPort module. Use the same terminal and execute the following commands:

```
cd Device*
perl Makefile.PL
make
make test
make install
```

5. Install the ControlX10::CM11 module. Use the same terminal and execute the following commands:

```
cd ../ControlX10*
perl Makefile.PL
make
make test
make install
```

4. Establish communication

Now that everything you need is installed, it's time to test the connectivity. The ControlX10 modules include a script to test connectivity by turning the light with the address A1 on and off twice. Using the command prompt you used to install the ControlX10 module, execute the test script with the following command:

```
perl eg_cm11.plx
```

If everything is working properly, you may see messy output that resembles the following:

```
-------

CM11 error, not a valid function code: 1100 at byte 4 value 00011100
Sending A1 On OFF
Bad checksum in cm11 send: cs1=138 cs2=110. Will retry
Mutex destroy failure: Device or resource busy
-------
Sending A1 On OFF
```

Of course, if the output doesn't return any errors, that's okay as well. The next time you execute the command, the output should be cleaner. If you have a light configured with the A1 address, it will flash on and off, pause for two seconds, and then flash on and off again.

5. Create the script

You now have completely flexible and extensible control over your home's lighting. Unless you want to simply flash your lights on and off, though, your computer doesn't yet have the logic it needs to accomplish your original goal of controlling the porch light based on events triggered by the motion detector and the time of day.

To accomplish this, you'll now create a script to listen for signals from the motion detector, and send commands based on the current time of day. This script must be running continuously.

You'll use the eg_cm11.plx script from the previous step as the foundation for a script to turn off the porch light. Save the script from Exhibit B as ~/homehacks/x10-controls.pl, or download it from *http://www.homehacking.com*. For you hackers, the later section "Understanding the Script" explains how the script works.

There are many applications out there to make it easy to edit Perl scripts. kedit works well, and is included with KDE.

---

6. Run the script

To run the script, open a terminal window and call Perl using the name of the script:

```
perl ~/homehacks/x10-controls.pl
```

Assuming that Perl and the required modules have been installed correctly, the script will start running and continue until you press Ctrl+C. Nothing will happen until it receives a signal from one of the motion detectors or the system time changes to midnight. So, to make sure everything is working correctly, press the "House/On" button on one of your motion detectors. You should see output that resembles the following:

```
Porch motion detected.   Received: C9CJ.
Turning on: B1
Turning on: B3
```

Of course, the output will vary depending on the time of day. Also, now that you've triggered the motion detector, the script thinks that it's dusk because you configured the motion detector to send signals only when it's dark.

If things don't work as expected, try moving your X10 computer interface and the wireless transceiver to different electrical outlets. You could even try connecting them to outlets right next to each other.

Take a look and see if the porch light turned on. If it did, congrats! Press Ctrl+C to stop the script running so you can schedule it to run automatically in the background.

WARNING

Note that you can run only one such script at a time, because only one script can control the serial port on your computer.

---

7. Schedule the script

For your script to run, your computer must be running. At some point, however, you're going to need to turn off or at least reboot your system. You don't want to have to restart the script each time the computer restarts, so you should configure your script to run automatically at startup. To do this, execute the following commands in a terminal window:

```
su
echo perl /usr/<username>/homehacks/x10-controls.pl >> /etc/rc.d/
rc.local
```

This adds the Perl command to run your new script to the *rc.local* file, which Linux automatically executes at startup. Restart your system, and the script will automatically run and allow you automated control over your porch light. You're done!

Understanding the Script

Unless your needs match mine exactly, you'll probably end up modifying the script to make it do what you want. There's a lot of code in that script, but the most interesting lines appear within the infinitely running while loop and the two subroutines. Everything before the while loop initializes variables, modules, and the serial port. This section of code contains variables that you may need to modify if you have used different house or unit codes:

```
my $lights_hc = "B";
my $porch_light_unit = "1";
my $floodlight_unit = "2";
my $interior_light_unit = "3";
my $motion_hc = "C";
my $porch_motion_unit = "9";
```

If you were creating a script that would be used by many people, you could store that information in a separate file, or pass it to the script using command-line parameters. For a hack that only runs in your house, however, it's easiest to store the information directly in the script itself. Table 2-3 describes the meanings of the different variables used in the script.

Table 2-3. Variable meanings for the x10-controls.pl script

Variable	Description
$lights_hc	The house code for your lights.
$porch_light_unit, $floodlight_unit, $interior_light_unit	The unit codes for your lights.
$motion_hc	The house code for your motion detector and wireless transceiver.
$porch_motion_unit	The unit code for your motion detector.
$porch_motion_on	The four-byte command string that the motion detector sends when it detects motion. This is created using the previously defined variables; by default it is "C9CJ".
$porch_motion_off	The four-byte command string that the motion detector sends when it hasn't detected motion for the time-out period. By default it is "C9CK".
$dusk_detected, $dawn_detected	The four-byte command strings that the motion detector sends at dawn and dusk. By default these are "C10CJ" and "C10CK".
$dusk, $night	Boolean variables (or as close as you can get in Perl) used to keep track of whether it is dusk, night, or neither. The script assumes it's daytime when it's launched.
$porch_light_on, $floodlight_on, $interior_light_on	Boolean variables that track whether someone has manually turned on a light. This way, if someone turns on the interior light manually, the script won't turn it off automatically after the motion time-out period has expired. However, the script can make this distinction only if the light was turned on using an X10 command. In other words, if the light was turned on from the physical light switch, the script may still automatically turn it back off.
$data	Stores unprocessed X10 commands. When the script starts, it may find several commands stored in the X10 receiver's memory. This isn't a bad thing—it may give the script a clue that dusk has recently fallen, or that someone manually turned on a light before the script started.
$OS_win	A variable used to determine whether the script is running on a Windows or a Linux system. Windows systems load the Win32::SerialPort module, while Linux systems need Device:: SerialPort.
$serial_port	A reference to the serial port device that must be provided to the ControlX10 module when communicating with the X10 computer interface.

There's a lot of code between the variables and the while loop that you don't need to understand to modify the script or write your own script—just copy and paste it. This code was taken almost directly from the sample script included with the X10 module.

Within the while loop, the following lines act as a simple scheduler to determine if it's midnight:

```
# If it's midnight, turn the lights off
@now = localtime;
if (($now[2] == 0) && ($now[2] != $before[2])) {
    print "Turning porch lights off because it is midnight.\n";
    light_off($porch_light_unit);
    $dusk = 0;
    $night = 1;
}
@before = @now;
```

$now[2] contains the current hour, and $before[2] contains the hour it was during the previous iteration. Therefore, if you wanted to cause something to happen at 6 A.M. instead, you could use this clause:

```
if (($now[2] == 6) && ($now[2] != $before[2])) {
```

To add additional scheduled tasks, simply add additional if statements between the @now = localtime; and @before = @now; statements.

The following line gathers the data from the X10 controller:

```
$data = $data.ControlX10::CM11::receive_buffer($serial_port);
```

Notice that the data is appended to previous data that was received. X10 commands may take several seconds to be transmitted. As a result, the data must be captured and analyzed across several different iterations of the while loop. $data is used to hold partial X10 commands until a complete command with both an address and a command is found.

When detecting data, keep in mind that unrelated X10 data may have been transmitted at the same time as useful commands. The X10 controller may also receive garbage that should simply be ignored. For that reason, when checking to determine if a particular address and command were transmitted, check only to see if the command you are interested in is contained somewhere within the received data. The following if clause does this:

```
if ($data =~ $porch_motion_on)
```

As a result, if the $porch_motion_on string you're looking for is "B1BJ", and the X10 controller receives garbage along with the signal and provides your script with the data "L1B1BJ", the if statement will still evaluate to true. If you were to look for an exact match using this clause:

```
if ($data == $porch_motion_on)
```

then garbage, or commands the script wasn't looking for, would cause the script to miss legitimate signals.

Within each if statement, calls to the light_on and light_off subroutines do the interesting work. This subroutine takes a unit code as an argument. This command:

```
light_on($porch_light_unit);
```

could also be written as:

```
light_on("1");
```

The subroutines automatically add the correct house code for the lights.

At the end of the while loop, you'll see several instances of if statements such as this one:

```
if ( $data =~ ($lights_hc.$porch_light_unit.$lights_hc."J") ) {
    $porch_light_on = 1;
    $data = "";
}
```

These if statements detect someone else turning on a light using an X10 command, and record the state of the light to a variable. These variables are referenced when turning lights off automatically to ensure that the script does not override someone's decision to manually turn on the light.

To understand how X10 commands are sent, examine the lights_on subroutine:

```
sleep 1;
ControlX10::CM11::send($serial_port, $lights_hc.$_[0]);
ControlX10::CM11::send($serial_port, $lights_hc."J");
```

The first line forces the Perl script to pause. Although this is not absolutely necessary, it does improve the script's reliability by avoiding a collision between the signal received from the motion detector and the signal being transmitted. The second line sends an X10 address, such as "B2", through the X10 controller. When the device with address B2 sees this message, it knows that it needs to respond to any commands that follow; any device that does not have the address B2 will know to ignore them. The third line sends the actual command: "BJ", which means, "Turn on."

The $lights_hc variable contains the house code, and the . operator concatenates two strings. $_[0] represents the first argument passed to the function, which is the unit code of the device being turned on.

Wrapping Up

Armed with only an X10 switch, an X10 controller, a computer, and a Perl script, I have turned a conventional porch light into an intelligent porch light (Figure 2-7). I can still turn it on and off from the switch, but I rarely need to because my Perl script meets my needs perfectly.

Figure 2-7. It may look like any other porch light, but it's computer controlled.

You probably have a bunch of ideas about how you want your new light to behave, but before you go too crazy, just live with the intelligent light for a week or so. You'll then have a better sense of how you want to tweak the script or rearrange the setup to better suit the needs of your home. Some specific things to think about are:

- Does the light turn on when nothing is there, or not turn on when you need it? If so, you may need to move the motion detector.

- Does the dusk detection of the motion detector work as you hoped? If not, you might be better off turning the light on at a specific time of day. This would require you to modify only a couple lines of the script.

- Has your electrical bill changed as a result? If it's changed for the worse, you might want to tweak the behavior to reduce the time the light is on.

- Does the script run reliably? If it fails because your computer is often offline, you might need to run it on a dedicated computer. You can use really, really low-end computer hardware to run this script, and the software is entirely free if you use Linux, so the dedicated computer could actually end up costing less than the X10 parts!

To determine if the project was worthwhile, stop the script. Do the other people in your household miss it?

Extensions

This project shows you the potential of the X10 computer interface to enable extremely intelligent lighting. It's only the beginning, though. Here are a couple ideas of how to extend the project:

- Create a log of all motion detected, day or night.

- Set up a camera and take a snapshot or video of people who approach the house.

- Automatically ring the doorbell when someone approaches.

- Create different schedules for different days of the week.

Exhibit A: Bill of Materials

All parts are available from large hardware stores, or home automation web sites such as *http://www.smarthome.com.*

Item	Quantity	Approximate cost	Part number
Serial Powerlinc computer interface	1	$35 and up	CM11A
X10 wireless transceiver	1	$20 and up	4005X or 400s
X10 motion detector	1	$20 and up	MS14A-C or MS13A
X10 switch	1	$13 and up	2031

Exhibit B: Script Source Code

```perl
#!/usr/bin/perl
use lib './blib/lib','./lib';

# Configure user-modifiable codes. "hc" means "housecode"
my $lights_hc = "B";
my $porch_light_unit = "1";
my $floodlight_unit = "2";
my $interior_light_unit = "3";
my $motion_hc = "C";
my $porch_motion_unit = "9";

# These variables just increase readability
my $porch_motion_on = $motion_hc.$porch_motion_unit.$motion_hc."J";
my $porch_motion_off = $motion_hc.$porch_motion_unit.$motion_hc."K";
my $dusk_detected = $motion_hc.($porch_motion_unit + 1).$motion_hc."J";
my $dawn_detected = $motion_hc.($porch_motion_unit + 1).$motion_hc."K";

my (@before, @now, $dusk, $night, $porch_light_on);
my ($floodlight_on, $interior_light_on, $data);
my ($OS_win, $serial_port);

# Load the proper SerialPort module based on platform
BEGIN { $| = 1;
    $OS_win = ($^O eq "MSWin32") ? 1 : 0;
    if ($OS_win) {
        eval "use Win32::SerialPort";
        die "$@\n" if ($@);
        $serial_port = Win32::SerialPort->new ("COM1",1);

    }
    else {
        eval "use Device::SerialPort";
        die "$@\n" if ($@);
        $serial_port = Device::SerialPort->new ("/dev/ttyS0",1);
    }
}
die "Can't open serial port: $^E\n" unless ($serial_port);
$serial_port->error_msg(1);
$serial_port->user_msg(0);
$serial_port->databits(8);
```

```perl
$serial_port->baudrate(4800);
$serial_port->parity("none");
$serial_port->stopbits(1);
$serial_port->dtr_active(1);
$serial_port->handshake("none");
$serial_port->write_settings || die "Could not set up port\n";

use ControlX10::CM11;

while () {
    # If it's midnight, turn the lights off
    @now = localtime;
    if (($now[2] == 0) && ($now[2] != $before[2])) {
        print "Turning porch lights off because it is midnight.\n";
        light_off($porch_light_unit);
        $dusk = 0;
        $night = 1;
    }
    @before = @now;

    # Grab the data from the X10 controller
    $data = $data.ControlX10::CM11::receive_buffer($serial_port);

    # Motion detected on porch.
    # Turn on porch and interior light, and possibly floodlight
    if ($data =~ $porch_motion_on)     {
        print "Porch motion detected.  Received: $data.\n";
        $data = "";
        light_on($porch_light_unit);
        light_on($interior_light_unit);

        # It is between midnight and dawn, so turn on the
floodlights
        if ($night) {
            light_on($floodlight_unit);
        }
    }

    # Motion detector on porch timed out. Turn off lights if necessary
    if ($data =~ $porch_motion_off) {
        print "No porch motion detected.  Received: $data.\n";
        # Turn off floodlights
        if ( !$floodlight_on ) {
            light_off($floodlight_unit);
        }

        $data = "";
        # Turn off porch and interior lights if it's not dusk.
        if ( !$dusk && !$porch_light_on ) {
            light_off($porch_light_unit);
        }
        if ( !$interior_light_on ) {
            light_off($interior_light_unit);
        }
    }

    # Dusk was detected. Turn on porch lights.
    if ( $data =~ $dusk_detected )     {
        print "Dusk detected.  Received: $data.\n";
        $data = "";
```

```perl
                light_on($porch_light_unit);
                $dusk = 1;
        }

        # Dawn was detected. Turn off porch lights.
        if ( $data =~ $dusk_detected )     {
                print "Dawn detected.  Received: $data.\n";
                $data = "";
                light_off($porch_light_unit);
                $night = 0;
                $dusk = 0;
        }

        # If someone manually turns the controlled lights on or off, make
note of it
        if ( $data =~ ($lights_hc.$porch_light_unit.$lights_hc."J") ) {
                $porch_light_on = 1;
                $data = "";
        }
        if ( $data =~ ($lights_hc.$floodlight_unit.$lights_hc."J") ) {
                $floodlight_on = 1;
                $data = "";
        }
        if ( $data =~ ($lights_hc.$interior_light_unit.$lights_hc."J") ) {
                $interior_light_on = 1;
                $data = "";
        }
        if ( $data =~ ($lights_hc.$porch_light_unit.$lights_hc."K") ) {
                $porch_light_on = 0;
                $data = "";
        }
        if ( $data =~ ($lights_hc.$floodlight_unit.$lights_hc."K") ) {
                $floodlight_on = 0;
                $data = "";
        }
        if ( $data =~ ($lights_hc.$interior_light_unit.$lights_hc."K") ) {
                $interior_light_on = 0;
                $data = "";
        }
}

# Release   the serial port
$serial_port->close || die "\nProblem closing serial port\n";
undef $serial_port;

sub light_on {
    print "Turning on: ".$lights_hc.$_[0]."\n";
    sleep 1;
    ControlX10::CM11::send($serial_port, $lights_hc.$_[0]);
    ControlX10::CM11::send($serial_port, $lights_hc."J");
}

sub light_off {
    print "Turning off: ".$lights_hc.$_[0]."\n";
    sleep 1;
    ControlX10::CM11::send($serial_port, $lights_hc.$_[0]);
    ControlX10::CM11::send($serial_port, $lights_hc."K");
}
```

Exhibit C

Exhibit C: Software Versions

Description	Version
Operating System	Windows XP SP1 Mandrake 9.1 Red Hat 9.2
Perl	5.8.0
ControlX10::CM11	2.09
Win32::SerialPort	0.19
Device::SerialPort	0.22

Remotely Monitor a Pet

3

Cost

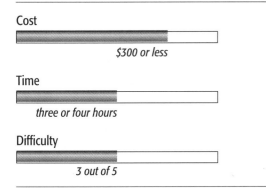

$300 or less

Time

three or four hours

Difficulty

3 out of 5

What You Need

- Three X10 lamp modules or wall switches

- Three indoor X10 motion detectors

- Three wireless cameras

- A wireless video receiver (compatible with wireless cameras)

- An X10 wireless transceiver

- X10 Powerlinc Serial Controller

- Eight AAA batteries

- A stable Internet connection that allows inbound connections (broadband helps)

- A computer running Linux

- A video capture card with composite video input

- Sticky poster adhesive

- A screwdriver

For a list of specific parts used in this project, refer to Exhibit A at the end of this chapter.

My wife, Erica, is an overprotective mother. We don't actually have any kids, though—just a cat. Sammy's not even the kind of cat that you really need to worry about; he's healthy, young, and built like a goat. But Erica still worries. Erica worries so much that we can't take an overnight trip without spending half the time wondering if the cat is okay.

Erica and I got married a couple of years ago and went on a honeymoon cruise. We hired a pet sitter to come and feed the cat on a daily basis, and to reassure Erica that everything was okay, I set up a cheap webcam and some motion detection software. It worked terribly.

Of course, it was still better than nothing—we were able to connect to the Internet from the very slow satellite link on the ship, and browse through a directory of webcam pictures to verify that Sammy was alive and that the pet sitter was feeding him. However, the motion detection software was very unreliable. The video from the webcam had so much noise that the motion detection software triggered almost constantly. It would even take pictures throughout the night, when there was total darkness and the camera couldn't capture an image. Worst of all, I actually *paid* for that software.

The camera was in the room with my computer, but the cat didn't spend much time in that room. So we had to look at hundreds of pictures to find a single one that actually had the cat in it. This was especially tedious because the webcam software just dropped the pictures into a folder. I used Windows 2000's Internet Information Server's directory-browsing capability to view the list of pictures from a browser, but this was slow because it didn't display thumbnails.

Clearly, it's time for something better. This time around, I'm going to set up a Sammy-monitoring system that can do the following things:

- Take pictures in three locations: the cat's food bowls, the cat's favorite window, and the cat's litter box.
- Take pictures only when there really is motion. No more false alarms.
- Turn lights on when necessary so the camera has adequate light to take a picture.
- Don't take pictures when it's too dark.
- Automatically process pictures to improve image quality.
- Allow me to browse thumbnails of the pictures from an Internet café.

And of course, it needs to be cheap. Figure 3-1 shows this project's conceptual architecture. As you can see, the pet triggers the motion detector, which sends a signal to your computer, which in turn will take a snapshot through the remote camera nearest the pet. Then, the picture will be timestamped and saved to a Web page, where you can view it anywhere in the world.

Project Overview

This project builds on the preceding projects by leveraging X10 switches, motion detectors, an X10 computer interface, and a custom Perl script. It also introduces several new components: wireless cameras, a video capture card, photo album software, and the Apache Web server software. Note that this project runs only on the Linux platform—just about any major Linux distribution should do fine.

Figure 3-1. The conceptual design is simple, but the execution will be complex.

OWNER WHO KNOWS
PET IS WELL WHILE AWAY

IMAGE RETRIEVAL

IMAGE CAPTURE

MOTION
DETECTOR

PET

With a little bit of effort, you could probably modify this project to run on a Windows system. The only component that I couldn't find was the Windows equivalent of the *webcam* tool that's part of XawTV. If you can find a command-line tool that saves a single picture file from your video capture card, you can make this project work in Windows.

The first step in this project is installing the hardware. If you want to be able to view pictures after the sun goes down, you'll need to install X10 light switches or modules to provide additional lighting for the cameras when a picture is going to be taken. An additional benefit of this is that it helps to simulate activity in the house—as your pet moves from camera to camera, the lights in different rooms will turn on, and your home will seem occupied (by more than a cat).

You'll then need to place three X10 cameras around your house. These wireless cameras transmit on the 2.4 GHz frequency, the same frequency used by 802.11b and 802.11g networks. The cameras don't seem to have any impact on the performance of my wireless network, though. Only one camera can transmit at a time, and fortunately, they are smart enough to turn themselves off when a different camera turns on. The cameras also turn off when there's no motion, so if they do interfere with your network, it will be only occasionally.

The three motion detectors will be installed in the rooms where the cameras are. When a motion detector is triggered, it will send an X10 signal that will be processed by three separate devices: the wireless camera in the same room, the light in the room, and the X10 computer interface (and the Perl script). This has the effect of changing the video feed into our video capture card to the active camera, turning on a light, and notifying our script that it's time to take a picture.

You'll need to connect your computer to the X10 network using a computer interface, as discussed in the "Connect the X10 computer interface" section of Chapter 2. If you don't already have one installed, you'll also need to add a video input card to your computer. Finally, you'll need to connect the X10 wireless video receiver to your video input card.

There will be some software to install, too. Hopefully, your Linux distribution will automatically detect your video capture card, but you'll need to install XawTV and the webcam component if they're not installed by default. You'll need Perl and a handful of modules for your script. And finally, to provide remote access to your pictures, you'll need to configure a web server (if you don't already have one) and a web-based photo album.

Beware of Humans

Of course, the traditional answer to pet monitoring is to get your neighbor to check up on your pets. But beware of human error—a good friend recently asked his neighbor to care for his pets while he was on vacation, and the neighbor *completely forgot*! My friend's dog and cat were severely malnourished when he returned from vacation.

Motion Detection

You want to take a picture only when your pet is active, so you need to know when your pet is moving and which room he is in. As you're probably well aware of by now, this feat can be easily accomplished using motion detectors.

For this project, you have two main considerations when choosing a motion detector: it needs to connect to your Linux computer (which is located in a different room) and it needs to be cheap. After looking around on the Web, I decided the best option was a wireless X10 motion detector. They cost only $20 each, they're wireless and battery powered, and a Linux computer can intercept their signals using a simple script.

1. Install X10 light switches or lamp modules

The webcams you'll be using in the Image Capture phase of this project can't see in the dark. In fact, they produce terrible pictures in anything less than bright sunlight. So, if you want to capture pictures of your pet moving around in the evening or in a room without bright natural light, you'll need to add some X10-enabled lighting.

If you've already replaced all the light switches in your house with X10 light switches, or if you're using night-vision cameras, you can skip to the next step. If not, and you want to capture pictures 24 hours a day, you'll need to replace the light switches in the relevant rooms with X10-enabled switches. For detailed instructions, refer to the "Replace the switch" section of Chapter 1.

You need all the lighting you can get. A desk lamp that can be pointed downward at the location where your pet will be is a great way to ensure that your pictures turn out well. If there's not enough light, the Perl script you'll create in the Image Capture phase will attempt to brighten the picture.

If you don't have built-in lighting in the room where you plan to put the camera, or if you just want to avoid wiring, you can use X10 lamp modules. To configure a lamp module, follow these steps:

1. Set the house code of the lamp module to C.

2. Set the unit code of the lamp module to 2, 3, or 4. Make note of the unit code you use in each room.

We're using 2, 3, and 4 because the wireless transceiver has the unit code of 1. While this doesn't stop you from using that address for other things, it will audibly click on and off each time a signal is sent to that unit code.

---

3. Plug the lamp you wish to control into the lamp module.

4. Position the lamp so that it casts light onto the area where your pet will likely be. The more light you can get on the pet, the better the pictures will turn out.

5. Plug the lamp module into the wall.

2. Install the wireless transceiver

The motion detectors used in this project are wireless, so you won't be forced to place them in less-than-ideal locations just to be near a power outlet. The wireless transceiver receives signals from the motion detector and relays them across the wired X10 network. For detailed instructions on configuring wireless transceivers, refer to "Connect the wireless transceiver" in Chapter 1.

3. Configure and install the motion detectors

Many motion detectors include the option to operate only in darkness; if your motion detector has this feature, be sure to configure it to operate at all times, regardless of the ambient light level. If you are using the X10 wireless motion detectors, follow these steps to configure them:

1. Press the Unit button once. The red light will flash.

2. Press and hold the House button. The green light will turn on. After about three seconds, the motion detector will report its dusk/dawn setting as follows:

   - The red light will blink once if the motion detector is set to detect motion at both day and night.

   - The red light will blink twice if it detects motion only when it's dark.

3. Release the House button. If the red light blinked twice, change the setting by holding the House button for three seconds until the red light blinks again. The red light will then report the new setting with one blink.

For instructions on configuring the house and unit codes of your motion detectors, refer to "Install and configure the motion detector" in Chapter 2. As always, you can configure any house and unit codes you like; however, the script in the Image Capture phase of this project uses a house code of C and a unit code of 2, 3, or 4 to match the unit codes of the cameras and lights.

You need to install one motion detector in each room that will have a camera. Since the motion detectors are wireless, you have much more flexibility when placing them than you will when placing the cameras. Follow

Figure 3-2. Carefully positioning the motion detector greatly reduces the number of false alarms.

Figure 3-3. Poster adhesive is an easy way to secure your motion detectors.

these guidelines when positioning the motion detectors:

- Place the motion detector so that it will be as close to your pet as possible. Figure 3-2 shows how I positioned a motion detector in the window frame of my cat's favorite window.

- Point the motion detector toward a wall. You want to avoid triggering it when you're walking past (even if just while getting ready for your trip), so do your best to isolate the small area where your pet is likely to be.

- Position the motion detector in an out-of-the-way location so that it isn't accidentally knocked over.

Rest the motion detector on a flat surface and secure it with poster adhesive. This is especially important if you have a cat, as cats like to bat at things. The adhesive works best if you stick small pieces in each corner of the back of the motion detector, as shown in Figure 3-3.

The motion detectors have a wider angle of view than the cameras, so if you find yourself getting a lot of false alarms, it may be that the motion detector is seeing movement outside the range of the camera. You can reduce the motion detector's range of view by covering part of the lens with opaque tape.

Image Capture

In this phase, you will configure the image-capture and archiving mechanism. This is the most complex phase of the project, and involves configuring wireless video cameras, a Perl script, and a handful of supporting tools.

1. Install the video capture card

Unlike traditional webcams, the wireless video cameras you'll be using for this project do not connect to your computer's USB port. They're actually intended to connect to a TV or VCR, so you'll need to add an old-timey analog video input interface to your computer. Fortunately, these are cheap and well supported by Linux. After all, lots of people use video capture cards to record TV shows, so quite a bit of energy has gone into making sure the software works well.

The wireless receiver has a composite connection, so make sure the card you choose supports that. I used the Hauppauge WinTV-GO-FM card just because I happened to have it lying around. This card uses the BT878 chipset, which is well supported by Linux; any card with that chipset should work equally well. There's no need to get an expensive video capture card, as it's not going to improve the performance or quality of your pet monitor, and you don't need sound support because the wireless cameras don't have microphones. Bottom line: don't spend more than $50 on your video capture card.

Once you've got your card, install it according to the manufacturer's instructions. Generally, this is as simple as turning off your computer, opening the computer case, and inserting the card into an empty PCI slot. Once Linux starts, install the drivers for the card. For more detailed instructions, refer to "Install the TV tuner card" in Chapter 7.

2. Install the wireless cameras

You're now ready to install the three cameras around your house. When positioning the cameras, follow these guidelines:

- Position the camera as close as possible to the place where your pet will be.

- Position the camera out of the way so that it doesn't get knocked over.

- Position the camera as low to the ground as possible. This will reduce the likelihood that it will take a picture of you as you're walking around the house. Even if you only intend to leave the system online while you're out of the house, you may find that you prefer to leave it on at all times to save yourself the trouble of setting it up before you travel.

- If possible, hide the camera in a bookshelf or below a cabinet.

- Though the cameras include screws to be permanently mounted, attach them temporarily with sticky stuff until you determine the optimal location.

- Point the antennae at your computer where the wireless video receiver will be.

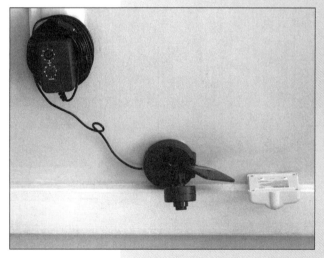

Figure 3-4. Careful camera positioning dramatically reduces the likelihood of publishing incriminating pictures of yourself.

One setup that I found to be particularly effective was to position the motion detector and camera on a chair rail, pointing directly down at the cat's automatic feeder (Figure 3-4). This reduces the number of false alarms triggered by people walking past.

Follow these steps to configure your wireless cameras:

1. Set the house code of the power adapter to C.

2. Set the unit code of the power adapter to 2, 3, or 4. (Make sure this unit code matches the one you used for the light in this room.)

3. Plug the wireless camera's power cord into the power adapter.

4. Position the camera, using poster adhesive to hold it in place. You'll probably end up moving the camera after you use it for a few days, so don't do anything too permanent.

5. Secure the power cord to the wall with tape.

6. Plug the camera into the wall.

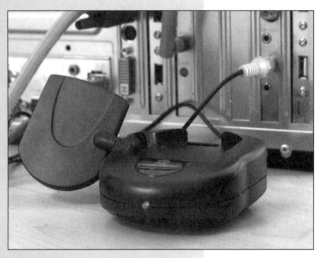

Figure 3-5. The antennae on my wireless receiver points down because my office is on the second floor.

3. Install the wireless video receiver

The wireless video receiver connects your computer to the wireless cameras using your video input card. You need to use the receiver that came with the wireless camera—if there's another kind that works, I'm not aware of it. Use the following guidelines when positioning the video receiver:

- Take advantage of the length of the composite cord, and position the receiver away from your computer.

- Point the antennae towards the cameras. Figure 3-5 shows how I positioned the antennae to receive signals from cameras on the lower floors.

- If you have cameras positioned all around the house, try pointing the antennae straight up.

Of course, there's only so much tweaking of the placement you can do before you get the software configured. After the software is set up, you can use XawTV to fine-tune the antennae placement.

4. Connect the X10 computer interface

If you haven't yet connected your X10 computer interface, connect it now. If you have more than one serial port on your computer, connect the X10 controller to the first one. Of course, you can connect it to whichever serial port you like, but you'll then need to modify the Perl script to communicate with the correct port.

Plug the power cable of the computer interface directly into a wall socket—do not plug it into a power strip or surge protector, and definitely don't plug it into a UPS. The more devices between your X10 computer interface and the power lines in your house, the more likely it is that the signals will be obscured.

5. Install core software

You've now got working cameras—you just need a script to pull them together. There are a couple of different ways you can create this script. The whole thing could be done with shell scripting, thanks to the excellent WISH project at Sourceforge (see *http://wish.sourceforge.net*). However, I chose to implement the script using Perl and the ControlX10::CM11 module primarily because Perl can run on a Windows system, and while the project is Linux-only, the script could easily be ported to a Windows environment.

Your Linux distribution probably comes with most of the software you need for this project. The procedures in this section show you how to install the software you need from your distribution CDs. The following instructions cover installing the correct packages for Mandrake 9.1 and Red Hat 9.2. Of course, by the time you read this, these versions will likely be outdated; if you're using a different version or a different distribution entirely, the version numbers of the packages may be different. Still, you should be able to find these packages fairly easily. If your distribution doesn't include these packages (it almost certainly has Perl), you can find the software you need at the following web sites:

- Perl: *http://www.perl.org*
- XawTV: *http://bytesex.org/xawtv/*
- ImageMagick and PerlMagick: *http://www.imagemagick.org*

In Mandrake 9.1, follow these steps to install the packages needed by this project:

1. Run *rpmdrake*.

2. Expand Development, and then select Development. You'll need the development tools to compile and/or install some of the tools needed for this project.

3. Select the "All packages, alphabetical" radio button. Then scroll down and select every package that starts with "xawtv".

4. Click Install and respond to any other prompts that appear.

In Red Hat 9.2, follow these steps:

1. Run *redhat-config-packages* and respond to any prompts that appear.

2. Within Applications, select Sound and Video. Click Details, expand Extra Packages, and select "xawtv" if it's not already selected.

3. Click Close to return to Add or Remove Packages.

4. Within Development, select Development Tools.

5. Click Update. When prompted, click Continue, and respond to any other prompts that appear.

6. Install Perl and X10 modules

Perl was almost certainly installed with your Linux distribution; if it wasn't, you can download and install it from *http://www.perl.org.* You'll probably also need to install some modules: the pet monitoring script needs to communicate with the serial port and X10 devices, and Image Display System (IDS), a Perl-based web photo album that we'll use to display the pictures in the Image Retrieval phase, also requires a couple of modules for working with pictures. Perl doesn't usually include these modules by default, so you'll need to download and install them before you can create the script.

1. Download the Device::SerialPort module to your home directory. The module is available at *http://search.cpan.org/~bbirth/* and is named *Device-SerialPort-*.tar.gz.*

You can find newer versions of these modules by digging through *http://www.misterhouse.net*; however, the versions at the given URL work fine.

---

2. Download the ControlX10::CM11 module from the same location. The module is named *ControlX10-CM11-*.tar.gz.*

3. Download the latest version of ImageMagick from one of the sources listed at *http://imagemagick.sourceforge.net/www/archives.html.* The file will be named *ImageMagick-*.tar.gz.* ImageMagick includes PerlMagick, which is the Image::Magick module required by IDS.

4. Download the Image::Info module from *http://search.cpan.org/~gaas/Image-Info/.* Click the Download link and save it in your home directory.

5. Download the CGI::Carp module from *http://search.cpan.org/~lds/CGI.pm/.* Click the Download link and save it in your home directory.

6. All these modules have a *.tar.gz* file extension and must be extracted before they can be installed. Open a terminal, change to your home directory, and execute the following commands:

```
su
tar -xvzf Device-SerialPort*
tar -xvzf ControlX10*
tar -xvzf Image-Info*
tar -xvzf ImageMagick*
tar -xvzf CGI*
```

7. Install the Device::SerialPort module by executing the following commands:

```
cd Device*
perl Makefile.PL
```

```
make
make test
make install
```

8. Install the ControlX10::CM11 module by executing the following commands:

```
cd ../ControlX10*
perl Makefile.PL
make
make test
make install
```

9. Install the Image::Info module by executing the following commands:

```
cd ../Image-Info*
perl Makefile.PL
make
make test
make install
```

10. Install the CGI::Carp module by executing the following commands:

```
cd ../CGI*
perl Makefile.PL
make
make test
make install
```

11. Install ImageMagick and the Image::Magick module. This will take a few minutes. Execute the following commands:

```
cd ../ImageMagick*/
./configure
make
make install
cd PerlMagick
perl Makefile.PL
make
make test
make install
```

7. Configure webcam

You now need to download a tool from the XawTV project. The *webcam* tool takes a snapshot from a video capture card and saves it as a JPEG file. Most people use *webcam* to upload pictures to an FTP server on a regular basis, but since you're configuring your own web server, you just need it to save each snapshot to the local computer and then stop running.

webcam is included with some distributions, but has disappeared from Mandrake 10.0. Just to be safe, start at *http://bytesex.org/xawtv/*, and download the latest version of XawTV to your home directory. Open a terminal, change to your home directory, and execute the following commands:

```
su
tar -xvzf xawtv*
cd xawtv*
./configure
```

```
make
make install
```

webcam needs to know which video input card to use (if you have more than one), and the format in which the wireless video receiver is providing input. It gathers this information from a text configuration file. The Perl script will provide *webcam* the path to this file, so you just need to create it. So, su to root and save the following information to a text file named */etc/petcam.config* in your home directory.

```
[grab]
device = /dev/video0
text = .
width = 640
height = 480
input = composite1
norm = ntsc
quality = 90
once = 1

[ftp]
dir  = /var/www/cgi-bin/ids/albums
local = 1
```

The above settings are probably the only ones you need to define; for a complete list of settings, execute the command info webcam. You'll be creating a custom Perl script to call the *webcam* tool, so you have the option of using different config files for different cameras. This would allow you, for example, to automatically rotate images from a camera you positioned on its side or upside-down.

Make sure everything is working by triggering one of the motion detectors. Then execute the following commands from your home directory:

```
mkdir /var/www/cgi-bin/ids/albums
su
webcam /etc/petcam.config
```

This should create a file named *webcam.jpeg* in what will be your root IDS directory (*/var/www/cgi-bin/ids/albums/*) and then stop running. Open the path */var/www/cgi-bin/ids/albums/webcam.jpeg* with your favorite browser, and you should see a picture of the video currently being received by your video capture card (Figure 3-6).

Trigger each of the motion detectors to make sure that the cameras are switching correctly, that the lights are turning on, and that the script is detecting motion. Then, point your browser at *file:///var/www/cgi-bin/ids/albums/*, and you should see a new photo directory with today's date.

Figure 3-6. The webcam tool creates a still image from the live video feed.

If it doesn't work right or if your picture is black, launch xawtv from the keyboard of your computer, and right-click it to configure it for the composite1 interface and ntsc video input. If you still don't see any picture, you may have one of the following problems:

- The XawTV configuration settings need adjusting. If you can fix the problem this way, update the *petcam.config* file with similar settings.

- Your wireless receiver isn't connected properly to your video capture card.

- Your cameras aren't communicating with the wireless receiver. Start by plugging in a camera in the same room as the wireless receiver. If this works, move the camera to another room and tweak the antennae on the camera and receiver until reception is improved.

- Your video capture card isn't configured correctly. Verify that the driver is installed and communicating properly with the card. If *webcam* outputs something along the lines of "open /dev/video0: No such device," the driver is probably the problem.

8. Create the script

You'll now create a script to listen for signals from the motion detector and grab a picture from the video capture card. This script will save the picture in the directory of the IDS album, which you'll install in the Image Retrieval phase. You'll likely end up capturing quite a few pictures throughout the course of a day (even if you have a lazy cat like I have), so you'll want to save each day's pictures in a unique folder. This script must be running continuously in the background.

Many applications make it easy to edit Perl scripts: kwrite, gedit, and emacs all work well.

Save the following script as *~/homehacking/pet-monitor.pl*. You can also download the script, along with any updates I've made, from *http://www. homehacking.com*.

```perl
#!/usr/bin/perl
use lib './blib/lib','./lib';
use Device::SerialPort;
use ControlX10::CM11;
use Image::Magick;
use strict;

my $motion_hc = "C";
my @motion_ucs = ("2", "3", "4");
my $album_path = '/var/www/cgi-bin/ids/albums';
my $webcam_config = '/etc/petcam.config';
my $serial_port = Device::SerialPort->new("/dev/ttyS0",1);

my $min_bright = 0.07;# Minimum brightness acceptable
my $min_color = 0.15; # Minimum brightness before forcing B&W
```

```perl
my $min_raw = 0.25;          # Minimum brightness to not equalize
my $apix = 200;              # Number of pixels to analyze (squared)
my $crop = 10;               # Number of pixels to crop off each side

my $motion_on = $motion_hc."J";
my ($data, $newpic, $dest_path, @now, @before, $unit, $image);
my ($grayimage, $x, $y, $bright, $w, $h, $wp, $bp, $px);

die "Can\'t open serial port: $^E\n" unless ($serial_port);

$serial_port->error_msg(1); # use built-in error messages
$serial_port->user_msg(0);
$serial_port->databits(8);
$serial_port->baudrate(4800);
$serial_port->parity("none");
$serial_port->stopbits(1);
$serial_port->dtr_active(1);
$serial_port->handshake("none");
$serial_port->write_settings || die "Could not set up port\n";

while ()
{
    # If the date changed, make a new folder
    @now = localtime;
    if ((($now[3] != $before[3])) || !$dest_path) {
        $dest_path = sprintf "%s/%04u-%02u-%02u", $album_path,
$now[5]+1900, $now[4]+1, $now[3];
        print "Creating a new folder: $dest_path\n";
     print `mkdir $dest_path\n`;
    }
    @before = @now;

    $data = $data.ControlX10::CM11::receive_buffer($serial_port);
    if (!$data) {
    sleep 1; # Let the processor rest if nothing has been detected
        next;
    }

    foreach $unit(@motion_ucs) {
        if ($data =~ "$motion_hc$unit$motion_on") {
            sleep 1; # Give the camera a moment to adjust
            print `webcam $webcam_config\n`; # Create image
            $image = new Image::Magick;
            $image->Read("$album_path/webcam.jpeg"); # Import image
            ($w, $h) = $image->Get('width', 'height');

            # Determine brightness of a crop of the center of the image
            $grayimage = $image->Clone(); # Create a temporary copy of
the image
            $grayimage->Crop(geometry=>($apix.'x'.$apix.'+'.($w/2-
$apix/2).'+'.($h/2-$apix/2)));

            # May need to change "$grayimage->Get('depth')" to "16"
            $grayimage->Quantize(colorspace=>'gray');
             $bp = (2 ** $grayimage->Get('depth'));

            for ($y = 0; $y < $apix; $y++) {
                for ($x = 0; $x < $apix; $x++) {
                  $px = 0 + $grayimage->Get("pixel[$x,$y]");
                    $bright += $px;
```

```
                    $wp = $px if ( $px > $wp );
                    $bp = $px if ( $px < $bp );
                }
            }
            # Determine a value for 100% brightness
            # May need to change "$grayimage->Get('depth')" to "16"
            $bright /= $apix * $apix * (2 ** $grayimage->Get('depth'));

            print "\nImage brightness: $bright\n\n";
            if ( $bright > $min_bright ) { # If the image is dark,
don't bother saving it
                # Crop out noisy edges
                $image->Crop(geometry=>($w-$crop*2).'x'.($h-$crop*2).'+
$crop+$crop');

                # Convert to BW if it's dark
                $image->Quantize(colorspace=>'gray') if ( $bright <
$min_color );

                # Equalize it if it's dim
                if ( $bright < $min_raw ) {
                    $image->Level(($bp*1.05).'/'.(1-$bright).'/
'.($wp*0.95));
                }

                # Save the image
                $newpic = sprintf "%02u%02u%02u-%s.jpg", $now[2],
$now[1], $now[0], $unit;
                print "Saving picture as: $dest_path/$newpic\n";
                $image->Write(filename=>"$dest_path/
$newpic",quality=>80);
            }
            eval "undef $_" for qw/$image $grayimage $bright $wp/;
            $data = "";
        }
    }
}

$serial_port->close || die "\nclose problem with serial port\n";
undef $serial_port;
```

9. Run the script

To run the script, open a terminal window and call Perl using the name of
the script:

```
perl ~/homehacking/pet-monitor.pl
```

You can run only one such script at a time, as only one script can control the serial
port on your computer.

Assuming that Perl and the required modules have been installed correctly,
the script will start running and continue until you press Ctrl+C. Nothing
will happen until it receives a signal from one of the motion detectors (when
the script captures a picture), or the system time changes to midnight

---

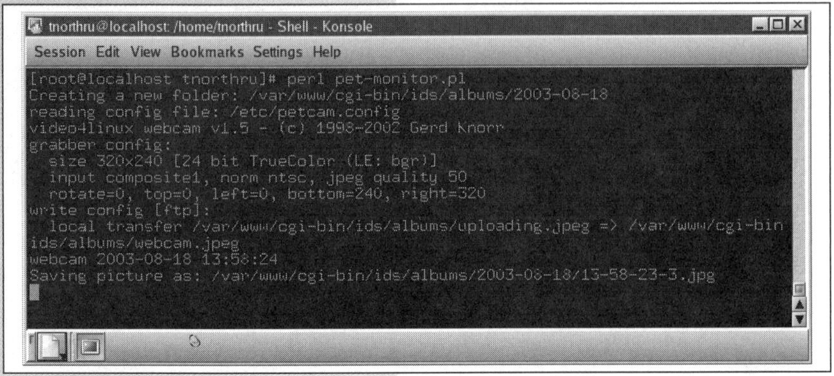

Figure 3-7. The output from the script lets you know that it's working.

(when the script creates a new folder). So, to make sure everything is working correctly, grab one of your motion detectors and press the "House/On" button. You should see output that resembles the screenshot shown in Figure 3-7.

You'll probably see the script take a picture immediately because you triggered the motion detector since connecting the X10 computer interface. The X10 computer interface keeps the last few messages in a queue.

> If things don't work as expected, try moving your X10 computer interface and the wireless transceiver to different electrical outlets. You might even try connecting them to outlets right next to each other.

10. Schedule the script

Your script relies on your computer running. You don't want to have to remember to restart the script each time the computer restarts, so you should configure your script to run automatically at startup. To do this, execute the following commands:

```
su
echo perl /home/username/homehacking/pet-monitor.pl >> /etc/rc.d/
rc.local
```

This adds the Perl command to run your new script to the *rc.local* file, which Linux automatically executes at startup. Restart your system, and the script will automatically run and snap pictures when your pet moves. You're done!

> If you discover that the script doesn't work when started automatically, you may need to grant additional rights to the */var/www/cgi-bin/ids/* directory and its subdirectories. To do this, su to root, and then run the command chmod 666 /var/www/cgi-bin/ids.

Understanding the Script

Unlike in some of the other projects, the script in this project will work for most people without any modification. However, you could extend it a great deal if you wanted to, so I'll describe what the different sections of code do and what the variables are. There's a lot of code in this script, but the most interesting lines appear within the infinitely running `while` loop and the subroutines. Everything before the `while` loop initializes variables, modules, and the serial port. This section of code contains variables that you may wish to modify if you have used different house or unit codes:

```perl
my $motion_hc = "C";
my @motion_ucs = ("2", "3", "4");
my $album_path = '/var/www/cgi-bin/ids/albums';
my $webcam_config = '/etc/petcam.config';
my $serial_port = Device::SerialPort->new("/dev/ttyS0",1);

my $min_bright = 0.07;      # Minimum brightness acceptable
my $min_color = 0.15;       # Minimum brightness before forcing B&W
my $min_raw = 0.25;         # Minimum brightness to not equalize
my $apix = 200;             # Number of pixels to analyze (squared)
my $crop = 10;              # Number of pixels to crop off each side
```

If you were creating a script that would be used by many people, you could store that information in a separate file or pass it to the script using command-line parameters. For a hack that runs only in your house, however, it's easiest to store that information directly in the script itself. Table 3-1 describes the meanings of the different variables used in the script.

Table 3-1. Variable descriptions for the pet-monitor.pl script

Variable	Description
$motion_hc	The house code for your motion detectors, wireless transceiver, wireless cameras, and lights.
@motion_ucs	The unit codes for your motion detectors, wireless transceiver, wireless cameras, and lights.
$album_path	The path to your album's IDS directory.
$webcam_config	The path to the configuration file that the *webcam* tool requires. This will be passed as a parameter to *webcam*.
$serial_port	A reference to the serial port device that must be provided to the ControlX10 module when communicating with the X10 computer interface.
$min_bright	The minimum image brightness that the script will accept. Anything below this threshold will probably be too dark to see anything. Possible values are between 0 and 1; a value of 0 will save all images. If you find that the script is reporting values greater than 1, change this value to 7.
$min_color	The minimum image brightness (between 0 and 1) that the script will save as a color picture. Anything below this threshold will be saved as black and white. The wireless cameras have a great deal of noise at low light levels, which is especially apparent after equalization. Desaturating the picture makes the image a bit clearer, though at these levels the image will still appear very grainy.

Variable	Description
$min_raw	Any pictures with a brightness below this level (between 0 and 1) will be processed with ImageMagick's Equalize function. This maximizes the contrast of all three color channels in the picture, which brightens dark images and serves to correct the color cast caused by artificial lights. If you prefer to have the Equalize function used on all images, increase this value to 1.
$apix	By default, the brightness of each picture is determined from a 200×200 square in the middle of the image. Change the $apix value to adjust the size of this square. Only the center of the picture is analyzed because noise tends to be more apparent at the top or bottom of the image, and the script assumes the camera is centered on the subject.
$crop	The number of pixels to crop from the top, bottom, and sides of the picture. The edges of the picture tend to be black or have excessive noise. Set this value to 0 to save the entire picture.
$data	This variable stores unprocessed X10 commands. When the script starts, it may find several commands stored in the X10 receiver's memory. This isn't a bad thing—it may give the script a clue that dusk has recently fallen, or that someone manually turned on a light before the script started.
$motion_on	The two-byte command string that the motion detector sends when it detects motion. By default it is "CJ".
$newpic	The filename of the picture being saved. You can change how this is determined, but each picture must have a unique filename.
$dest_path	The folder currently used to store pictures. This changes once per day.
$bright	The brightness of the picture. 0 is a completely black picture; 1 is a completely white picture.
$wp	The white point of the picture. This is the brightness of the brightest pixel in the 200×200 crop of the center of the picture. This variable is used only if you later apply the Image::Magick Level function to adjust the contrast of the image.
$bp	The black point of the picture. This is the brightness of the darkest pixel in the 200×200 crop of the center of the picture.

There's lots of code between the variables and the while loop that you don't need to understand to modify or write the script—just copy and paste it. If you need to run the script on a Windows box, refer to Chapter 2.

Within the while loop, the following lines act as a simple scheduler to determine when the date changes and create a new directory. It also initially establishes $dest_path if it hasn't yet been defined. The current year, month, and date are used as the name of the directory to make sorting more straightforward. $now[3] contains the current date, and $before[3] contains the date of the previous iteration. IDS automatically detects that the new directory has been created, and shows it as a new photo album.

```
@now = localtime;
if ((($now[3] != $before[3])) || !$dest_path) {
    $dest_path = sprintf "%s/%04u-%02u-%02u", $album_path,
$now[5]+1900, $now[4]+1, $now[3];
    print "Creating a new folder: $dest_path\n";
    print `mkdir $dest_path\n`;
}
@before = @now;
```

If you wanted to cause something to happen at 6 A.M., for example, you could use this clause:

```
if (($now[2] == 6) && ($now[2] != $before[2])) {
```

To add additional scheduled tasks, simply add additional `if` statements between the `@now = localtime;` and the `@before = @now;` statements.

The following line gathers the data from the X10 controller:

```
$data = $data.ControlX10::CM11::receive_buffer($serial_port);
```

Notice that the data is appended to previously received data. X10 commands may take several seconds to be transmitted, and as a result, the data must be captured and analyzed across several different iterations of the `while` loop. The `$data` variable is used to hold partial X10 commands until a complete command with both an address and a command is found.

When detecting data, keep in mind that unrelated X10 data may have been transmitted at the same time as useful commands; the X10 controller may also have received garbage that should simply be ignored. Therefore, when checking to determine if a particular address and command were transmitted, only check to see if the command you are interested in is contained somewhere within the received data. The following `if` clause does this:

```
if ($data =~ "$motion_hc$unit$motion_on")
```

That is, if the `$motion_hc$unit$motion_on` string we're looking for is "C2CJ", and the X10 controller receives garbage along with the signal and provides our script with the data "L1C2BJ", the `if` statement will still evaluate to true. On the other hand, if you were to look for an exact match using this clause:

```
if ($data == "$motion_hc$unit$motion_on")
```

then garbage, or commands the script wasn't looking for, would cause the script not to detect a valid command.

The `foreach` loop iterates through each of the camera unit codes you've defined in the `@motion_ucs` array. If an "on" command is contained within the `$data` variable for a particular camera, the `snap_photo` subroutine is called and the `$data` variable is cleared to make sure the same command isn't detected twice.

> Because a `foreach` loop is used, adding an additional camera is as easy as adding an extra unit code to the `@motion_ucs` array, such as `my @motion_ucs = ("1", "2", "3", "4");`.

Within the foreach loop, the script waits before taking the next picture to give the wireless camera a moment to warm up. Then, the script calls the *webcam* tool to create a snapshot.

The script then uses the Image::Magick module to read the picture, analyze the brightness, adjust the levels if necessary, and then output the picture to the correct folder. Adjusting the levels of the picture dramatically improves the quality of pictures taken in low light. You could certainly reduce the size and quality of the picture before saving it to improve performance when viewing the pictures remotely; however, IDS does a great job of doing this on the fly, so you might as well save it with whatever (generally mediocre) quality the cameras can produce.

> Image::Magick can do many different things to improve image quality, so check out the docs at *http://www.imagemagick.org/www/perl.html*.

If you find that the script is reporting an image brightness of greater than 1, it's probably because Image::Magick is reporting an image depth lower than the image's actual bit depth. After upgrading to a new version of the libraries, I discovered that it was reporting an 8-bit image depth, but the image was actually 16 bits. To fix the problem (an ugly fix, admittedly), I replaced both instances of `$grayimage->Get('depth')` in the script with `16`—the actual number of bits per pixel in the image. I'm guessing this is a bug, because another user has complained of the same problem. Hopefully, it'll be fixed by the time this is published, so I'll leave the original code in place.

The script uses the current time and the camera number to create the filename. The format is *hhmmss-#.jpg*, where # is the camera number. The hours are in 24-hour format.

Image Retrieval

The last phase of this project will enable you to retrieve your pictures from across the Internet. You will set up a web server on your computer, configure your software and hardware firewalls to forward web traffic, and finally install IDS.

1. Install Apache

Many of the projects in this book rely on being able to remotely access your computer. For example, in order to monitor your home security system while on vacation, you'll need to be able to pull up a web browser at an Internet café and connect to your home computer. Connecting your home system to the Internet has a lot of potential: you could fire up your air conditioning if you're coming home early from work; you could listen to your home music collection over the Internet; or you could even schedule a show to record from your desk at work if you forget to set the VCR.

> You don't even need a broadband connection to do this; you can do it over dial-up. It'll just be a bit slower.

To enable this, you need to harden your system and then install and configure web server software. If you're an Internet geek, you probably already know how to do this. If you're some other type of geek, though, you may need some guidance. This section will teach you the basics of self-hosting a web server, including understanding DNS, dynamic IP addressing, and security. As in previous chapters, all the software and services are free, so you won't have to spend a dime!

1. Harden your system

Large-scale attacks on Linux web servers are not as common as those on Windows web servers, but there are still a few widespread worms that will infect an unpatched Linux web server connected to the Internet. And of course, your computer isn't even safe if it's *not* a server—worms and viruses infect client-only PCs all the time. Nonetheless, before you set your system up as a server, you should mentally acknowledge that you're increasing your vulnerability. That said, I'll do my best to make sure you connect your system to the Internet safely.

> In fact, chances are good that when you've completed this project, your computer will be more secure than it is right now.

The first step is to update your distribution with the latest patches. Many vendors provide a graphical tool to make this easier. In Red Hat, this is *up2date*; in Mandrake, it's */usr/sbin/ MandrakeUpdate* (see Figure 3-8). Let the tool scan your system, and apply all the security updates.

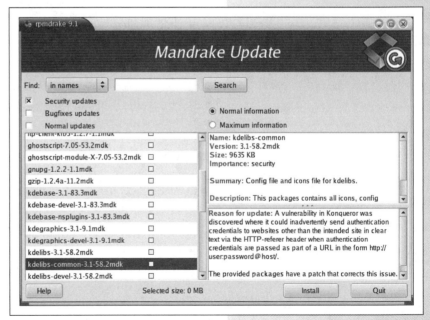

Figure 3-8. Install security updates before you set up your computer as a server.

Chapter 3, Remotely Monitor a Pet

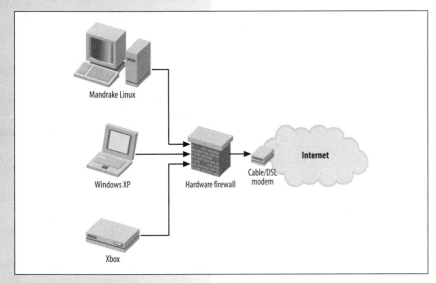

Figure 3-9. A hardware firewall, or even a router with filtering capabilities, can do a lot to improve your security.

If you don't have a router with packet filtering capabilities yet, set one up between your internal network and the public Internet, as shown in Figure 3-9. By default, routers with firewall capabilities block all incoming traffic and allow all outbound connections. Even if you've secured your PC's software, a filtering router is important because it protects your computer while you're in the process of setting it up. The simplest of these devices cost less than $100, and they're well worth the investment. Not only do they filter traffic without relying on your software's security, but they often include a switch to network multiple computers, and may even act as a print server.

I use a Linksys cable/DSL router, but several other vendors, such as the ones below, offer similar products.

- Linksys Routers (*http://www.linksys.com/Products/*)

- Netgear Routers (*http://www.netgear.com/products/details/FR114P.php*)

- SMC Routers (*http://www.smc.com/index.cfm?sec=Products&pg=Product-List&cat=4&site=c*)

Next, set up a software firewall (also known as a personal firewall or a host-based firewall). While having two firewalls may seem redundant, it's really not. Relying on firewalls only at the perimeter doesn't protect you from dangers that lie inside your own network—many, many networks have been infected by worms that have snuck past the firewall on a single computer. If you have a laptop, software firewalls are even more important, because your system could be attacked when you're traveling.

Linux has a very nice firewall built in, and most distributions give you the option of setting it up to drop all incoming packets by default. Make sure that this firewall is set up before you install potentially vulnerable software on your computer. Both Mandrake and Red Hat provide graphical tools to configure the firewall: in Mandrake, launch the drakfirewall tool, and in Red Hat, launch redhat-config-securitylevel. In either tool, configure the firewall to not allow any incoming traffic (unless, of course, you've already intentionally set up your computer as a server).

2. Configure a static IP address

Most people who use a router to access the Internet allow their router to assign private IP addresses using DHCP. In order to reliably use your computer as a server, though, the computer needs to have the same IP address each time it starts. In this step, you'll configure a manually assigned IP address. (You can skip to the next step if your computer's IP address is assigned directly by your ISP, or if you have already manually configured a static IP address.)

If your IP address is not in one of the following ranges, you probably have a public IP address and shouldn't change it. Contact your ISP if you're not sure.

- 10.0.0.0–10.255.255.255
- 172.16.0.0–172.31.255.255
- 192.168.0.0–192.168.255.255

First, make note of your computer's configuration. Open a terminal, su to root, and execute the command /sbin/ifconfig eth0 | grep Mask. Output will resemble the following:

```
inet addr:192.168.0.160  Bcast:192.168.0.255  Mask:255.255.255.0
```

Your Linux distribution probably has graphical tools to configure your IP address, and you're welcome to use them if you know how. It's just easier to document the command-line tools because they're the same for all distributions.

Make note of the inet addr and Mask fields: inet addr is your current IP address, and Mask is your netmask. Next, identify your DNS servers using the command cat /etc/resolv.conf. Output will resemble:

```
nameserver 204.127.202.19
nameserver 204.148.227.79
```

You probably won't need to change this file, but make note of your DNS numbers just in case you lose the settings along the way. Finally, identify your default gateway using the command /sbin/route -n|grep '^0.0.0.0'. Output will resemble:

```
0.0.0.0   192.168.0.1   0.0.0.0   UG   0   0   0 eth0
```

The second IP address identifies your default gateway. Keep the terminal window open so you can refer to this information later.

Next, you need to determine an IP address on the same network so that your router won't try to assign to a different computer. Unfortunately, different routers handle this differently. My Linksys router assigns the IP addresses 192.168.1.100 through 192.168.1.150, and uses the IP address 192.168.1.1. So, anything between 192.168.1.2 through 192.168.1.99, or 192.168.1.151

through 192.168.1.254 will work. So I'm going to choose the IP address 192.168.1.203, but you should refer to your router's documentation to identify which IP addresses are available to be assigned on you network.

Once you identify an available IP address, execute the following commands to configure your static IP address and default gateway to be set automatically at startup:

```
echo /sbin/ifconfig eth0 inet ip-address netmask netmask >> /etc/rc.d/
rc.local
echo /sbin/route add default gw default-gateway >> /etc/rc.d/rc.local
```

For example, I used the commands:

```
echo /sbin/ifconfig eth0 inet 192.168.1.203 netmask 255.255.255.0 >>
/etc/rc.d/rc.local
echo /sbin/route add default gw 192.168.1.1 >> /etc/rc.d/rc.local
```

Reboot your computer, and you're done! Notice that you didn't need to reconfigure your DNS servers; the *etc/resolv.conf* file should have remained in place when you configured a static IP address. If you have problems connecting to hosts on the Internet after you reboot, verify that *etc/resolv.conf* is still in place and contains the IP addresses of your DNS servers.

3. Install Apache

Now that your system is nestled safely behind at least one firewall, you're ready to start installing the almost-certainly-vulnerable version of Apache that came with your distribution. You can download the latest version from *http://httpd.apache.org*, but you may spend some time struggling with dependencies. The easiest thing to do is to install Apache using your Linux setup disks, and then update it with the latest version.

In Mandrake 9.1, follow these steps to install the packages needed by this project:

1. Run rpmdrake.

2. Expand Server and select Web/ FTP, as shown in Figure 3-10.

3. Click Install and respond to any other prompts that appear.

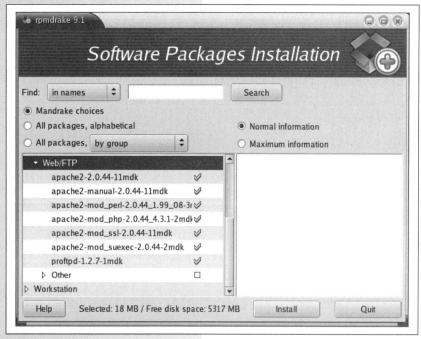

Figure 3-10. Using Mandrake's package installer to add Apache.

In Red Hat 9.2, follow these steps:

1. Run redhat-config-packages and respond to any prompts that appear.

2. Within Servers, select the Web Server package (Figure 3-11) if it's not already installed.

3. Click Update. When prompted, click Continue, and respond to any other prompts that appear.

4. Update Apache

Now, launch *up2date*, */usr/sbin/ MandrakeUpdate*, or your distribution's update tool, and install any updates available for Apache. This may seem a bit redundant since you just installed updates, but the new software almost certainly requires

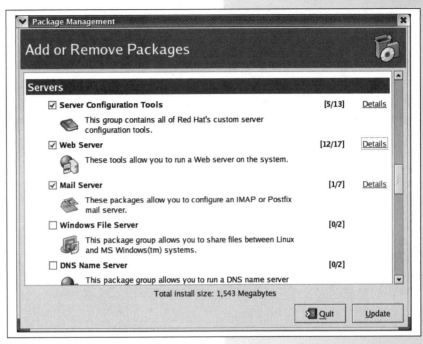

Figure 3-11. Using Red Hat's Web Server package to install Apache.

some patches. Check your version of Apache using either the command /usr/sbin/apachectl extendedstatus or /usr/sbin/apachectl -v. Then, visit *http://httpd.apache.org* and verify that you do indeed have the most recent version.

5. Configure Apache

The vast majority of web servers use TCP port 80, so worms that prey on web servers traditionally search for vulnerable hosts by querying that default port. If you're running a web server that the general public needs to be able to find, you basically need to use that port as well. However, the projects in this book are intended for only certain people to access, so you should change this default port number. This will prevent the average worm from finding your system, even if you are vulnerable. It won't prevent someone who is willing to do a resource-intensive full port scan from finding your web server, but you'll be shielded from the vast majority of attacks.

The port number is defined in Apache's configuration file using the Listen configuration directive. Changing the port number is as simple as editing this file and restarting Apache. The filename varies by Linux distribution, but the file itself is almost certainly contained in your */etc/httpd/conf/* directory. Identify the file using the following command:

```
grep -Hi '^ *listen*' /etc/httpd/conf/*.conf
```

Edit the configuration file to change port 80 to a number between 1024 and 10000 that you can easily remember. If there are multiple Listen directives, you probably only need to change the Listen 80 directive.

Make note of the port you choose, because you'll need to configure the firewall to permit that port number.

Installing Apache using the built-in tools sets it to start automatically in Mandrake 9.1, but not in Red Hat 9.2. To verify that Apache starts automatically, restart your system. Open a terminal window and execute the following command:

```
ps -A | grep httpd
```

You should see at least one line listed, showing that *httpd* or *httpd2* (the Apache process) is running. If not, there are several ways you can set Apache to start automatically; the easiest is to add the apachectl start command to your *rc.local* file. To do this, issue the following commands in a terminal window:

```
su
echo /usr/sbin/apachectl start >> /etc/rc.d/rc.local
```

Then issue the command /usr/sbin/apachectl start to start Apache immediately (you'll need it running for the next step).

Many distributions include graphical tools for controlling which services start automatically, but it's often easier just to edit the config files.

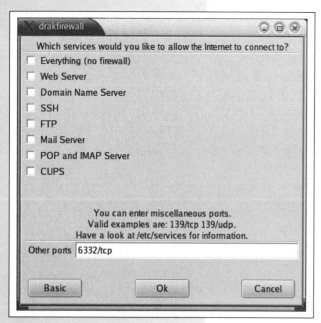

Figure 3-12. Using drakfirewall to open a custom port.

2. Open the firewalls

You need to open the TCP port you specified for the Apache Listen directive on both your host-based firewall software and your filtering router. Start with the software firewall. As usual, the easiest way to configure this is using the graphical tool that came with your distribution.

In Mandrake 9.1 (or similar), follow these steps to open a custom TCP port in your firewall:

1. Launch the drakfirewall tool.

2. Click the Advanced button.

3. In the "Other ports" field, enter **CustomPort/tcp**. For example, if you chose 6332 as your custom port number, you would type **6332/tcp**, as shown in Figure 3-12.

4. Click OK.

In Red Hat 9.2 (or similar), follow these steps:

1. Run setup.

2. At the first screen, select "Firewall Configuration."

3. Select Customize.

4. Tab down to "Other ports" and type *CustomPort*:tcp, as shown in Figure 3-13. For example, if you chose 6332 as your custom port number, you would type **6332:tcp**.

5. Click OK twice, then Quit.

At this point, if everything has worked properly, you should be able to enter the URL *http://localhost: TCP_Port/* in your browser and see a web page served directly from your computer. Of course, there's no useful content on this site yet, but you'll take care of that in later projects.

Since you're using a custom port number (not TCP port 80), you need to specify the port number as part of the URL by adding a colon and the port number to the server IP address or hostname. For example, if you are using TCP port 6332 and your IP address is 192.168.1.203, you would type the URL *http://192.168.1.203 :6332/* into your browser's address field. You should see Apache's welcome screen, as shown in Figure 3-14. Different distributions have different test screens.

You can access the web server from your LAN, but you won't be able to access it from the outside world until you configure your router to forward packets with your custom TCP port to your computer's IP address. The

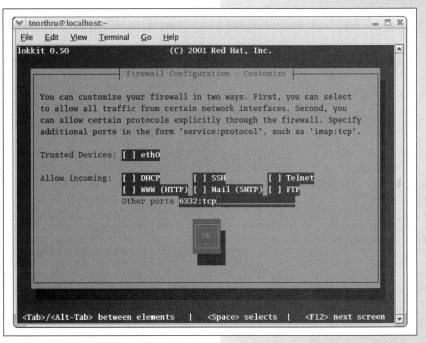

Figure 3-13. Adding custom ports to Red Hat's firewall.

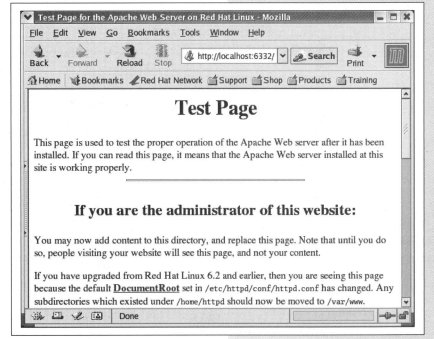

Figure 3-14. Congrats, you've got Apache working!

Chapter 3, Remotely Monitor a Pet

procedure for configuring this is different for every router, so consult your manufacturer's instructions. On my Linksys router, I do the following.

If you do not have a router on your LAN, you can skip this step.

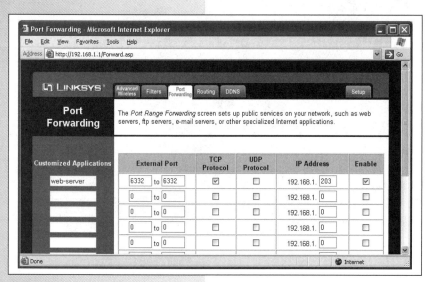

Figure 3-15. The Port Forwarding configuration page for my Linksys router!

1. Enter *http://192.168.1.1/* into a web browser, and provide the administrative username and password when prompted.

2. Click the Advanced tab.

3. Click the Port Forwarding tab.

4. Type the custom TCP port number in both of the External Port fields of a new row in the Customized Applications table. Select the TCP Protocol checkbox. Type the private IP address of the computer running IIS in the IP Address field, and select the Enabled checkbox (Figure 3-15).

5. Click Apply.

Now that your computer and router have been configured to allow remote access to your web server, all you need to do is determine your public IP address and (optionally) configure a domain name.

3. Determine your IP address

Earlier, you used the `ifconfig` command to examine your IP address configuration. If you determined that you did not have a private IP address, then you can skip this step—you already know your IP. If you do have a private IP address, you'll have to figure out what your public IP address is to connect to your computer from the Internet.

To learn your IP address, visit one of these sites from your home computer: *http://www.whatismyip.org*, *http://www.whatismyip.com*, or *http://www. whatismyip.net*. Unfortunately, there's a catch: the IP address that you have now may not be your permanent address. Most ISPs offer dynamic IP addressing, which means that your IP address may change from time to time. My personal experience with ISPs is that cable modem and DSL IP addresses rarely, if ever, change; however, it's important to consider the possibility when configuring DNS for your site. If you use a dial-up connection, your IP address will almost certainly change each time you connect to the Internet.

4. Get a domain name

At this point, you are successfully hosting a web site on your PC. However, it's only accessible by the IP address, which is not exactly easy to remember. Most people prefer to identify their site on the Web using a domain name, so if you don't already own a domain name, it's time to get one. There are many different organizations that can sell you a .com, .net, or .org domain name; for a complete listing, go to *http://www.internic.net/regist.html*.

> Owning a domain name is good for other reasons as well. Most importantly, you can use the same email address for as long as you own the domain name. I use *tony@northrup.org* as my permanent email address, and forward it to whatever mailbox my ISP has given me this month.

Simply owning a domain name isn't enough—you also need someone to provide ongoing DNS services. Providing DNS services is a little like an active telephone directory service—a DNS service provider on the Internet needs to take responsibility for your domain name, and provide your home IP address to anyone who enters your domain name into their browser. If your ISP uses dynamic IP addresses, you will need a way to automatically notify your DNS service provider of the changed IP address.

> I use zoneedit.com for my DNS service provider. They're free.

There are many companies who offer dynamic DNS management service for a small fee, and many others who provide the service completely free of charge. These providers often offer software that runs on your computer to notify them if your IP address changes. For a listing of these organizations, check out *http://www.technopagan.org/dynamic/* or *http://www.geocities.com/kiore_nz/dynamicdns.htm*. You can also try searching the Web for "Dynamic DNS Management."

The company you select to manage your DNS address will provide you with IP addresses for their primary and secondary nameservers. These nameservers are the actual computers on the Internet that will perform your address-book lookups for people surfing your site. You'll provide those two IP addresses to your domain name registrar, and your computer will then be accessible using your domain name.

5. Connect to your web server

To connect to your home web server from a remote location, open a browser and enter a URL in the following format:

```
http://domain-name-or-ip:TCP_Port/
```

So in my case, where I used the TCP port 6332, purchased the domain name northrup.org, and assigned the hostname www to my home network's public IP address, I would enter the following URL:

```
http://www.northrup.org:6332/
```

If you did not purchase a domain name, simply use the IP address instead, such as:

```
http://208.201.239.37:6332/
```

Your web server won't have a default page at this point, but that's okay; in fact, it's probably for the best. You don't ever need to set up a default page—instead, just type the path to the application you've installed. Later projects in this book will walk you through the process of configuring a virtual directory to contain each project, and accessing that project from a browser.

6. Install Image Display System (IDS)

Image Display System is a set of Perl scripts that displays a web interface for directories full of pictures. It's a good choice for this project because:

- It doesn't require a database.

- It's fairly easy to set up.

- It's free.

- I know one of the guys who worked on the project.

To set up IDS, follow these steps:

1. Download the latest version of IDS from *http://sourceforge.net/projects/ ids/* (Version 0.82 as of the time of this writing). Save the **.tar.gz* file to your home directory.

2. Determine your ScriptAlias by issuing the following command:

   ```
   grep '^ *ScriptAlias' /etc/httpd/conf/*.conf
   ```

   In Mandrake 9.1, Mandrake 10.0, and Red Hat 9.2, this is */var/www/cgi-bin/*. Make sure the *dir* line in the */etc/petcam.config* file contains this same value, plus */ids/albums*.

3. Open a terminal window and execute the following commands. These will extract IDS to its own directory within your web server's *cgi-bin* directory and rename it to *ids*. (Be sure to substitute your own username and *cgi-bin* directory.)

   ```
   su
   cd /var/www/cgi-bin
   cp ~username/ids*.gz .
   tar -xvzf ids*.gz
   rm ids*.gz
   mv ids-* ids
   rm -rf ids-*
   ```

4. You now need to update Apache's configuration file with information about IDS's folders. To do this, use your favorite editor to open the */etc/httpd/conf/*.conf* file (which may be named *httpd.conf* or *commonhttpd.conf*) and add the following lines to the end of the file. (You can type these in, or you can copy and paste them from *http://ids.sourceforge.net/documentation/ids-apache.html*).

```
<Location /cgi-bin/ids/album-data>
    SetHandler default-handler
</Location>

<Location /cgi-bin/ids/albums>
    SetHandler default-handler
</Location>

<Location /cgi-bin/ids/image-cache>
    SetHandler default-handler
</Location>

<Location /cgi-bin/ids/site-images>
    SetHandler default-handler
</Location>

<Location /cgi-bin/ids/themes>
    SetHandler default-handler
</Location>

<Location /cgi-bin/ids/admin/templates>
    SetHandler default-handler
</Location>
```

5. And that does it for the IDS configuration. You'll need to restart Apache to make the configuration settings take effect, so issue the following commands:

```
su
/usr/sbin/apachectl restart
```

6. Open a browser and enter the URL *http://127.0.0.1/cgi-bin/ids/index.cgi*. You should see the IDS default page, with a one-picture sample album available for viewing (Figure 3-16).

If IDS isn't working, you probably don't have all the dependencies set up properly. The easiest way to diagnose this is to switch to */var/www/cgi-bin/ids* in your terminal window and execute the command `perl index.cgi`. Perl should display the name of any missing modules, and you should be able to find those modules at *http://www.cpan.org*.

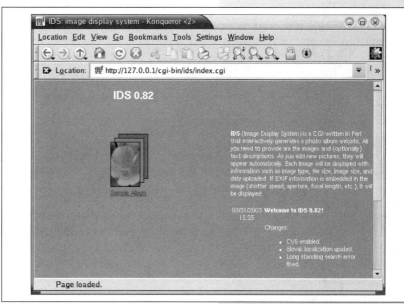

Figure 3-16. The IDS default page.

I chose IDS for this project because it's easy to set up and doesn't require any configuration. However, if you want to do it, it is very configurable; just point your browser at *http://localhost:tcp_port/cgi-bin/ids/admin/index.cgi.* For more detailed control over the configuration, read the IDS documentation. At the very least, you should password-protect the admin pages.

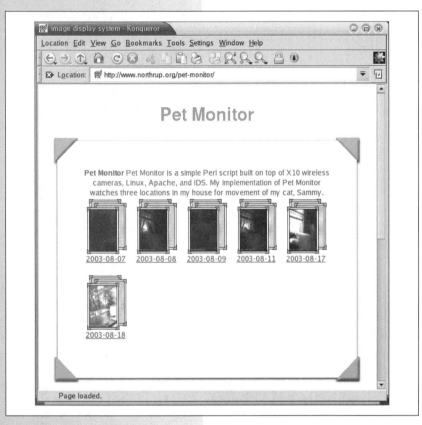

Figure 3-17. The pet monitor works!

Spend a few minutes customizing IDS's interface by visiting the admin pages at *http://127.0.0.1/cgi-bin/ids/admin/index.cgi*, and you can set up a pretty slick frontend. Figure 3-17 shows the current setup of my pet monitor interface. IDS is very configurable, so if you're not happy with some aspect of it, you can probably change it. Refer to the documentation for more information.

Wrapping Up

In addition to allowing you to enjoy your vacation without worrying about your pet, this project has accomplished several other useful things:

- Implemented intelligent, wireless video monitoring throughout your home.

- Connected your home (and your pet) to the Internet.

- Enabled remote monitoring of your home.

- Enabled your computer to respond to movement throughout your house.

If you've positioned the motion detectors and cameras well, you can safely leave the script running even when you're at home, though of course you'll want to change the X10 settings on your lights so that they're not turned on and off by motion. Remember to keep an eye on your disk space, though, especially if your cat turns out to be active just about the whole night. (Even though I can't see pictures taken at night without the lights, it's interesting to use the motion detectors to track my cat's movements.)

Extensions

One of the nice things about using a script for a project like this is that it's easy to modify and extend. Some of the things you might want to do include:

- Save both a JPEG snapshot and a few seconds of video. You could even capture video until you receive the "off" signal from the motion detector indicating that movement is no longer being detected.

- Have the script send an email to your pager if no motion is detected around feeding time.

- Archive pictures older than a week by shrinking them to 320×240 and increasing the JPEG compression.

- Organize the pictures for constant use by creating separate folders for months and years.

If you check this book's web site at *http://www.homehacking.com*, you'll probably discover that I've updated the script with some of these improvements.

Exhibit A: Bill of Materials

Most parts are available from home automation web sites such as *http://www.smarthome.com*. X10 wireless cameras are available only from *http://www.x10.com*.

Item	Quantity	Approximate cost	Part number
Serial Powerlinc computer interface	1	$35 and up	CM11A
X10 motion detector	3	$20 and up	MS14A-C or MS13A
X10 wireless cameras	3	$170 for all of these items	XCam2
X10 wireless transceiver	1		4005X or 400s
Wireless video receiver	1		VR36A
Composite video input card	1	About $40	WinTV-GO-FM, 00191
X10 lamp module	3	$10-$15 each	2000
Kwik-Fix Stick-E-Tak poster adhesive	1	$3	QSA2-01

Exhibit B: Software Versions Used

Description	Version
Mandrake Linux	9.1
Red Hat Linux Personal Edition	9.2
Apache	2.0.48
XawTV	3.90
ImageMagick	5.5.7
PerlMagick	5.5.7
Image::Info	1.15
CGI::Carp	1.05
Image Display System	0.82
Perl	5.8.0
ControlX10::CM11	2.09
Device::SerialPort	0.22

Make Your House Talk

4

Cost

$40 - $200

Time

two and a half hours

Difficulty

3 out of 5

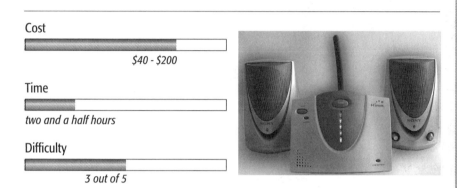

What You Need

- Wireless audio transmitter and receiver

- X10 Powerlinc Serial Controller

- Two X10 appliance modules

- A computer running Windows

- An Internet connection

For a list of specific parts used in this project, refer to Exhibit A at the end of this chapter.

Who wouldn't want to wake up to the voice of a strange man under the bed? Well, perhaps nobody. But let me sweeten the pot a little: the voice under the bed knows what the weather is like outside, and doesn't even have a knife!

Every day before I get dressed, I have to walk to my computer, open a web browser, and check the weather online. What a hassle! I'd like to know the weather without leaving my bed so that I know how to get dressed.

There are a few different ways I could do this:

- I could hire a man to come to my house every morning, check the temperature, and read me the weather report.

- I could buy a wireless thermometer from Radio Shack, stick it outside my house, and place the display in my bedroom.

- I could listen to one of those cheesy local radio stations that read the weather every five minutes.

- I could make my computer talk, and teach it to throw its voice into my bedroom.

When one option is a talking computer, is there really a choice? Figure 4-1 shows the components we will use to build this project. A script will start every morning, retrieve weather information from the Internet, convert it into speech, and then send the audio through remote speakers in my bedroom.

Project Overview

Obviously, there are a variety of different thermometers available that will tell you the temperature outside. However, I don't want to just stick a thermometer on the outside of my house—that's far too boring for me. Instead, I'm going to make my computer look up the weather every morning, and read it to me in my bedroom through some wireless speakers.

This project has four phases, which correspond to each of the layers in our conceptual design:

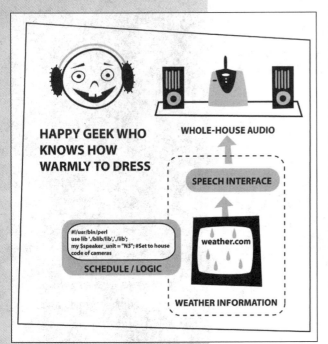

Figure 4-1. A conceptual design for translating weather information into spoken word.

- Weather Information

- Speech Interface

- Remote Audio

- Control/Scheduling Mechanism

Each of these components is modular, so you can complete them in any order you like. You can even pick and choose the components you want to do—for example, if you're creating a web page and want to show the current temperature, you can scavenge from the Weather Information phase. If you want to add speech to a chat room, explore the Speech Interface phase.

Weather Information

There are many different ways to look up the current weather on the Internet—you probably use a browser to read one of the many web pages showing weather information. Such web pages tend to have a lot of stuff besides the current temperature, though, such as pretty icons illustrating the current weather, a toolbar, and advertisements (see Figure 4-2).

Of course, your brain is smart enough to ignore all of these distractions and focus on the current temperature. That's not so easy for a computer to do. A computer can certainly download the page, but digging through all of the information in the source code to retrieve the current temperature is difficult (see Figure 4-3). It can be done, though, using a technique called *screen scraping*. Screen scraping downloads a web page and extracts just the information needed by an application.

Unfortunately, screen scraping isn't an ideal way for two computers to communicate. It's challenging to program because you have to create a script that digs through raw HTML and looks for some way to consistently determine where in the HTML file the current temperature is located. It's certainly doable, but it's also unreliable—whenever the layout of the page changes, your program will break, and you'll have to figure out the HTML all over again.

But thanks to web services, two computers on the Internet can communicate in a much more computer-friendly way: by using Extensible Markup Language (XML). XML is just a text format that allows computers to exchange a wide variety of information. XML libraries exist for all major development environments now, so you can consume XML information in just about any application.

Here's what the current temperature on the Weather.com site looks like in XML:

Figure 4-2. My eyes can easily find the temperature on this page...

Figure 4-3. ...but finding it buried in the HTML is a bit more difficult.

```
<SOAP-ENV:Envelope
    xmlns:SOAP-ENV="http://schemas.xmlsoap.org/soap/envelope/"
    xmlns:xsi="http://www.w3.org/2001/XMLSchema-instance"
    xmlns:xsd="http://www.w3.org/2001/XMLSchema">
  <SOAP-ENV:Body>
     <ns1:getTempResponse SOAP-ENV:encodingStyle="http://schemas.
xmlsoap.org/soap/encoding/" xmlns:ns1="urn:xmethods-Temperature">
        <return xsi:type="xsd:float">47.0</return>
     </ns1:getTempResponse>
  </SOAP-ENV:Body>
</SOAP-ENV:Envelope>
```

It's not so easy for a human to read, but for a computer, it's simple. Most of the XML above is dedicated to describing the Simple Object Access Protocol (SOAP) envelope and the XML schema, which shows the client parsing the XML file exactly how to parse it. Note that the current temperature, expressed as a floating-point number, is contained in the tag `<return xsi:type="xsd:float">47.0</return>`.

Slashdot offers their news articles in both XML and RDF Site Summary (RSS) formats. Check out *http://slashdot.org/index.xml* and *http://slashdot.org/index.rss*. It's very simple to grab and parse these using just about any programming environment.

In this first phase of the project, you'll create a small application to retrieve weather information from the Web using SOAP, extract the current temperature, and output the current temperature to the console. Later, you'll grab this output and use it in your speech application.

1. Create the temperature retrieval application

This step assumes you have Microsoft Visual Studio .NET and the .NET Framework installed. If you don't want to use Visual Studio, you can compile this application using free tools that Microsoft provides. Or, even easier, visit *http://www.homehacking.com/* and download the executables.

1. Launch Microsoft Visual Studio .NET.

2. Go to File → New → Project.

3. In the New Project dialog, click Visual C# Projects, and then click Console Application.

4. In the Name field, type `GetTempFromZip`. Click OK.

5. Click the Project menu, then click Add Web Reference.

6. Click the Project menu, then click Add Reference.

7. In the URL field, type `http://www.xmethods.net/sd/2001/TemperatureService.wsdl`, then click Go.

8. Visual Studio requests the WSDL file you specified, and then parses it to determine what methods are available and how to communicate with them. It then provides you with a list of methods, as shown in Figure 4-4. Click Add Reference.

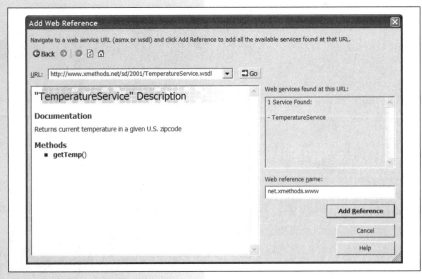

Figure 4-4. Using web services is much easier than screen scraping.

9. Replace the default *Class1.cs* code with the following:

```csharp
using System;
using System.Diagnostics;
using System.Xml.Serialization;
using System.Web.Services.Protocols;
using System.ComponentModel;
using System.Web.Services;

namespace GetTempFromZip
{
    class Class1
    {
        [STAThread]
        static void Main(string[] args)
        {
            net.xmethods.www.TemperatureService tempSvc = new net.
xmethods.www.TemperatureService( );
            Console.WriteLine( tempSvc.getTemp( args[0] ) );
        }
    }
}
```

10. On the Standard toolbar, click the list that currently shows Debug, and then click Release. This ensures that you are using the release build configuration.

11. Click the Build menu, then click Build Solution.

Time to test it out. Open a terminal and switch to the directory your project was configured to build in (by default, this will be *C:\Documents and Settings\username\My Documents\Visual Studio Projects\GetTempFromZip\bin\Release*). Then execute the following command:

```
GetTempFromZip 01801
```

Your computer will contact the *xmethods.net* web service, retrieve the current temperature for my ZIP code, output it to the console, and exit. Of course, if you don't care about how warmly *I* need to dress, you can pass the program your own ZIP code instead.

Web services make it really, really easy to use data from the Web in an application. In fact, there are only two interesting lines of code in this application:

```csharp
net.xmethods.www.TemperatureService tempSvc = new net.xmethods.www.
TemperatureService( );
Console.WriteLine( tempSvc.getTemp( args[0] ) );
```

These lines create a new TemperatureService object, and then call the getTemp method using the ZIP code. The ZIP code is passed to the application as an argument, which is represented by args[0] (the variable args is declared with the line static void Main(string[] args)). The .NET Framework then performs a web services request in the background and returns the results, which are written to the console.

> This could easily be a much longer application—if you wanted, you could provide usage information, comments, and exception handling. In fact, if you don't pass it a parameter, it'll throw an unhandled exception. But hey, it's just a hack.

Be sure that any computer you run this application on has the .NET Framework installed. You can get the .NET Framework from the Recommended Updates section of Windows Update at *http://windowsupdate.microsoft.com*.

Speech Interface

Talking computers are the coolest thing. When I was a kid I had this software for my Commodore 64 that would talk, and I would spend hours making it say stupid, stupid things. (Hey, if you grew up in Pflugerville, Texas, you'd probably have been driven to such nonsense too.)

First, the good news: computers can still talk! Now, the bad news: they still don't talk very well, and putting voice synthesis into a script isn't as easy as I would have hoped.

> That said, AT&T Natural Voices is fantastic. It can be trained to the point that you can hardly tell that it's not a human being. It's not free, but if really good synthesized speech is important to you, it might be worth the cost.

A great deal of development time has been devoted to improving computer voice synthesis, largely because it provides an interface for physically challenged people who can't use a monitor. There is also a crowd of people who believe voice will be the way people interact with computers in the future. I'm not sure that voice is ever going to be that popular, though I do appreciate it that my PDA speaks driving directions to me. Otherwise, I'd rather just read something from the screen than have the computer read it aloud.

This project requires a command-line tool that can be called from a script to speak a phrase. I couldn't find a free tool on the Web that worked well, so after a great deal of research, I decided I was going to have to write my own program. Microsoft provides a speech API with Windows, so I decided to take advantage of that by using C# and Visual Studio .NET.

This little speech app has a lot of uses. If you're an IRC freak like myself, you can add voice to your favorite channel. I use Mirc as my chat client, and the following remote script speaks every line that someone types (as long as it's not more than 29 words):

```
on 1:TEXT:*:#banter:/run -np C:\homehacking\ReadWeather\Say $nick
says $1 $2 $3 $4 $5 $6 $7 $8 $9 $10 $11 $12 $13 $14 $15 $16 $17 $18
$19 $20 $21 $22 $23 $24 $25 $26 $27 $28 $29
on 1:ACTION:*:#banter:/run -np C:\homehacking\ReadWeather\Say $nick
$1 $2 $3 $4 $5 $6 $7 $8 $9 $10 $11 $12 $13 $14 $15 $16 $17 $18 $19
$20 $21 $22 $23 $24 $25 $26 $27 $28 $29
```

If you are using Linux for this project, I would use the Festival speech synthesis system and the Perl voice synthesis modules. You can download Festival from *http://www.cstr.ed.ac.uk/projects/festival/*. The Perl modules that work with Festival can be found at CPAN, at *http://search.cpan.org/ ~rcaley/speech_pm_1.0/*. You can theoretically use Festival on Windows, too, though I couldn't find any documentation that had been updated since Windows was still called "NT."

1. Find SAPI.DLL

You'll need the Microsoft Dynamic Link Library (DLL) that contains the Speech Application Programming Interface (API). It's called SAPI.DLL, and if you have a recent version of Windows or Office, you probably already have it. You can do a search for the file *sapi.dll*, or you can open a command prompt and execute the command dir /s \sapi.dll.

If you find this file, make note of its location—you'll need to identify it when you write your C# application. If you have multiple versions, make note of where the newest version lives. If you can't find the file or just want to make sure you have the latest version, download the Speech SDK or the Speech Application SDK from *http://www.microsoft.com/speech/*. (Be warned—the SDKs are a huge download.) The only file you need to extract is the *sapi.dll* file; once you've dug it out, store it in your *%systemroot%\system32* directory.

2. Create the speech console application

This step assumes that you have Microsoft Visual Studio .NET and the .NET Framework installed. If you don't want to use Visual Studio, you can compile this application using free tools that Microsoft provides, or, even easier, you can visit *http://www.homehacking.com/* and download the executables.

1. Launch Microsoft Visual Studio .NET.

2. Go to File → New → Project.

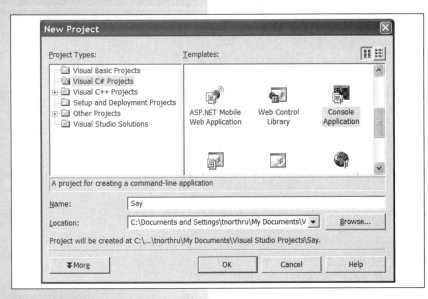

Figure 4-5. Creating a console application that talks.

3. In the New Project dialog, click Visual C# Projects, then click Console Application.

4. In the Name field, type **Say**, as shown in Figure 4-5.

5. Click OK.

6. Click the Project menu, then click Add Reference.

7. Click the COM tab, then double-click the highest version of the Microsoft Speech Object Library available. If it's not in the list, click the Browse button and locate your *sapi.dll* file.

8. Click OK.

9. Replace the default *Class1.cs* code with the following:

```csharp
using System;

namespace Say
{
    using System.Threading;
    using SpeechLib;
    class Class1
    {
        [STAThread]
        static void Main(string[] sentence)
        {
            string toSpeak = "";
            foreach(string word in sentence)
            {
                toSpeak = toSpeak + word + " ";
            }
            toSpeak = toSpeak.Trim();

            if ( toSpeak.Length > 0 )
            {
                Console.WriteLine("Saying: \"" + toSpeak + "\"");

                SpeechVoiceSpeakFlags SpFlags =
SpeechVoiceSpeakFlags.SVSFlagsAsync;
                SpVoice Voice = new SpVoice();
                Voice.Speak(toSpeak, SpFlags);
                Voice.WaitUntilDone(Timeout.Infinite);
            }
            else
            {
                Console.WriteLine("What you talkin 'bout,
Willis?");
            }
        }
    }
}
```

10. On the Standard toolbar, click the list that currently shows Debug, then click Release. (This ensures that you are using the release build configuration.)

11. Click the Build menu, then click Build Solution.

And that's it—the Say console application is ready to go. Let's test it out. Open a terminal and switch to the directory your project was configured to build in (by default, this will be *C:\Documents and Settings\username\My Documents\Visual Studio Projects\Say\bin\Release*). Then execute the following command:

```
Say Eric John Parucki is my God.
```

Your computer will swear allegiance to Eric, and it's wise that you do it, too.

Notice that there are two files in the *Release* directory: *Say.exe* and *Interop. SpeechLib.dll*. Visual Studio wrapped up the *sapi.dll* library so that your .NET Framework application could access it. Copy both files to the *C:\ homehacking\ReadWeather* folder (remember to move both files if you end up moving the application to a different directory). If you move the application to a different computer, make sure the computer has the .NET Framework installed; you can download the .NET Framework from *http:// windowsupdate.microsoft.com*.

Everyone knows you're making your computer say dirty things, so just stop it.

Whole-House Audio

In this phase, you'll create a system for distributing audio from your computer to your bedroom. In Chapter 9, Create Time-Shifted FM Radio, I use an FM transmitter to send sound to the radio located in my bedroom. I don't want the weather announcements to depend on me having the radio turned on, though, so I'm going to add a second set of speakers under the bed.

Like most of you, I have several boxes of computers parts in the basement. Among those parts, I have two or three sets of cheap computers speakers that came with something-or-other that I bought once-upon-a-time. This is the perfect opportunity to get some life out of those speakers. My computer isn't in my bedroom, though, so I'll need to use a wireless link to connect the speakers.

The wireless link and the speakers will be used for only a few seconds per day, and they occasionally make clicking and static sounds. Therefore, I want them to turn on only when they're being used, and off otherwise.

1. Install X10 appliance modules

You don't want to leave your speakers and wireless audio devices on all the time, so you're going to plug them into X10 appliance modules so that you can turn them on and off from a script on the computer. Follow these steps to connect the appliance modules:

1. Set the house code of the appliance modules to N. If you're already using a different house code, feel free to set it to that code, but you'll then need to edit the Perl script.

2. Set the unit code of the appliance module to 3 (or any other unit code). Make note of which unit code you use in which room.

3. Plug in one appliance module near your computer and the other in your bedroom (or wherever you'll be listening to the computer audio). You'll be connecting two devices to the appliance module in your bedroom, so connect an extension cord or power strip to that module.

2. Install speakers

You almost certainly have a spare set of speakers lying around somewhere—it doesn't matter how cheap they are. In fact, you don't even need two speakers—a single speaker will do just fine. The only requirement is that they have to turn on automatically when power is applied. If they have a "soft" power button that needs to be pressed each time you plug them in, they won't work with your X10 interface.

Position the speakers wherever you want them; I placed them on the floor under my bed, pointing directly up. Then, plug the power supply into the power strip that you connected to your X10 appliance module. Turn the speakers on and adjust the volume to a moderate level (unless you like being shouted at in the morning).

3. Install wireless audio

Now, connect the wireless transmitter to your computer's sound card. The Kima wireless audio set that I'm using included a pass-through for a local set of speakers, so all I needed to do was unplug my desktop speakers, plug them into the Kima, and then plug the Kima into my sound card where the speakers had been connected. Plug the transmitter into the X10 appliance module—hopefully it'll turn on automatically, like my Kima transmitter did. If it doesn't, turn it on manually, then unplug it and reconnect it to power. If it defaults to being off, you'll have to bypass the X10 appliance module and leave the transmitter turned on all the time.

Next, plug the wireless receiver into the power strip connected to the X10 appliance module, alongside your speakers (my setup is shown in Figure 4-6). Turn on the receiver and speakers. And that should do it—you are now ready to test out the wireless audio by making a sound on your computer. Open a terminal and execute the command:

```
C:\homehacking\ReadWeather\Say Slashdot rules my
life
```

Scheduling and Logic

There are many different ways you can tell your computer to read you the weather. The Control Distribution phase of Chapter 9 shows you how to do it with an IR remote. If you'd rather use a wall switch or an X10 remote, review Chapter 2—the Perl script can listen for X10 signals and launch the script on demand.

Figure 4-6. Speakers dug up from the basement, and a wireless receiver.

For this project, I decided to keep things simple and launch the script at a regular time every day. (My favorite user interface is when the user remains completely passive.)

1. Install the Firecracker, Perl, and Perl X10 modules

As described in Chapter 12, install the Firecracker wireless X10 interface, Perl, and the Perl X10 modules.

2. Create the script

You need to turn on your wireless speakers, call your C# application to retrieve the current temperature, create an English sentence, and send that sentence to the C# application that synthesizes it into the spoken word. As with most projects, Perl is my choice for gluing multiple components together. Type up the following script and save it as *C:\homehacking\ SpeakWeather.pl*, then download it, along with any updates I've made, from *http://www.homehacking.com*.

Various applications make it easy to edit Perl scripts, but Notepad works just fine too.

```
#!/usr/bin/perl
use lib './blib/lib','./lib';

my $speaker_unit = "N3"; #Set to house code of cameras
my $zipcode = "01801";

my ($OS_win, $serial_port);

# Load the proper SerialPort module based on platform
BEGIN { $| = 1;
```

```perl
$OS_win = ($^O eq "MSWin32") ? 1 : 0;
if ($OS_win) {
    eval "use Win32::SerialPort";
    die "$@\n" if ($@);
    $serial_port = Win32::SerialPort->new ("COM1",1);
}
else {
    eval "use Device::SerialPort";
    die "$@\n" if ($@);
    $serial_port = Device::SerialPort->new ("/dev/ttyS0",1);
}
}
die "Can't open serial port: $^E\n" unless ($serial_port);
$serial_port->error_msg(1);
$serial_port->user_msg(0);
$serial_port->databits(8);
$serial_port->baudrate(4800);
$serial_port->parity("none");
$serial_port->stopbits(1);
$serial_port->dtr_active(1);
$serial_port->handshake("none");
$serial_port->write_settings || die "Could not set up port\n";

use ControlX10::CM17;

$CurrentTemp = `GetTempFromZip $zipcode`;
chomp $CurrentTemp;

# Send on signal to speakers
&ControlX10::CM17::send($serial_port, $speaker_unit . 'J');
print `Say Good morning. The current temperature is $CurrentTemp
degrees.`;
&ControlX10::CM17::send($serial_port, $speaker_unit . 'K');

# Release  the serial port
$serial_port->close || die "\nProblem closing serial port\n";
undef $serial_port;
```

You need to define two variables at the beginning of the script. Set $speaker_ unit to the house and unit code of the X10 appliance switches that you connected to your wireless transmitter, receiver, and speakers. Set $zipcode to your ZIP code.

3. Run the script from the command line

To run the script, open a terminal and switch to the directory you saved it in (I suggested *C:\homehacks*). Then simply type the name of the script:

```
ReadWeather.pl
```

Assuming that Perl and the required modules have been installed correctly, the script will run, send the signal to turn on the speakers, retrieve the current temperature using web services, and read it as part of a sentence.

4. Schedule the script

For your script to run, your computer needs to be running, but at some point you're going to need to shut your system off or at least reboot. Follow these instructions to configure your script to run automatically at startup:

1. Go to Start → All Programs → Accessories → System Tools → Scheduled Tasks. The Scheduled Tasks window appears, as shown in Figure 4-7.

2. Double-click Add Scheduled Task and click Next.

3. Click Browse and select the *C:\ HomeHacking\ReadWeather.pl* Perl script. Click Next.

4. Click Daily as shown in Figure 4-8, and then click Next.

5. Specify the time you want the computer to speak, then click Next.

6. Enter the username and password you use to log onto the system. Alternatively, if you're concerned about security or don't want the window open when you're logged in, you can create a new user account with limited privileges, and specify that account. Click Next.

7. On the last page, select "Open advanced properties for this task." Click Finish.

8. The Properties dialog for the ReadWeather task will appear. In the Run field, select your Perl script from the *C:\homehacking\ReadWeather* folder. Click OK.

9. Since you made a change to the task, you'll need to provide your account information again. Click OK.

10. Test the task out by right-clicking it and clicking Run. You should hear the current weather announced. You're done!

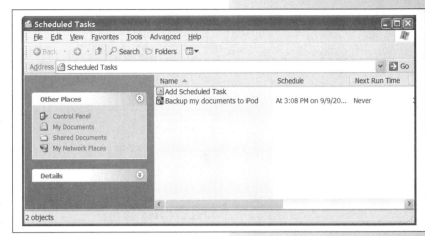

Figure 4-7. Use Scheduled Tasks to program your script to run each time your computer starts.

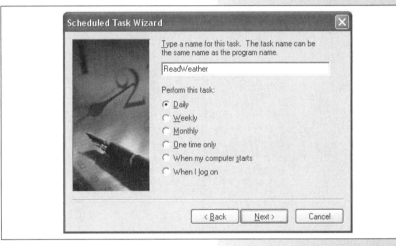

Figure 4-8. Simply scheduling your script to run daily can make your life a lot easier.

Wrapping Up

The modular approach to this project actually ended up making it much more complex than it needed to be. It's certainly possible to create a single C# application that checks the weather, turns on the wireless speakers, and reads the weather aloud. However, I want you to create your own application and have it say whatever you want, so I made it as easy as possible to replace parts of my solution. Separating the individual components allows you to replace one or more of the components, as needed for your customizations.

Extensions

If you're anything like me, you'll quickly realize that you want more information than just the current temperature. Browse through the web services listed at *http://www.xmethods.net/* for interesting data feeds. (Most of these don't actually work, though, so test them out before writing any code to connect to them.) You may also want to switch to an on-demand control mechanism so that the cold, mechanical voice doesn't wake you up on weekends and holidays when you forget about it.

I've gotten very excited about the potential of voice synthesis and remote audio components of this project. For example, you could use these technologies to do the following:

- Read your email to you in the morning.

- With motion detectors and wireless speakers placed throughout the house, keep track of the room where there was last motion. When you receive an instant message or an important email and you're not near your computer, turn on the remote speakers in the same room as you and read you the message.

- Read the Slashdot news headlines, or any other RSS newsfeed.

- Check the traffic report and wake you up early if traffic is bad.

- Check the weather report, wake you up early if it snowed so that you have time to clear your driveway, and, for the love of God, apply power to the coffee maker to get some coffee ready before you have to go out there and shovel.

Exhibit A: Bill of Materials

Most of the parts listed here are available from home automation web sites such as *http://www.smarthome.com*. X10 wireless cameras are available only from *http://www.x10.com*.

Item	Quantity	Approximate cost	Part number
Serial Powerlinc computer interface	1	$35 and up	CM11A
Cheap computer speakers	1 pair	$5 and up, or free in your basement	
Kima KS-100	1	About $40	KS-100
X10 appliance modules	2	$13	2001

Exhibit B: Software Versions

Description	Version
Windows OS	XP SP1
.NET Framework	1.1.4322
Microsoft Visual Studio .NET 2003	7.1.3088
Speech API	5.2.4210.0
Perl	5.8.1
ControlX10::CM17	0.07
Win32::SerialPort	0.19

Home Entertainment

II

Part II of this book shows you how to connect your home entertainment systems to your computer. In Chapter 5, you'll control your computer with a remote control, enabling you to switch MP3s without getting off the couch. In Chapter 6, you'll do just the opposite—you'll turn your computer into the ultimate programmable remote control. In Chapters 7 and 8, you'll build your own personal video recorder (a device like a TiVo) using either Windows or Linux. In Chapter 9, you'll extend TiVo-like capabilities to your FM radio, enabling you to pause, rewind, and fast-forward live radio while still listening through your current radio. In Chapter 10, you'll make your MP3 collection accessible from the Web, so that you can listen to your favorite digital music at work without investing in an iPod.

In this part

Remotely Control Your Computer

5

Cost

$15

Time

two hours

Difficulty

3 out of 5

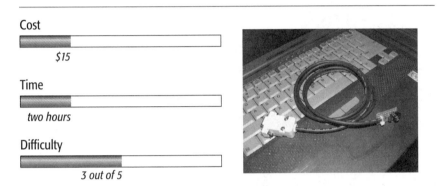

If you've skipped ahead and completed either of the HTPC projects, you've already gotten a taste of what it's like to control your PC using an infrared remote. But what if you don't like the remote that came with the TV tuner? Maybe you'd prefer to use the remote from your TiVo, or the one that came with your stereo that has ten trillion buttons. Or maybe you have a different application you'd like to control using a remote. An audio player like XMMS or MediaPlayer would clearly benefit from remote control. If you build the IR receiver module described in this chapter, you can do all this and more.

And if that's not enough, by training your PC to understand the remote you choose, you can cause complex scripted actions to occur in response to a single button press. For example, pressing the play button on your remote can not only start a DVD, it can also dim the lights prior to starting the movie. You can even have it start the popcorn!

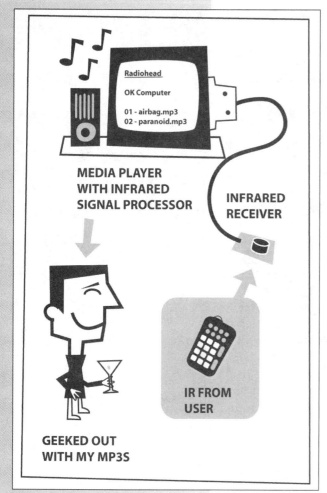

Figure 5-1. Conceptual diagram of the infrared computer control system.

Figure 5-1 shows the components of the project we'll be building in this chapter.

Project Overview

For this project, you'll be building a serial port infrared receiver using off-the-shelf parts you can pick up at your local electronics hobby shop. Don't worry if you don't fully understand how to read schematics—this will be as simple as pie. However, if you're still nervous or just not interested in building the hardware yourself, you can purchase a ready-made serial port IR receiver for under $20.

The difficulty in this project is primarily found in building the hardware. That's not to say that it will be difficult for everyone. If you have even rudimentary soldering skills, building the simple circuit board should not be any trouble. If you haven't done much soldering but you're willing to make mistakes (and possibly purchase the parts more than once), that skill can be acquired during this process. And hey, you can probably see from the pictures just how poor my soldering skills are, and I still managed to make it work.

There are two versions of this project that rely on the same home-brew receiver: one using Linux, the other using Windows. For the Linux version, you'll use open source software to bring it to life. The Linux Infrared Remote Control project (LIRC) began as a hardware/software implementation of the very same circuit you'll be building (or buying) in this project. In fact, if you've completed the Linux-based home theater PC project in Chapter 8, you've already seen it. It's LIRC that drives the IR remote that came with the TV tuner card.

There's also a Windows port of LIRC that you'll be combining with another application called Girder for the Windows version of this project.

The Infrared Receiver

Let's begin by assembling the IR receiver. I was able to get everything I needed at my local Radio Shack, with the exception of the voltage regulator. I had to go to another electronics supplier in my area for that. If you live in New England, You-Do-It Electronics is a great source for electronic components but, alas, they don't carry IR receiver modules, so there's no one-stop shopping here.

As just mentioned, you can purchase completely assembled receivers online and jump right to the software phase of this project. Exhibit B lists some sources if you want to go this route.

1. Prepare the perfboard

You'll be using perfboard to mount your components. Perfboard is a resin-based material with a grid of predrilled holes that line up with the pin spacing on many electronic components. You'll probably want to start by trimming the perfboard down a bit. I used a Dremel rotary tool with a fiberglass reinforced cut-off wheel to remove a 5/8" × 1 1/4" chunk from the board, leaving a 5 × 11 array of holes on the piece I was working with. I then used a drill with a 1/16" bit to enlarge and elongate some of the holes, as shown in Figure 5-2. You'll fasten the cable to the assembly using a nylon wire tie through these slots. I also sanded the cut edges smooth and slightly rounded over the corners, but this is by no means required.

2. Assemble the components

You'll now place the remaining components on the board and solder the connections. If you were able to find the exact components that are listed in the Bill of Materials, you can lay out the parts as shown in Figure 5-3.

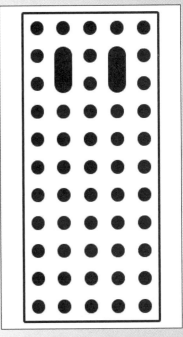

Figure 5-2. Cut your perfboard to this size and create two slots.

WARNING

This layout is based on the IR receiver module from Radio Shack, part number 276-640. There are numerous alternatives, and you can see a complete list of IR receiver modules that are known to behave well with this circuit at *http://www. lirc.org/receivers.html*. However, beware of varying pin assignments—not all manufacturers have chosen the same configuration, and they don't necessarily work exactly as shown here. Just remember that the function assigned to each pin is more important than whether it's pin 1, 2, or 3.

Also be careful of varying names. Some manufacturers refer to *Out*, *Gnd*, and *Vcc* as *Data*, *-*, and *+*, respectively (and the schematics all over the Internet have gone along with the latter designations). I'm using Radio Shack's labels because I'm guessing you have a Radio Shack nearby.

I bent the leads after inserting them in the perfboard to hold the pieces in place until I soldered. I tried to bend them in such a way as to make soldering the connections easier, overlapping as many as I could (see Figure 5-4).

Now that you have most of the parts in their final resting places, it's time to make the connections more permanent. Fire up your soldering iron and glob on some solder, as I did in Figure 5-5. (Don't laugh—it works!)

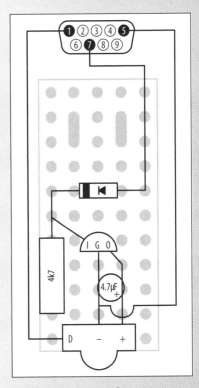

Figure 5-3. Component layout.

Figure 5-4. Bend the leads to hold the parts together for soldering.

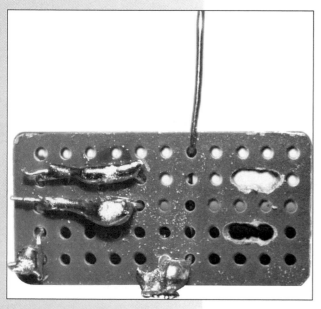

Figure 5-5. Apply solder to this side.

3. Assemble the connector and cable

Serial ports come in two flavors: 9-pin and 25-pin. I chose the 9-pin variant because I haven't seen a 25-pin serial port since floppies were...well, floppy. Begin by stripping about 3/4" of the outer sheath from the cable, being careful not to cut into the insulation on any of the internal wires. Then strip about 1/8" from the three internal wires.

Take a close look at the crimp-on terminals. See how the crimp end has two pairs of ears to crimp? One set is intended to crimp around the bare wire, while the other should be crimped on the still-insulated part of the wire. This allows the contact to be anchored more securely on the wire to prevent pullouts.

> Keep track of which wires are which so you can connect them to the right place on both ends. My wires were red, black, and brown, so I decided to use the red to carry the voltage, the black as ground, and the brown for the data. You can do whatever makes sense to you as long as you know which wire is which when you complete the assembly.

You can use a pair of needle-nose pliers to do the crimping. There are also special tools available that are designed specifically for crimping these contacts securely in place; they do a much better job at creating a solid connection, but at over $100 a pop they make more sense for full-scale production use.

> You might find the feel of those do-it-yourself D-Sub connectors kind of toy-like. For a real professional look (at a higher cost) you can purchase a standard serial extension cable at your local computer store. These will have molded-on connectors with a one-to-one pass-through for each pin on the connector to the other end. Simply lop off one end to expose the wires.
>
> To determine which wires correspond to the contacts you're interested in (1, 5, and 7 for this project) use a continuity tester (see Chapter 1) to test for continuity between the contacts.

Now that the contacts are firmly connected to the wires, simply insert them into the back side of the connector. To help you locate the correct holes, most manufacturers mold tiny numbers into the plastic. Push the Vcc contact (red in my case) into position 7, the ground (black) in 5, and the data lead (brown) in 1. Be sure to push them all the way in. You might detect a tiny click when the contacts are fully inserted; even if you don't, you'll know you've hit the mark when a gentle tug doesn't pull it back out. (Don't pull too hard, though—you may end up pulling the wire out and leaving the contact behind.)

Finally, finish the connector off by enclosing it in a hood. Begin by attaching the small retention clip around the cable. This will transfer any pulling forces to the hood rather than the contacts, reducing the chance of pulling your connections apart. Position the clip in such a way as to allow a small amount of slack in the wires and make sure it's clamped down tightly (see Figure 5-6). Once you're done with that, close the hood up with the other half and screw it in place. You'll now shift your focus to the other end of the cable.

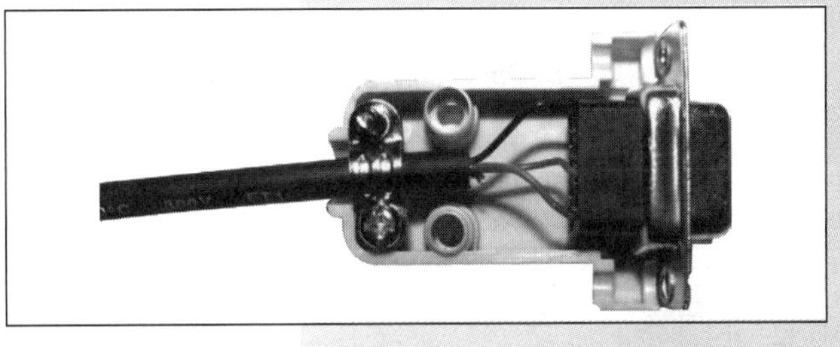

Figure 5-6. Make sure the retention clamp is positioned such that there's no tension in the wires.

4. Attach the cable to the receiver module

You're now in the home stretch of the hardware portion of this project. Begin by stripping about one inch of the outer sheath from the cable, again being careful not to disrupt the insulation on the inner wires. Before stripping the insulation from the inner wires, you're going to secure the cable itself to the module. Lace a nylon cable tie through the slot you created in the perfboard such that the buckle is on the component side of the assembly. Now run the three wires through individual holes on the component side of the perfboard and tighten the cable tie to hold it together. Finally, cut the free ends of the wires to appropriate lengths, and strip enough of the insulation to solder the wires to the circuit and complete the connections. You can see the completed device in Figure 5-7.

Figure 5-7. The completed assembly.

This completes the hardware portion of the project. Congratulations! The real fun stuff starts with the software.

Infrared Signal Processor (Linux)

Now that you have a completed IR receiver module, you're going to want to make it control your computer. In this section, you'll be building the infrared signal processor. Conveniently, there is free software available that's meant to do just that. The Linux Infrared Remote Control project (LIRC) was created specifically for the hardware you've just built, but over the years it has been significantly expanded to support an impressive array of devices (including the IR remote that comes with the Hauppauge PVR-250 used in the HTPC projects later in this book). There are also ports to Windows and Mac OS X.

Take a look at the driver model in Figure 5-8. The model is made up of two major layers: hardware and software. The hardware layer (i.e., the serial port IR module you just built or purchased), is responsible for receiving IR signals and transmitting them to the serial port. Of course, these signals need something to "listen" for them; this is where the software comes in. LIRC uses a kernel module to connect to the serial port, intercept these signals, and pass them, unaltered, up to the decoder daemon (*lircd*). This is where the real action is—the daemon decodes the raw input and dispatches messages to other applications as directed by the *.lircrc* resource file.

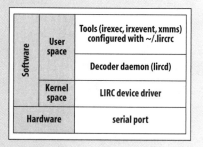

Figure 5-8. The LIRC driver model.

Of course, before you can complete all the configuration requirements and test the hardware for successful operation, you need to install the software.

1. Install the software

The first thing to do is head over to *http://www.lirc.org* and download the latest source archive. For this project, I'll assume you've downloaded it to a subfolder of your home folder called *homehacking*.

```
$ cd ~/homehacking
$ tar -xjvf lirc*
$ cd lirc*
$ ./setup.sh
```

A dialog will appear to walk you through the configuration of the driver. By default, COM1 (*/dev/ttyS0*) will be selected as the serial port.

If you decide to use COM2 (*/dev/ttyS1*) or any other serial port:

1. Press Enter to advance to the Driver Configurations screen.

2. Press Enter again to select the home-brew serial port driver.

3. Use the arrow keys to navigate to the appropriate port and press Enter to continue.

4. Press Enter again to accept the default driver-specific options.

Next, select Save Configuration And Run Configure to create the *makefile*.

There's one more thing you need to do before compiling LIRC. Compilation will fail if the compiler doesn't find a config file in your kernel source directory. The documentation at LIRC's web site tells you that you need to compile your own kernel, and then leaves you on your own to figure it out. In reality, you can bypass this requirement by simply copying a config file for your particular architecture from the *configs* subdirectory of your kernel source into the kernel source directory and naming it *.config*. For the AMD Athlon CPU in my system, the following accomplished this task:

```
$ su
# cp /usr/src/linux-2.4/configs/kernel-2.4.20-athlon.config /usr/src/
linux-2.4/.config
```

WARNING

The specific location of the kernel config files may vary by distribution and kernel version. Also be aware that there are specific configuration files for each processor type with varying numbers of processors and amounts of memory. Choose the config file that's most appropriate for the system you're working with. The example shown here is specific to my single AMD Athlon XP 2800+ processor with 512MB of RAM.

Now you can build LIRC:

```
# make
# make install
```

When the install is complete, the basic pieces will be in place to begin controlling your PC using an IR remote. There's still some work to be done, though. First, part of the installation routine created some devices in */dev* that need to have their permissions modified to allow access. You can fix this by executing:

```
# chmod 666 /dev/lircd
```

You also need to edit */etc/modules.conf* to include the kernel module for the serial port receiver. Add the following line to the file:

```
alias char-major-61 lirc_serial
```

The last thing to do is update */etc/ld.so.conf* to include */usr/local/lib*, which will help the runtime linker find the *lirc_client* library. Commit the change by running:

```
# /sbin/ldconfig
```

At this point, everything should be in place to allow LIRC to receive and decode IR signals from a remote. However, it's a good idea to get confirmation of this, and LIRC has several programs to help out. You can use *mode2* to test if the input is being received. *mode2* prints the pulse/space length to stdout when signals are received by the module.

```
# mode2
```

Troubleshooting LIRC

Unfortunately, you won't know if you made an error when building the hardware until you actually install and properly configure the LIRC drivers. Before you go back to square one, let's assume that you've correctly assembled the device and begin by troubleshooting the software.

- If you see an error like this:

```
mode2: error opening /dev/lirc
mode2: Device or resource busy
```

check to see if another application is already using */dev/lirc*. You can do this by executing the following as root:

```
/sbin/fuser -v /dev/lirc
```

- If you can get LIRC to work only when you're logged in as root, you probably haven't set the permissions on the device to allow access by others. Do this by calling:

```
chmod 666 /dev/lirc
```

- If you can't seem to compile LIRC and receive an error like:

```
[…]
make[4]: Entering directory
'/usr/src/linux'
make[4]: *** No rule to make
target 'lirc_serial.o', needed
by 'modules'.
[…]
```

then you probably haven't copied a config file into the correct location. You can find the config files in a subdirectory of your kernel source tree called *configs*. Copy the one for your architecture into the root of the source tree and name it *.config*.

(continued)

Now press some buttons on your remote. If you see a stream of codes scroll across the terminal, the installation was successful; if you don't, there are many things that could be getting in the way. See the Troubleshooting LIRC sidebar for some tips to help you resolve the problem. When you're done testing, press Ctrl-C to terminate the program.

Now that you've determined that the hardware and software are working, the next step is to create an environment that makes use of the signals.

2. Configure the remote

LIRC has predefined configuration files available for a large number of IR remotes; you can find them at *http://www.lirc.org* or in the LIRC source tree's *remotes* subfolder. If your remote has a predefined config file, simply copy it to */etc/lircd.conf*. If it doesn't, you're going to have to create one yourself. Happily, LIRC provides a tool called *irrecord* to make it easy for you—launch it by entering:

```
# irrecord myremote
```

and following the on-screen prompts. This will create a file in the current directory called *myremote* that contains all the information necessary for *lircd* to interpret the signals. If you're familiar with the type of remotes that learn by receiving another remote's signals, you can think of *irrecord* as doing something similar. The resulting file should then be copied to */etc/lircd.conf*.

When you're asked to name the buttons on the remote, you can greatly simplify your life by sticking with the obvious. For example, if there's a Power button on the remote, go ahead and name it *power* for the configuration. This will make it a lot easier to configure your applications to respond to buttons.

---

3. Configure the audio player

As an example of using the IR remote, let's configure an audio player such as *XMMS* (X Multimedia System) to respond to events triggered by pressing buttons on the remote. You'll need to install XMMS if your distribution doesn't include it; however, most do, so I won't cover installing it here.

See *http://www.xmms.org* for more information and downloads related to XMMS.

Controlling XMMS with a remote requires you to install a plug-in that enables XMMS to receive and act upon LIRC messages.

1. Download the plug-in from *http://rpmfind.net/linux/RPM/freshrpms/ redhat/9/xmms-lirc*.

2. Install it by running `rpm -Uvh xmms-lirc*`.

Next, you need to create a *.lircrc* file that tells *lircd* what to do when you press buttons on your remote. Begin by configuring *lircd* to start XMMS when the Power button is pressed. Create a text file called *.lircrc* and add the following lines to it:

```
begin
    remote = myremote
    prog = irexec
    button = power
    config = xmms &
    mode = xmms
    flags = once
end
```

This tells *lircd* that when the Power button is pressed, to send the command `xmms &` to the program `irexec` and switch to `xmms` mode. In order to receive the message, of course, *irexec* must be running. To test if it's working, do the following:

1. Save *.lircrc* to your home directory.

2. Restart the daemon by running `/sbin.service lircd restart`.

3. Run `irexec &`.

4. Press the Power button on your remote.

If all is well, XMMS will launch; you still won't have the ability to control it with the remote, though. We'll take care of that right now. Let's start by setting up the remote to close XMMS when you press the Power button again.

Pressing the Power button when XMMS is not running will tell *lircd* to enter *xmms* mode. (Recall the discussion of modes earlier in the chapter.) Within *.lircrc*, the modes are contained within blocks framed by `begin` *mode* ... `end` *mode* pairs. Since you're calling the mode *xmms*, all the configuration for that mode will fall between `begin xmms` and `end xmms`. So to exit XMMS from within that mode, add the following lines to your *.lircrc* file:

```
begin xmms
    begin
    prog = xmms
    button = power
    config = QUIT
    flags = mode
    end
end xmms
```

This tells the daemon to pass the command `QUIT` to the program `xmms`. The `flags` parameter tells the daemon to exit the current mode. For the remaining commands you'll be sending to XMMS, you won't be exiting the *xmms*

Troubleshooting LIRC
(continued)

- You may have a simple conflict with devices attached to the serial port. You can correct this by calling:

  `setserial /dev/ttySx uart none`

  where `ttySx` is *ttyS0* for COM1, *ttyS1* for COM2, and so on.

When you've ruled out all of the software-related issues, you may have to come to the conclusion that the hardware is faulty. If you have access to a Windows box you can try configuring WinLIRC to test the hardware. It's far simpler to configure and works right "out of the box" if the hardware is good. Unfortunately, if you do determine that the device itself isn't working, there's little you can do to find out why. Since it's such a simple device, the best course of action may be to just rebuild it... which is exactly what I had to do on my first attempt.

MP3 Support for Red Hat 8/9

As you are probably aware, the MP3 format is not open. Legally, anyone using an MP3 decoder should have paid a royalty to the patent owner, Fraunhofer. For this reason, Red Hat has intentionally removed the MP3 decoder from XMMS in order to avoid incurring unnecessary costs and potential patent violations. However, you can replace that functionality by installing the MP3 decoder manually.

1. Download *xmms-mpg123* from *http://staff.xmms.org/priv/redhat8.*

2. Install it by entering:

```
Rpm -Uvh xmms-mpg123*
```

mode. For example, to assign the command PLAY to a play button, place the following code inside the *xmms* mode block (but outside of any nested button blocks):

```
begin
    prog = xmms
    button = play
    config = PLAY
end
```

By now the format should be getting familiar; you just need to keep a few simple details in mind. prog specifies the name of the application that should receive the messages; button is the name of the button specified in *lircd.conf*; and config is the actual message to be delivered. For a complete list of the possible commands you can send to XMMS using LIRC, see the *xmms-lirc* documentation in */usr/share/doc/xmms-lirc/README*.

Infrared Signal Processor (Windows)

You've got your LIRC IR receiver ready to go and you want to use it to control your software—but you don't run Linux. You might reasonably assume that the Linux Infrared Remote Control package runs only on Linux; however, you'd be wrong. There's a port of LIRC for Windows named *WinLIRC*.

A completely unrelated IR receiver project already scooped the name *WIRC*; that program runs only on Windows 9x and Me and was specifically designed for the Packard Bell FastMedia receiver. It's not compatible with the receiver we've built in this project.

1. Install and configure the WinLIRC driver

Download WinLIRC from *http://winlirc.sourceforge.net* and extract it someplace where you'll be able to find it. There is no installation routine. I extracted WinLIRC to *c:\program files\winlirc*, and the steps that follow use that directory.

You now need to configure WinLIRC to understand the remote control you'll be using. WinLIRC will work with thousands of remote controls, so the one you have will likely be compatible. I'll be using one that was left over from an old cable box.

There are many remote control configuration files available at *http://www.lirc. org*. If you find one that matches your remote, simply download it to the *WinLIRC* directory and rename it *winlirc.rc*.

When you launch WinLIRC for the first time, you'll probably receive an error complaining that it failed to initialize. This is expected because you haven't created the configuration file yet. Click OK and the configuration screen will appear, as shown in Figure 5-9.

2. Test the receiver

Click on Raw Codes to test your receiver. When the Learn Remote screen appears, press any of the buttons on your remote. If your receiver is working you will see a series of codes scrolling by, similar to those listed here:

```
space 3421710
pulse 3220
space 3514
pulse 716
space 2672
pulse 703
space 2652
pulse 725
space 913
pulse 757
space 2646
pulse 716
space 2646
pulse 731
space 950
```

3. Teach the driver your remote

The next thing do is to train the driver to associate names with the codes emitted by your remote when you press buttons. For example, pressing the Power button will emit a code that is different from the Volume Up button. WinLIRC will allow you to attach names like POWER and VOLUP to those codes. Close the "Learn Remote (Raw Codes)" dialog to return to the main configuration window and click the Learn button. Click Yes to confirm that you want to overwrite the existing configuration file, and the Learn Remote dialog will reappear. To create the configuration file:

1. Enter a name for the remote in the input box and click Enter. This name can be anything you want but must not include any spaces.

2. Accept the default margin of error by leaving the input box blank and clicking Enter.

3. Click Enter again to skip the manual gap and signal length input.

4. You'll be asked to press a button. Press any button on the remote with the remote pointed towards the receiver. (Don't hold it too close, though.) If the receiver picks up the signal it will ask you to press the button repeatedly, with a one-second pause in between, to obtain ten readings. This will be used to establish what type of remote you have.

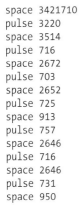

Figure 5-9. WinLIRC configuration settings.

If at First You Don't Succeed...

If you don't see anything when you run the Raw Codes module of WinLIRC, there's probably something wrong with the hardware. The first receiver I built didn't work; I rebuilt it with the same components and it still didn't work.

Finally, I bought all new parts and got it working using a prototype board. A prototype board is a board with an array of holes that are connected electrically in rows. This allows you to plug components in and make connections between them either by inserting leads in the same row or by using jumper wires. Once you have your circuit working, it's simple to transfer it to something more permanent.

Incidentally, after I got the receiver working, I swapped all the new components with the old components and it continued to work. This led me to the conclusion that I'd been making errors in the assembly all along. Oops.

5. Enter a name for the button you're going to start with and click Enter to begin training. Instructions will be given for the type of remote you have.

If you have a signal-repeating remote with no special repeat code, pressing a button can quickly amount to multiple transmissions of the code. For these types of remotes, 64 samples of each button will be taken by holding down the button being learned until told to stop. If you have a nonrepeating remote or if there is a special repeat code, only eight samples are needed with a pause in between each one.

---

6. If you're satisfied that the button was learned (i.e., the number of matches is substantially greater than the number of faults), click Yes to keep it. Otherwise, click No and try again.

7. Repeat Steps 5 and 6 until all the buttons have been learned.

8. Leave the input box blank and click Enter to complete the process and write out the configuration.

9. Click OK to close each of the Success message boxes.

10. Click Analyze to analyze the codes. Your remote might support only raw code and the analysis will fail, but don't worry—it will still work.

11. Click OK to close the configuration window.

You've now enabled the receiver to make sense of the signals it sees. Now you will take those codes that WinLIRC receives and make them perform some actual work. The software that enables this, the Girder program, is free for noncommercial use and can be downloaded at *http://www.girder.nl*. Get the most recent version of the installer and save it somewhere you'll remember. You'll also need to download the WinLIRC plug-in.

Install Girder using the installer you downloaded. The installation is very straightforward; simply accept all the defaults to get it working. Also extract the plug-in to the Girder plug-in folder, which defaults to *C:\Program Files\girder32\Plugins*.

Now you're ready to launch Girder. You'll find that a program group has been made for you on the Start menu, or you can open a Run dialog and execute *c:\Program Files\girder32\Girder.exe*. Once it's loaded, you'll see a screen like Figure 5-10.

The first thing to do to configure Girder is to enable the WinLIRC plug-in.

1. From the Girder File menu, select Settings.

2. Select the Plugins tab from the Settings dialog.

3. Scroll down in the list box until you find WinLIRC and ensure that there's a checkmark next to it.

4. Click Apply to load the plug-in. (The status should display "Plugin is loaded in memory...".)

5. Click OK to return to the main Girder window.

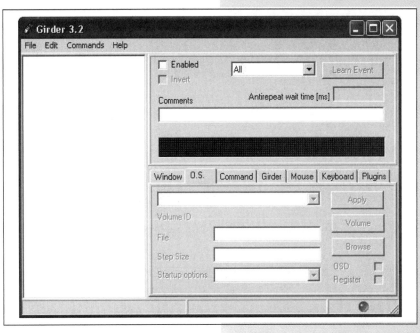

Figure 5-10. The unconfigured Girder interface.

Girder is a framework in which you can program how your computer should respond to various buttons being pressed on your remote, but in fact it's a whole lot more than that. It can respond to a vast array of events, including SNMP, voice recognition, email, and so on. This project covers only a limited application of Girder, but just keep in mind that it's capable of much more.

4. Configure the audio player

You'll now teach your IR system to control an audio player. You'll start by programming Girder to load Windows Media Player when the Power button on the remote is pressed, and then unload it when it's pressed again. (Note that even though we're using Windows Media Player here, the general idea carries forward to any program.)

1. Right-click in the empty tree view that takes up most of the left-hand side of the Girder window and select Add Toplevel Group.

2. Press F2 and rename the new top-level group *MediaPlayer* (or some other descriptive name).

3. Right-click on the newly created *MediaPlayer* group and select Add Multigroup.

4. Press F2 and rename the new multigroup *Power*.

5. Right-click the *Power* multigroup and select Add Command.

6. Press F2 and rename the new command *Load MediaPlayer*.

7. On the properties page that fills the bottom right-hand side of the Girder window, select the O.S. tab.

8. Select Execute from the drop-down list and click Browse to navigate to the *MediaPlayer* executable (*C:\Program Files\Windows Media Player\ wmplayer.exe*).

9. Click Apply.

10. Right-click the *Power* multigroup and select Add Command.

11. Press F2 and rename the new command *Unload MediaPlayer.*

12. From the properties sheet of the *Unload MediaPlayer* command, select the Window tab.

13. Select Close from the drop-down list and click Target.

14. In the Target Selector window in the Settings control group, uncheck Send to Foreground Task and check Executable. Enter *wmplayer.exe* in the text box.

15. Click OK to close the Target Selector box.

16. Click Apply.

At this point, the two commands you created will be executed successively. You need a way to tell Girder to run *Load MediaPlayer* the first time and *Unload MediaPlayer* the second time. This can be accomplished by using states.

17. Right-click *Load MediaPlayer* and select State Settings.

18. Enter a State Count of 2 and a Begin State of 1. Click OK.

19. Right-click *Unload MediaPlayer* and select State Settings.

20. Enter a State Count of 2 and a Begin State of 2. Click OK.

You've now established that there are two states that should be toggled whenever you execute this multigroup command, but you still need to associate this behavior with a button press event from the remote.

21. Click the *Power* multigroup to select it.

22. Click the Learn Event button and press the button on your remote you want to associate with this action.

23. Rename the new event by pressing F2 and typing *Power Button.*

24. If your remote is the signal-repeating type with no special repeat code, you might need to specify an antirepeat wait time. 500 milliseconds should suffice.

Now, every time you press the Power button on your remote, Media Player will toggle in and out of existence. But simply starting and stopping Media

Player hardly suffices as controlling by remote—you're going to want to do much more. Configure the Play button according to the following instructions.

1. Right-click the *MediaPlayer* top-level group and select Add Command.

2. Press F2 to rename the new command *Play*.

3. Select the Command tab from the right-hand properties sheet.

4. Start Media Player. You'll be using it to teach Girder exactly what to do when you press the Play button on the remote.

5. Return to Girder and click the Capture button from the Command tab.

6. Click Start Capture from the System Wide Capturing dialog. You'll see messages appear in the list whenever you click anything.

7. Arrange the windows so you can see Media Player and the System Wide Capturing dialog at the same time.

8. Click the Play button in Media Player and watch the System Wide Capturing dialog for entries that appear to be associated with the Play button. Figure 5-11 shows the highlighted captured event. The SmartFill option tells Girder to attempt to automatically populate the application target information.

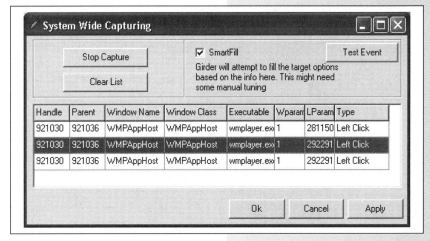

Figure 5-11. Capturing command events in Girder.

9. Select the correct message and click the Apply button.

10. Click OK to exit the System Wide Capturing dialog.

11. Test the command by right-clicking the *Play* command and selecting Test Command. If nothing happens, you may have selected the wrong message, or perhaps Girder has not correctly identified all the necessary target information. If it works, skip to Step 16.

12. Click the Target button to open the Target Selector dialog.

13. Drag the Target icon onto Media Player's Play button to gather any missing target information.

14. Click Apply.

15. Click OK to close the Target Selector dialog.

16. Click the Learn Event button to associate a remote button with the command.

17. Click the button on your remote that you want to associate with the command. (The Play button is an obvious choice.)

18. To prevent multiple signals from being processed, select the Event String entry below the *Play* command and enter an antirepeat wait time of 500 milliseconds.

19. Test the command with your remote.

You can use the same technique to process the remaining functions like Stop, Rewind, Pause, and so on. Because Girder uses a binary file format for its configurations, a listing cannot be included in this book; however, you can download a command group from the web site at *http://www. homehacking.com*.

Wrapping Up

Controlling your PC via an infrared remote allows you to seamlessly integrate PC functions with everyday life. Music and video applications are a great start. Tell the other people in your household that anything they can imagine is probably configurable, and be open to their suggestions about improving whatever you come up with. Sometimes what makes perfect sense to a geek can be utterly meaningless to "regular" people.

Extensions

Now that you have a remote-controlled PC, there's virtually no limit to what you can do. If you have a home theater PC (see the project Building an HTPC) and an X10 computer interface, you can have X10-controlled lights dim when you press the Play button on your remote. Think of it as movie time.

You can also build an IR transmitter and send IR codes from your PC to any infrared-controlled device. Imagine being able to ditch the vast majority of your remotes and control multiple devices with just one. For instance, watching TV at my house used to require at least three devices to be powered on. More than just a nuisance, it meant that I was the only one that knew how to operate the TV. So I built a transmitter to allow a single power button to turn on all the necessary components. Read all about it in Chapter 6, Control Your Home Theater.

Exhibit A: Bill of Materials

You'll need all of the following items if you are going to build your own IR receiver.

Item	Quantity	Part number
Prepunched perfboard, .100" × .100" spacing, 0.042" hole diameter	1 sheet	Radio Shack 276-1395 A
38 kHz IR Receiver Module	1	Radio Shack 276-640
4k7 (4.7 kΩ) resistor	1	Radio Shack 271-1124
1N4148 diode	1	
4.7 μF capacitor	1	Radio Shack 272-1024
78L05, 100mA voltage regulator (TO-92 casing)	1	NTE 977
9-pin female D-Sub connector	1	Radio Shack 276-1428
D-Sub connector hood	1	Radio Shack 276-1539
3-conductor cable	Variable	

Exhibit B: Ready-Made IR Receivers

If building your own infrared receiver is not your bag, check out these alternatives:

Description	Source
Ready-made home-brew receiver (just like the one described in this project)	*http://www.zapway.de*
Irman	*http://www.evation.com*

Control Your Home Theater

6

Cost

$40

Time

eight hours

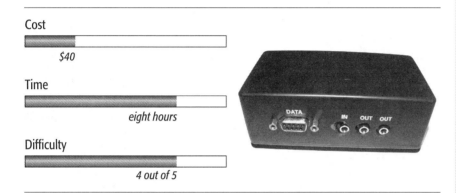

Difficulty

4 out of 5

What You Need

- PC running Microsoft
- Windows with available serial port
- UIRT2 kit
- 40-watt soldering iron with pencil tip
- 60/40 resin core solder
- 3-stranded conductor shielded cable for receiver
- 2-stranded conductor shielded cable for transmitters
- Shrink tubing
- 5V DC power supply
- Panel-mounted DC power jack
- Girder with UIRT plug-in
- Infrared remote with all the buttons you want to use
- Rotary tool (like a Dremel)

For a list of specific parts used in this project, refer to Exhibit A at the end of this chapter.

In my home theater (and very likely in yours), the simple act of watching TV requires controlling several separate devices. I need to turn on the TV, the cable box, and the receiver individually, and ensure that the correct sources are selected. It was a pain, so I got a programmable universal remote and mapped all the functions to it. Unfortunately, certain members of my household couldn't figure out how to switch modes with the remote. They seem to have the idea that the Power button should turn everything on at once, and they get frustrated when they try to change the channel on the cable box but the TV changes its channel instead because the remote was set to TV mode. And believe it or not, they can't imagine that they're doing something wrong!

To help these hapless individuals, I tried a remote with the ability to learn macros. This way I could program the Power button to turn on all the necessary devices. Sadly, this failed as well, because the remote had to be held in such a way that all the signals could reach the devices as it chugged through the macro. My family would prefer to press the button, and then immediately toss the remote on the couch next to them.

I then considered using a reasonably priced remote that transmits RF signals to a base station, which in turn retransmits IR signals to my home theater components. This allowed me to press a button to start a macro with no line-of-sight requirement. The problem was that RF signals get mysteriously lost in my house. And the device was limited to four macros.

For information on RF remotes, refer to Chapter 9, Create Time-Shifted FM Radio.

Salvation finally came in the form of the Universal Infrared Transceiver (UIRT2). This device receives IR signals, processes them via a PC, and performs any of an impressive array of tasks. I'm using it with Girder to retransmit IR signals. You might remember Girder from the IR PC control project. Now the "Power" button turns on all three devices. My family finds the new system intuitive to use—they just point the remote at the TV, which is where the receiver is, and press one button to turn everything on or off. And that's not all—they can also switch to various modes such as TV, PVR, or DVD, and both the receiver and the TV switch to the correct sources. Back in the dark ages, they would be constantly tracking me down to switch modes for them, and they never did learn how to do it themselves. But they can understand a button on the remote labeled "DVD," and now everybody's happy—especially me. Figure 6-1 shows the components of this project.

Figure 6-1. The components of IR (infrared) control.

Project Overview

In this project you're going to build a UIRT2 Type B device and enclose it in a project box with its own power supply. You'll be configuring software that enables you to interpret the signals received by the UIRT through a receiver you'll build yourself, and you'll also transmit IR signals using IR emitters you'll build.

If you'd prefer to not build your own, you can contact Luc Degrande. Luc is the man behind the UIRT2, and is willing to assemble and test one for you for a small fee. I recommend building it yourself, though; it's much more satisfying to make something work when you've built it by hand. And if I can pull it off with my mediocre soldering skills, you certainly can too!

The IR Transceiver

This phase of the project revolves around the assembly of a Universal Infrared Transceiver (UIRT2). There are basically two types of UIRT2 modules available: Type A and Type B.

Type A is an external version that connects to your PC via a serial cable and has an IR receiver and a pair of emitters mounted directly on the board. Type B also communicates over a serial cable and is meant to be mounted internally using one of the expansion bays of your PC case. The main difference between the two, at least to my mind, is that the Type B device supports IR receivers and emitters connected by cable. This allows you to place the receiver and emitters in separate locations, which is ideal if you plan to keep your home theater components in a cabinet.

Technically speaking, you could mount the emitters and receiver for a Type A device on a wire as well. However, I'd only recommend this if you accidentally purchased the wrong version or can absolutely not afford the extra $7.70 for Type B.

---

1. Assemble the UIRT2 circuit

You can order a complete kit from Luc's web site, which is listed in the Bill of Materials in Exhibit A. The first thing to do when you receive your package is ensure that all the parts are there, as listed in Table 6-1.

Fast Track to Soldering

Even if you haven't done any soldering before, don't be afraid to
get started. With a little help, you
can soon be soldering at least well
enough to complete this and similar
projects successfully. The first step to
good soldering is choosing the right
stuff.

Begin with a soldering iron—not a
soldering gun—in the 30-40 watt
range. Anything hotter runs the risk
of damaging your components or
printed circuit board; anything cooler
and you'll be waiting all day for the
solder to melt. You should also steer
clear of acid-core solder—the acid
corrodes leads and traces and can
create conductive bridges between
traces that you won't be able to see.
Instead, use a thin rosin-core solder. I
use .032" diameter solder for projects
like this. Coating the soldering tip
with solder will dramatically improve
its performance.

Preparation is also important. You
should clean any surfaces you plan
to solder together—this means both
the pad on the circuit board and the
leads on the components. You can
use a lint-free cloth with lacquer thinner to wipe off any residue.

When placing the components, I
like to bend the leads after inserting
them to hold the part in place. Then
apply heat to both the pad and the
lead for a couple of seconds. Once
it's hot enough you can apply solder
to the connection, not the soldering
iron. The solder should flow around
the connection. When you've added
enough solder, remove the soldering
iron.

(continued)

Table 6-1. UIRT2 parts list

Part	Quantity	Description
D1, D2	2	1n4148 diode
ZD1	1	5v6 zener diode
R1, R9	2	1KΩ resistor: brown, black, red, gold
R2, R3, R8,R14	4	10KΩ resistor: brown, black, orange, gold
R4	1	3.3KΩ resistor: orange, orange, red, gold
R5, R6	2	10Ω resistor: brown, black, black, gold
R7	1	4.7kΩ resistor: yellow, violet, red, gold
C4, C5	2	22μF capacitor with 2.5mm lead spacing
U1	1	PIC16F84A-20/P
U2	1	uln2003a
C1, C3	2	100μF capacitor with 5mm lead spacing
C2	1	100μF 25V electrolytic capacitor
IR emitters	2	Vishay Telefunken TSAL6200
IR receiver	1	Vishay TSOP4838, 38 kHz
Shunt1	1	3-pin header
WOL +5V	1	Connects to WOL on motherboard
DB9 female connec-tor, nuts, and bolts	1	Provides data connection to PC
Jumper	1	Switches unit between programming and oper-ating modes
X1	1	10 MHz crystal (**Note: Do not install until after the PIC is programmed!**)
Serial cable	1	Connects UIRT2 to PC serial port
Capacitor	1	0.1μF capacitor
Ferrite core	1	Reduced interference

WARNING

Sometimes Luc makes small improvements and modifications to his design, so
the components shipped with your UIRT2 may differ slightly from the list here.

You're going to solder the components in place in the order they're listed in
the table. This way, you start with the lowest profile parts, making it easy
to hold things in place while you solder. The diagram in Figure 6-2 should
help you determine the placement of all the parts. Do all your soldering on
the side of the board that has the traces. (If you're new to soldering, see the
"Fast Track to Soldering" sidebar.)

Some of the components must be placed in a particular orientation. The three diodes, the two integrated circuits, and the electrolytic capacitor (C2) fall into this category, and have distinguishing marks to help you out (see Figure 6-2). The diodes have a black band around one end. The ICs have a notch at one end indicating the end Pin 1 is near; the printed circuit board that the UIRT2 is built on has rectangular pads where Pin 1 belongs. The electrolytic capacitor has a black stripe down one side that shows you where the cathode (-) lead is. Orient the stripe toward the edge of the board, putting the anode (+) on the side marked with a + in Figure 6-2.

When you install the DB9 connector you should connect it to the board with the supplied nuts and screws before soldering. If you tighten the screws after soldering, you might break or weaken the solder joints. Also, it's important *not* to mount the crystal yet; you need to program the PIC first.

2. Program the PIC chip

Now that you've mounted all the parts (except for the crystal) it's time to program the PIC (Programmable Integrated Circuit). You'll be using an ICSP tool developed by Danijel Pticar Mauri and firmware written by John Rhees; you can download both from *http://users.skynet.be/sky50985*. You'll also need a +12V and a +5V power source and a ground, all of which can be obtained from an unused disk drive power connector. You can find +12V on the yellow wire and +5V on the red wire; the two black wires are ground. You can also use the Wake On LAN (WOL) header of your motherboard if you're fortunate enough to have one. Connect the UIRT2 to your PC as follows:

1. Place the jumper on the UIRT2 Shunt1 to connect Pins 1 and 2.

2. Power down your PC and open the case.

3. Connect a +12V power source to the VPP header on the UIRT2, right next to Shunt1. (You can find +12V on the yellow wire of a spare power connector.) A jumper wire with a micro-clip is great for this if you have one; if not, any wire will do.

4. If you have a WOL header and a WOL cable, plug one end of the cable into the header on the motherboard and the other end into the WOL header of the UIRT2. Consult your motherboard's documentation if you're not sure which pin is which. If you don't have a WOL header, you can connect the +5V and GND pins from the UIRT2 to a spare peripheral power connector. (You'll find +5V on the red wire; either

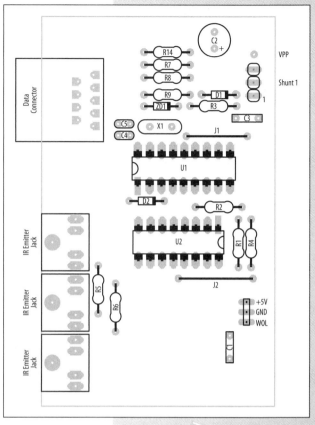

Figure 6-2. Component layout (some pads have been removed for clarity).

Fast Track to Soldering

(continued)

Be careful not to stress the connection before it cools. After the solder cools completely you can snip off the excess leads with diagonal cutters.

When you've completed soldering all the connections, clean up any remaining rosin with a solvent-like lacquer thinner. That's all there is to it!

black wire will provide ground.) Jumper wires with micro-clamps are a great help.

5. Connect the provided serial cable to the DB9 connector on the UIRT2 and an available serial port on your PC.

6. Start up the PC.

7. Run the ICSP program you downloaded earlier.

8. Select the correct COM port from the COM Port group.

9. Click the Open Hex button and browse to the firmware file you downloaded. Click Open.

10. Click the Program UIRT button to begin programming the PIC.

11. When the programming is complete it will display the message "Programming finished. Put jumper back." Click OK.

12. Shut down the PC and disconnect all the cables.

13. Move the jumper on Shunt1 to pins 2 and 3, closest to C2, to put the UIRT2 into operational mode.

You may now mount the crystal. If you plan to install your UIRT2 in your PC, you can also attach the supplied bracket: just secure it to the DB9 connector using the two provided connector retainers, and skip Step 3. Alternately, if you're going to mount UIRT2 in a project box like I did, then read on.

3. Mount the UIRT2 in a project box

The UIRT2 draws a +5V current from the WOL header on the motherboard. My motherboard doesn't have a WOL header. I could draw my +5V from various other sources, and if you'd rather do that, go ahead. I decided to mount my UIRT2 in a separate box with its own dedicated power supply instead, probably just because it's extra geeky. This section will show you how to do it.

Start by going to your local electronics hobby store—Radio Shack will do fine—and find a project box that is just large enough to accommodate the board. The box I ended up with had dimensions of 2.5" × 4.5" × 1.5".

Project boxes are available in a variety of materials and designs. You'll be cutting into the sides of the box to pass the various connectors through, so be sure to get one that will accommodate that. A plastic box is an excellent choice if you have a drill and a Dremel tool. Also, be sure that there are no seams where you'll be making your cutouts.

Once you've got your box, it's time to cut openings for the connectors on the UIRT2; Figure 6-3 provides a detailed layout. A Dremel rotary tool is great for cutting plastic or thin metal. The box I chose had ridges in the wall to accommodate small project boards; however, I won't be using those, and the ridges made the walls much too thick to allow the D-sub connector to protrude well. Figure 6-4 shows where I used the Dremel tool with a sanding wheel to remove the ridges from the wall with the cutouts.

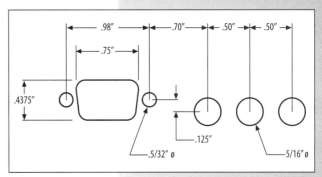

Figure 6-3. Cutout placement in a project box.

Be sure to align the cutouts so that the board will mount with the component side facing the removable cover. I didn't think of this ahead of time, so now if I need to reprogram the PIC I need to remove the board from the box. It's not a huge problem, but it would be nice if it weren't necessary.

You might also notice in some of the photos that the cutouts on my finished box are a little sloppy. Figure 6-3 was drawn after I did that (I couldn't find my calipers to get good dimensions) and should provide better results.

As I've already mentioned, you need to provide +5V DC power to the device. I used an HP PocketPC power adapter, which provides +5V DC at 2A with the positive terminal on the pin and ground on the ring. The specifications are usually listed right on the power supply, so look through your stash for one that's +5V. You can also purchase one for under $30 from just about anywhere that sells PDAs.

Figure 6-4. You may need to grind down the wall thickness to allow the D-sub connector to protrude sufficiently.

Once you've got your power supply, you need to find a DC power jack that matches the connector on it. For the PocketPC AC adapter I used, a 5.15MM O.D. × 1.65MM I.D. connector works well. You need to make a small wiring harness for it, as shown in Figure 6-5. Connect the pin terminal on the jack to the +5V terminal of the WOL connector, and connect the ground of the WOL connector to the ring terminal of the jack. Then drill a hole for the jack in the side of the box (mine ended up being about 5/16" in diameter).

Figure 6-5. Build a tiny power harness using a WOL cable.

My power supply, like most others, has the positive terminal on the pin. Other power supplies have the positive terminal on the ring instead. Be sure to verify that you are connecting the positive terminal to the +5V pin of the WOL connector.

Figure 6-6. You can label your connections and add rubber feet for a professional look.

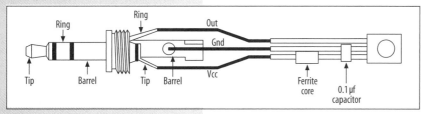

Figure 6-7. Adding a capacitor and ferrite core to the receiver reduces interference.

Figure 6-8. Applying shrink tubing to the completed receiver assembly creates a finished appearance.

It's now time to mount the board in the box. First you need to mount the power harness to the box, and then plug the WOL connector to the header on the UIRT2. Next, mount the board using the two barrel-nut screws that came with the D-sub connector.

If you want to get extra fancy, you can label the inputs and outputs with dry transfers. You can also mount rubber feet on the bottom of the box. Figure 6-6 shows the finished product.

4. Build the external connections

The best thing about the Type B UIRT2 is that the receiver and emitters are mounted on the end of cables and plug into the device with standard stereo phono connectors. This allows you a great deal of flexibility in terms of placement.

Building the cables is pretty simple. First up is the receiver cable. I wanted mine to be long enough to run through my wall from my equipment cabinet, so I bought 25 feet of shielded 4-conductor cable. (You actually only need 3-conductor cable, but I couldn't find that at my local Home Depot.)

Figure 6-7 shows how the receiver assembly goes together. Some people complain about interference with the receiver, so Luc recommends adding a .1 µF capacitor between the voltage and ground terminals of the IR receiver as well as a ferrite core inline with the voltage lead. Some people choose not to use the ferrite core with no detrimental effect, but I figure that as long as Luc is providing it with the kit, I might as well use it. Once you've soldered everything together, you should insulate the leads with electrical tape to prevent them from touching each other. You can optionally cover the whole assembly in shrink tubing for a finished look, as shown in Figure 6-8.

You also need to create the emitter cables, as shown in Figure 6-9, using basically the same techniques: applying electrical tape to keep the leads from touching, and optionally using shrink tubing.

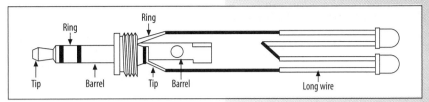

Figure 6-9. Connect the two IR LEDs to the jack, being careful not to reverse the polarity of the emitters.

Finally, connect the UIRT2 to the PC using the serial cable that was supplied with the kit. Connect the power supply, and you're ready to start teaching it some tricks!

The IR Signal Processor

Now that you've built the UIRT2, you need to teach your PC how to control it. There's no better way to do this than with the free Girder program. Girder can respond to any input, not just infrared signals, and translate that input into action. For this project you'll focus on receiving infrared signals from a single remote and retransmitting sequences of infrared signals to control multiple devices.

1. Obtain and install Girder

Girder is a free download from *http://www.girder.nl*. I recommend downloading the installer version rather than the zip file version. Installing it is as simple as clicking Next a bunch of times and accepting a license agreement along the way.

You're also going to need to download the UIRT plug-in—not the UIRT USB plug-in—to control the UIRT2. This plug-in comes as a zip file that contains only one DLL, which you should extract to the Girder plug-ins folder (usually found in *c:\Program Files\girder32\plugins*).

Before you can actually start programming Girder, you need to enable the UIRT plug-in.

1. Start Girder from the Start menu.

2. Choose Settings from the File menu.

3. Select the Plugins tab.

4. Scroll down the list of plug-ins and check the box next to UIRT Driver.

5. Click the Settings button and ensure the correct COM port is specified. Click OK.

6. Click Apply on the Settings page. The Status message should change to "Plugin Is Loaded In Memory."

That's it. Now let's pull everything together.

Receiver and Emitters

You have one receiver and at least one emitter, and in many cases that should be all you need. You might need another emitter assembly if you will be controlling two zones (e.g., closet and theater, or front and rear) or if you need to mask a device's built-in receiver from the remote control.

You'll find yourself in the latter situation if one of the devices you want to control is natively controlled by the remote you'd like to use. In this case, you'll obviously want to prevent the device from responding directly to the remote, and instead take its cues from the UIRT2. You could cover the device's IR receiver with black electrical tape, but now the UIRT2 won't be able to speak to it either. To remedy this, you'll have to build a second emitter assembly and place the LEDs under the tape. Now the device's receiver is insulated from commands emitted by the remote and will respond only to the UIRT2.

If you do need another emitter, all the parts are available from *http://www.newark.com*. You'll need a 3.5mm stereo phono plug, a length of shielded two-conductor cable, and a pair of Vishay TSAL6200 IR LEDs.

You'll also want to think about placement. How long can you make the cables? Mine are each 50 feet long! Some people complain about problems with runs much shorter than mine. You should see results like mine if you use shielded cables and never run them parallel to power lines.

(continued)

2. Program Girder to control IR-controlled equipment

As I mentioned at the beginning of this chapter, controlling my home theater system required the use of three remotes, and no one but me had the first clue of how to operate them. Happily, you can teach Girder how to turn on or off each device, and then associate that with a single button on a single remote. For example, here's the manual sequence of events that needed to happen to turn on my system:

1. Press the Power button on the TV remote.

2. Press the Power button on the receiver remote.

3. Press the Power button on the cable box remote.

I'd like to have the Power button on the receiver remote do all these things at once. The reason I chose the receiver remote is that it's the only one with a single-mode power button. What do I mean by that? Well, many remotes are designed to operate multiple devices: you select the device button for the device you'd like to control and the buttons begin serving codes specific to that mode. My receiver remote, on the other hand, has a main power button that doesn't change with mode, as well as a separate mode-specific power button. I'm pretty sure that even my family can remember to press the big orange button.

You'll start by creating a *top-level group* in Girder.

1. Choose Add Toplevel Group from the Edit menu.

2. Choose Rename from the Edit menu and name the group something like **Home Theater**.

3. Choose Edit → Add MultiGroup to add a new multigroup object.

4. Choose Edit → Rename and rename the group **Power**. You'll contain our individual commands in this group.

5. Select Edit → Add Command and name it **TV Power**.

6. Repeat Step 5 two more times, naming the new commands **Receiver Power** and **Cable Power**.

7. Select TV Power from the tree view and switch to the Plugins tab at the right of the configuration area.

8. Ensure that the UIRT Driver plug-in is selected and click the button marked Settings. The UIRT Driver configuration page will appear.

9. Click the Learn button.

10. When the Learn IR Code dialog box appears, press and hold the Power button on your TV remote. If the progress bar doesn't move all the way

to the end you may have to press the button repeatedly to learn the signal. When it's complete, the box will automatically close.

11. Time to test it! Press the Test button to see if the emitter can control the television.

12. Click OK.

13. Repeat Steps 7 through 12 for the AV receiver and the cable box. You should end up with a configuration resembling Figure 6-10.

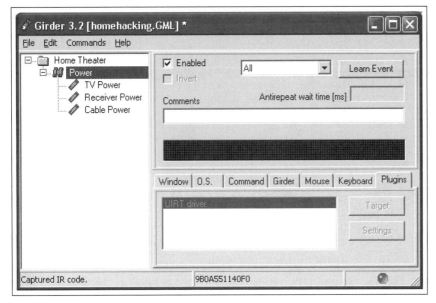

Figure 6-10. Create three commands in one multigroup to have them behave as one command.

14. Now select the Power multigroup and click the Learn Event button.

15. Press the button on the remote that you want to assign this function to. The macro will run immediately.

16. Test it again. It should run through the macro every time you press the button.

You may find that your configuration does not run reliably. This often occurs when you have remotes that repeat their signals continuously, which confuses Girder. But you can filter out the repetition for a specified amount of time by setting an antirepeat wait time in milliseconds. Try 500ms to start; you can tweak it up or down if it's still having problems or if it seems to lag behind your command. You can also tweak the Repeat setting of each UIRT command; the default is 4, but some devices respond better to a single signal by setting the Repeat to 1.

Place one emitter someplace where its light will be seen by all the devices you want to control. In my case, the projector is at the rear of the theater, and all the other devices are in a wall-mounted cabinet to the left of the projection screen. By placing the emitter with the projector in view of its IR receiver, signals can reach both zones with one emitter. This also allows me to conceal it as part of the projection system.

The remote I've chosen to use is the one that natively controls my AV receiver. So I've built a second emitter assembly that's taped directly over the IR receiver on the AV receiver with black electrical tape.

When placing the receiver, try to keep it centered on the viewing area. People naturally point the remote at the TV and don't want to have to remember to point elsewhere. My theater has a fixed screen, so I placed my receiver on the wall behind it so that it was just slightly exposed. If your setup doesn't make it easy to conceal the receiver, consider embedding it in something that fits your décor—it could be anything from a model ship to a Beanie Baby.

3. Switch inputs on multiple devices simultaneously

On my system, going from one viewing mode to another means switching inputs on my AV receiver and TV. To remedy this using Girder, I can use the technique described earlier to create a multigroup with the individual commands required to change to a given mode, and then associate the multigroup with a button on my remote.

There's also another way to do this if you are more comfortable in a scripting environment than using a tree-based programming model like Girder's. Fortunately, Girder allows you to use a real scripting language called LUA, which is similar to VBScript or JavaScript.

Let's get started. First off, to manually switch from TiVo to DVD, I would take the following steps:

1. Switch the TV to its component inputs using the TV remote.

2. Switch the AV receiver to DVD using the receiver remote.

In order to be able to send those commands, I need to teach them to Girder:

1. Add a new top-level group called **Mode Changes**.

2. Add two new commands: **tv_mode_component** and **receiver_mode_dvd**.

3. Select tv_mode_component from the tree view and switch to the Plugins tab to the right of the configuration area.

4. Ensure that the UIRT Driver plug-in is selected and click the button marked Settings. The UIRT Driver configuration page will appear.

5. Click the Learn button.

6. When the Learn IR Code dialog box appears, press and hold the component video input selection button on your TV remote. If the progress bar doesn't move all the way to the end, you may have to press the button repeatedly to learn the signal. When it's complete, the box will automatically close.

7. Press the Test button to see if the emitter can control the television.

8. Click OK.

9. Repeats Steps 3 through 8 for the receiver_mode_dvd command with the mode selection button of the receiver's remote.

You'll now assign Girder events to the two new commands.

10. Select tv_mode_component from the tree.

11. Select Girder Event from the drop-down list to the left of the Learn Event button.

12. Click the Learn Event button.

13. Enter **tv_mode_component** in the Girder Event box and click Select.

14. Select receiver_mode_dvd from the tree.

15. Click the Learn Event button.

16. Enter **receiver_mode_dvd** and click Select.

You now have two commands with events associated with them. The next step is to create a script that triggers the events.

17. Add a new command to the tree and name it **theater_mode_dvd**.

18. Select the Girder tab from the settings area.

19. Choose Variable Manipulation Script from the drop-down list.

20. Click the Script button and type the following small script:

```
TriggerEvent("tv_mode_component", 18)
TriggerEvent("receiver_mode_dvd", 18)
```

21. Click the Apply button to close the script editor.

22. Select All from the drop-down list to the left of the Learn Event button.

23. Click the Learn Event button to start listening for IR signals.

24. Press and hold the button on your remote that you would like to associate with the mode change until the progress bar reaches the end and the dialog box closes. If the progress bar is not progressing, try pressing the button repeatedly.

Now, when you press that button on your remote, your AV receiver will switch to DVD mode and the TV will switch to the component video inputs. You can use these principles to set up similar scripts to switch to other modes.

My DVD player and cable box both connect to my AV receiver using component video connections. They share an output that goes to my TV, and switching between DVD and TV doesn't require the TV input to change. But what if your situation isn't that simple?

For example, say you're watching cable TV and you decide to watch a movie. The component video input on the TV is already active. If enabling DVD mode indiscriminately tells your TV to switch to component video inputs, your TV will assume that since it's already using component video inputs it should cycle to the next component input. By "managing state," you can switch the TV input only when necessary.

Think of your TV as being in one of two states with respect to the inputs you're using: component video or S-Video. Similarly, the receiver can be in one of three states for modes that require the TV: DVD, VCR, and TV. In LUA, all variables are *global*: the state of a variable defined in one script is available to all scripts unless declared using the local keyword. So, you can create two state variables to indicate what the current state is. To keep track of which input on the TV is currently active, create a variable called **tv_mode**; create another variable, **receiver_mode**, to watch over the state of the receiver's modes. We'll use strings as the values of the variables in this project, but integers or even bitfields would work fine, too. The following table shows the two state variables and their possible values.

Variable	Possible values
tv_mode	component
	s-video
receiver_mode	dvd
	vcr
	tv

Now, instead of blindly trying to switch my TV from component input, the script can check to see if it's already in the desired state. For example, to enable DVD viewing mode, the script needs to ensure that the component video inputs are active and that DVD mode is active. The following code will make a change only if the desired condition isn't met.

```
if ( tv_mode ~= "component" ) then
    TriggerEvent("tv_mode_component", 18)
    tv_mode = "component"
end

if ( receiver_mode ~= "dvd" ) then
    TriggerEvent("receiver_mode_dvd", 18)
    receiver_mode = "dvd"
end
```

This code doesn't cover all the possible values, but you would handle all the other modes in the same way. Using these very simple techniques, you can create an elaborate control system using only the UIRT2, a computer, and little ingenuity.

Wrapping Up

Perhaps you've picked up a new skill along the way or gained a little confidence with some you recently acquired. Your equipment and needs probably differ from mine, but hopefully you now understand the basic techniques of controlling IR devices.

Whatever system of control you come up with, there are some important things to keep in mind. For one thing, Girder is a very powerful application—if it's not doing what you want it to do, there's a good chance you haven't looked hard enough. Consult the Girder forum (*http://www.girder. nl*) for ideas and solutions. The Girder community has been around for quite a while now, so the problem you're having has likely already been solved and the solution freely available. Don't reinvent the wheel if you don't need to. And if there really isn't any way to do what you want to do, consider developing a plug-in that solves the problem and sharing it with the Girder community.

Another important thing to remember is that even though you are the designer and maintainer of your control system, that doesn't always make you right. Listen to the other members of your household for ideas—they may even help you find bugs or gaps in your logic. Remember, you're the geek. If they want things to work differently, do it their way (or both if possible). You will find it much easier to adapt to their way than to teach them yours.

Extensions

Girder is much more than the control language of the UIRT2—it has the ability to interact with many varied systems. For example, you can use Girder to respond to CD/DVD insertion events, perhaps powering up devices such as the stereo or television. Maybe inserting a DVD automatically dims the lights after giving you time to reach your seat. Or you could have Girder insert a short film from your collection before and then start the movie after, just like in the old days!

You can even use Girder in a client/server mode that allows multiple machines to communicate with each other. You might envision a scenario where you have a rack-mounted media server with massive storage and multiple TV tuner cards gathering all of you favorite shows. You could have a small PC with a 7-inch touch-screen panel acting as a dashboard for your home theater system; you could have another PC, or perhaps the media server, driving the UIRT2 to control the IR devices. The Internet Event Client/Server plug-ins allow these devices to relay events to other Girder-enabled computers to orchestrate more complex control designs. You could use the touch-screen interface to specify a television show to be scheduled and recorded by the media server. The possibilities are nearly endless.

Exhibit A: Bill of Materials

Item	Quantity	Source
UIRT Type B Kit	1	http://users.skynet.be/sky50985
3-stranded conductor shielded cable for receiver	As required	Home Depot
2-stranded conductor shielded cable for transmitters	As required	Home Depot
Shrink tubing	As required	http://www.youdoitelectronics.com
5V DC power supply	1	http://www.youdoitelectronics.com
Panel-mounted DC power jack	1	http://www.youdoitelectronics.com
Girder with UIRT plug-in		http://www.girder.nl

Build a Windows-Based Home Theater PC

7

Cost

$150 - $1000

Time

six hours

Difficulty

4 out of 5

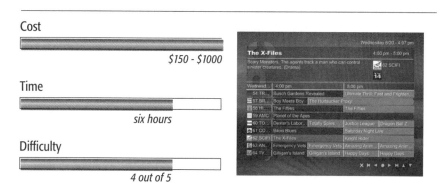

In 1997, Mike Ramsey and Jim Barton came up with a concept that would forever change the way people interacted with their televisions. The product of their vision, TiVo, created an entirely new category of electronic appliances called *personal video recorders*, or PVRs. These devices allow you to automatically record your favorite television shows without having to program the exact time and date and without using videotapes. You can even pause live TV if you get a phone call during you favorite show, or rewind if you missed something.

But why stop there? TiVo was built using standard computer hardware, so it stands to reason that you could build your own from scratch. If you did build your own PVR, you could use it for things that computers are meant to do, such as playing music and games. It would also be nice to load video from your camera and view your digital pictures. Add these features to your PVR and you've got a *home theater PC*, or HTPC. This project, conceptualized in Figure 7-1, will show you how to create your own HTPC with some special features that are not even available from TiVo, ReplayTV, or Microsoft.

What You Need

- A PC with an available PCI slot (a complete list of the components I used is available in Exhibit A)

- A TV tuner card

- Windows XP CDs

- An Internet connection (note that downloading the components will take a very long time if your connection is provided by a telephone modem)

For a list of specific parts used in this project, refer to Exhibit A at the end of this chapter.

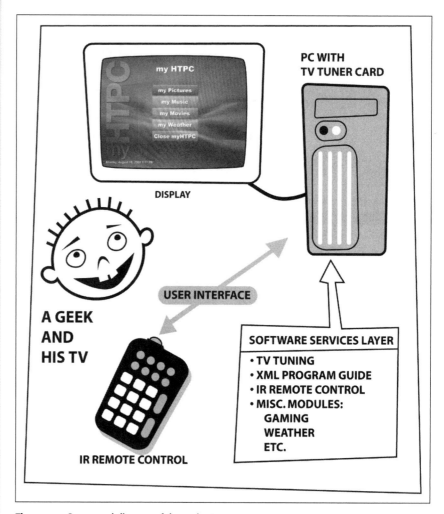

Figure 7-1. Conceptual diagram of the main HTPC components.

Project Overview

This project is fairly complex and definitely not cheap if you're starting from scratch, but will result in an HTPC with many features not currently supported by any of the commercially available PVRs. Here's what this HTPC will offer:

- Free programming guide.

- Nonproprietary file format allows easy video editing. Permanently remove advertising from your recorded shows!

- Ability to archive to SVCD or DVD.

- Ability to watch video files from other sources with automatic metadata lookups.

- Gaming front-end for use with MAME, NES, SNES, and many other emulators as well as PC games.

- Integrated weather information display.

- Integrated music library with the ability to rip or play CDs with CDDB support. (TiVo requires a separate computer and Home Media Option for this.)

- Integrated photo library with support for downloading directly from your camera. (TiVo requires a separate computer and Home Media Option for this as well.)

- Ability to Pause/Fast Forward/Rewind live and recorded television shows.

All this is not to say that TiVo isn't a great product. In fact, both my coauthor and I have one and would recommend them to anyone. However, all but the last four of the features in this list are not available with TiVo.

This chapter begins with a guide for building a personal computer from scratch, including pointers on how to select each component from the many options available in the marketplace. From there we'll take on the task of turning it into a full-fledged home theater PC with Windows XP as the base operating system.

Be prepared to dig in up to your elbows in this project. If your hardware varies at all from what's listed in Exhibit A, it's possible that some things won't work with your configuration. However, lots of people have gotten this project to work with all sorts of hardware configurations, and there's a fair amount of community support for getting yours working, too.

If you're really ambitious, perhaps you'd prefer the Red Hat Linux-based solution in Chapter 8. It's built entirely on free software, but you'll be subjected to a lesser degree of driver support.

If you decide not to build a new PC as the basis for your PVR, skip to Step 7, "Install the TV tuner card." Otherwise, gather your parts and let's start building!

The Hardware Platform

Let's first turn our attention to the Platform aspect. This section presents a very detailed description of how to build a PC from scratch to form the foundation upon which you'll build the PVR. If you plan to use an existing PC for your PVR or if you'll be using different components than those listed in Exhibit A, you you may need to deviate from this guide. Variations in driver support make it impossible to define a perfect recipe for all situations.

129

The hardware I used in this project was selected for one of three reasons. The first criterion was whether I already had the parts. Geeks like me tend to amass quite an array of spare parts, and I had most of them sitting in my spares bin. For items I needed to purchase, I looked for inexpensive parts that would do the job I needed them to do. Finally, to give me options for reusing the hardware if I changed my mind about the system, I chose manufacturers with a policy of supporting Linux drivers. See Exhibit A for a complete list of the parts I used.

Note that my components were selected with budget as a primary concern; if your budget has more elbow room, you might want to place performance at a higher priority.

1. Select your components

There are several things to consider when selecting your hardware components. The following sections offer a few guidelines.

Chassis

If you plan on building the Linux version of this project and would like to use different hardware than what I've recommended, visit *http://pvrhw. goldfish.org/tiki-pvrhwdb.php* to see a database of machines built by others. This is a great place to start if you're not sure which components to buy and would prefer to build on proven designs.

Choosing a PC chassis is almost as much a matter of taste as functionality. Consider where this PC is going to be living. Will it be used primarily as a PC, or will it be part of your home entertainment system? Will it be in a place where noise might be a problem? PCs generally have a lot of fans and move enough air to be audible during the quiet portions of television shows or movies. On the other hand, if your HTPC is going to be located away from the viewing area in a well-ventilated equipment closet, fan noise will be less of a concern than being rack mountable.

Many choices for the home theater PC chassis come with no power supply, which allows you to choose one that is both properly sized for your CPU and has the appropriate connectors for your motherboard. Possibly just as important, it gives you the option of choosing a quiet (or silent) power supply. Many retailers are carrying silent power supplies these days, so finding one shouldn't be a problem.

CPU

Encoding and decoding video streams can be very CPU-intensive. You can expect decent performance from an AMD Athlon XP 1800+ or better or any Pentium 4. I've designed this rig to use a hardware encoder to dramatically reduce the CPU load during recording of television shows. This allows me to use the machine while recording as a background task, while also allowing me to stay on the low end of the CPU scale both in terms of performance and cost.

CPU cooling

Like the chassis, the cooling of your CPU should be chosen according to how you'll be using the machine. If noise is a concern, look for a heatsink/fan combo that is specifically designed for silence. I chose a Zalman CNPS-5100CU, which comes with an adjustable fan speed controller. When the fan is run at its lowest setting, the manufacturer claims noise output to be only 20dB. If your CPU came with a heatsink/fan, it was probably designed for cooling without regard for noise levels. There's no need to replace it if this is acceptable in your application; on the other hand, if you want super cooling with minimal noise and you can afford to spend a little money, maybe a water cooler is what you need.

Motherboard

The motherboard you choose will primarily depend on the CPU you choose. AMD and Intel CPUs do not use the same sockets or chipsets. Aside from processor type, there are several other factors to take into account. For example, many motherboards come with numerous integrated peripherals like built-in audio, video, and networking. The more of these components you can find integrated, the fewer you'll need to add. Generally speaking, you can get a lot of functionality for less money when you choose a motherboard with many integrated components, but you give up some of the flexibility of choosing individual components.

> If you decide that you don't like the integrated components or you can't find drivers for them, you can always disable them in the BIOS and install add-on components.

Memory

These days, motherboards run with a variety of bus speeds and there's a memory module for each one of them. The motherboard I used has a front side bus speed of 400MHz so I could use PC 3200 DDR memory, but the AMD 2400+ runs at 266MHz. I'm not using the full speed of the bus with the CPU, so I should match the memory to the CPU and choose PCDDR memory. To figure out which memory to use, multiply the core speed of your CPU by 8. For example, $266 \times 8 = 2128$, which is approximately 2100.

As far as how much memory you should use, the more the merrier. Memory prices are pretty low, so I wouldn't use less than 512MB. And the fewer memory chips, the better—if you can use one chip instead of two, you can later upgrade your system without removing any existing memory.

Video card

When choosing a video card, you'll first need to determine how you intend to use the card and figure out how much money you're willing to part with. Depending on your needs, you could spend as little as $30 or as much as $500.

Do you plan to connect your PC to a television? If so, the television's inputs will be a primary consideration. Most televisions have composite, S-Video, or component inputs. A composite input is a single RCA connector and is usually color-coded in yellow. This is generally considered to be the absolute minimum acceptable input for decent picture quality because the complete video signal is combined into a single channel.

S-Video gives a noticeable improvement in image resolution over composite. S-Video has separate channels for dealing with black and white information and color difference information. If your television has component inputs, sometimes referred to as RGB inputs, then you will see a small improvement over S-Video when watching DVDs because this is the native format in which DVDs are encoded. Finally, newer digital display devices such as plasma or LCD televisions usually sport a Digital Video Interface (DVI) connector. If you intend to connect your PC to one of these devices, either now or in the future, you should select a video card that has a DVI output.

> If you're going to use DVI, you'd better have your computer right next to your TV. A 33-foot DVI cable can cost you as much as $650!

What about gaming? You'll find it difficult to find a video card these days that doesn't support gaming, but if you're a hardcore gamer, look for cards that support OpenGL and DirectX. The latest video chips from ATI and nVidia can display real-time 3-D graphics comparable to the cinematic renderings in movies like *Toy Story*, which results in an extraordinarily realistic gaming experience.

Lastly, the interface to your motherboard will play a major role in the decision process. If your motherboard has an AGP connector, you'll certainly want to choose an adapter that fits that specification. Otherwise, you'll have to choose a PCI card.

Hard drives

Capturing and storing video requires a lot of storage space. To build a decent HTPC, you need at least 60GB of free disk space. DVD-quality video files use up about 2GB per hour of recording, so 60GB should be able to store 30 hours. Your HTPC will also be hosting several media types, so basically you should get the largest hard drive you can afford. Another option is to get a pair of large drives and create a "stripe set," which makes the two disks appear as one volume to the operating system.

You *can* have too much storage. I upgraded my TiVo with the biggest hard drives I could find, and now it's storing shows from eight months ago that I'll never watch. Indexing all those shows makes it very slow. As wonderful as TiVo is, it's not a powerful PC. Unless you try building your HTPC on a very old PC you shouldn't have this problem.

Hard drives are yet another source of noise. If you find the noise a problem, look into purchasing a noise-dampening device.

Infrared receiver

The open source community has written some excellent utilities that enable you to control your applications using a standard infrared remote control. The one we'll be using is built into the TV tuner card, but if you elect to use a different card or you'd rather use a different remote, you can purchase an infrared receiver that connects to your computer through a serial interface. Or better still, you can build your own! We show you how in the Serial IR Receiver project in Chapter 5.

2. Prepare the motherboard

Now that you've got all your components, it's time to prepare the motherboard. Before mounting the motherboard in the chassis, you should install the CPU and fan. Start by lifting the handle on the socket to unlock it; you'll need to flex it a little to clear the locking tab. Take a moment to look at the CPU. You'll notice a small triangle or arrow in one corner, as shown in Figure 7-2. This arrow should be pointing to the hinge pin of the locking lever when the CPU is oriented properly. Carefully line up the CPU with the holes in the socket. Insert the CPU and close the socket lever to lock the CPU in place.

WARNING

The type of socket shown here requires no force to insert the CPU. If yours isn't sliding in easily, it might be oriented the wrong way. Make sure the small arrow in the corner points to the locking lever's hinge pin. If you're certain that it's oriented correctly, take a closer look at the CPU's pin array. Are any of the pins bent? If so, you can attempt to straighten them, but be careful. The pins are easily broken off if bent too much. If no pins are bent, your CPU may just need a gentle nudge into place.

Proper Handling of Components

Electronic components tend to be sensitive to static electrical discharge, and poor handling can lead to damage. Pick up some anti-static wristbands at your local computer store or at Radio Shack, and be very sure to follow the manufacturer's instructions on usage. (Are we required to say that? Maybe. But I fried a motherboard and CPU through improper grounding during the writing of this chapter. It really does happen!) If you insist on not using a wristband, at least take the time to touch the bare metal chassis before picking up any components.

Figure 7-2. Make sure the CPU is correctly oriented and locked in the socket.

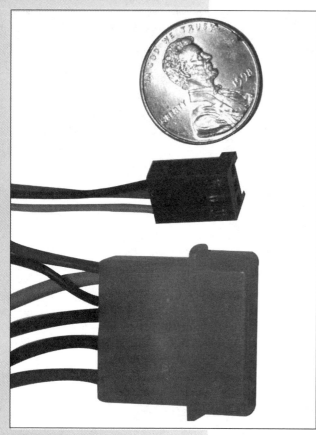

Figure 7-3. 3-pin (top) and 4-pin(bottom) fan power connectors.

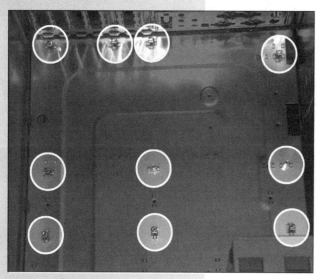

Figure 7-4. Mount stand-offs on the chassis to align with the mounting holes on the motherboard.

I won't tell you which heatsink/fan you should use, since the software is not dependent on these items and CPUs are often bundled with a heatsink/fan anyway. Whichever CPU cooling solution you choose, make sure it's approved for your CPU, and follow the manufacturer's guidelines for installation. Finally, plug the CPU fan into an appropriate power source. My fan has a 3-pin power connector that plugs into the header marked CPUFAN1; your CPU fan might have a standard 4-pin power connector that connects directly to the power supply harness. Take a look at Figure 7-3 to see what I mean.

The last thing to do before installing the motherboard is to insert the memory into the sockets. If you look closely at the edge of the memory module that has all the contacts, you'll see an off-center notch. This aligns with a ridge in the socket that prevents it from being inserted backward. Making sure the module is oriented correctly, press it firmly into place until the locking tabs at both ends close. It's generally easier to get one end of the module inserted and locked before pushing the other end in. My system uses two 256MB modules for a total of 512MB.

3. Install the motherboard in the chassis

Motherboards can be mounted to the chassis in several different ways. If you take a look at your motherboard you'll see several mounting holes that should line up with whatever mounting devices your chassis provides. The chassis I used came with stand-offs that clip into perforations in the sheetmetal. Figure 7-4 shows where I inserted these clips so that they would line up with all of the holes in the motherboard. Once the clips are positioned, align the holes on the motherboard with the threaded holes in the clips and insert the screws.

Next, you need to make the power and signal connections between the motherboard and chassis. There are several wires with small connectors that have labels like HDD LED, PWR LED, and RESET that you will need to plug into the headers on the motherboard for the front-panel switches and indicators. Figure 7-5 shows you where to plug in each connector.

> Polarity is important only for the LED connectors. If the indicators on your front panel do not light properly, chances are you have the polarity reversed.

The connector on my chassis for the power LED was not configured to align with the pins on the header, so I had to perform some minor surgery. If you have the same problem, look for the tiny flaps on the back of the connector that serve to lock the connector pins in place. Slide the tip of a hobby knife under one of the flaps so you can remove the misaligned pin by tugging on the wire, and then reinsert the pin in the correct slot (see Figure 7-6).

You can now connect the power supply to the motherboard. My motherboard came with two power connectors: one is the standard ATX power connector that all ATX motherboards and ATX power supplies have, and the other is the result of a revision to Intel's ATX specification that calls for a separate 12V supply directly to the CPU. If your power supply doesn't have this second connector, don't worry—the CPU will draw its current from the standard ATX power harness. You may also have an additional 6-pin AUX connector on your motherboard and power supply; if so, connect that as well. My power supply also came with a 3-pin connector (like the one on the CPU fan) that has two conductors. I plugged this into the header marked PWRFAN1 so that the BIOS can monitor the speed of the power supply fan, but this is nonessential as well.

4. Install the video card

Your motherboard will have a number of slots, with one slot (usually brown) set further from the back of the chassis than the rest (see Figure 7-7). This is the AGP slot. Insert the edge connector of the AGP video card into the slot and press it firmly into place.

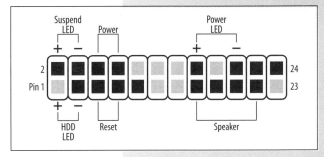

Figure 7-5. Layout of the front-panel power and indicator LED header on my motherboard.

Figure 7-6. Remove and rearrange pins by lifting the tab with a hobby knife.

Figure 7-7. Identify the AGP port on the motherboard.

Now is a good time to conduct a basic test. Plug in a power cord, keyboard, mouse, and monitor, and start up the system. You won't get far, as you have no boot device, but this should give you an operational baseline if successful.

If the system complains about anything other than an inaccessible boot device, remove the power source and fix the problem. If the machine won't start at all, check your power connections and the power switch connection. If any of the front-panel LEDs fail to light, reverse the polarity by giving its connector a 180° turn.

If there's no video, try reseating the video card. If you hear a series of beeps, chances are your memory needs to be reseated. If you still can't determine the problem, your motherboard might not be properly grounded, or you might have fried it or the CPU during handling.

If the machine goes through POST (Power On Self Test), you're good to continue. Turn the power back off and unplug the power supply.

> As a general rule, your computer only needs a video card, a CPU, and memory to perform its POST. Ensuring that it can POST with only these components during assembly means that you can eliminate these components as suspects if problems arise later.

5. Install the IDE devices

You're going to install two hard disk drives and one CD/DVD burner in this machine. One hard drive will be dedicated to the operating system, and the other will be used for datafiles such as recorded TV shows and music.

> In general, 5400 RPM drives are suitable for capturing video streams, and have the added benefit of being much quieter and longer lived than higher-RPM drives.

Set all your drives to Cable Select. For most drives this is accomplished by using jumpers in a small pin array at the end of the drive where the data and power cables connect. Most manufacturers will place some sort of guide right on the device; you may have to look very closely. One of my drives just has small codes etched into the circuit board to guide me. Once you've set the jumpers to Cable Select, you can install the drives into the chassis following the chassis manufacturer's guidelines.

Now plug the blue connector of the IDE cable into the first IDE channel's connector on the motherboard. These connectors are keyed to prevent them from being inserted backward. Plug the middle (slave) connector to the CD/DVD burner, and plug the last (master) connector into the operating system drive. Figure 7-8 shows the three connectors on a typical 80-pin IDE cable. Take a second IDE cable and plug it into the second IDE channel on the motherboard, and plug the other end of the cable into the data drive (the middle connector will be left unused). Connect the disk drives to the power harness, and finally, plug a CD audio cable into the jack on the CD/DVD burner and connect the other end to the motherboard's CD audio input header.

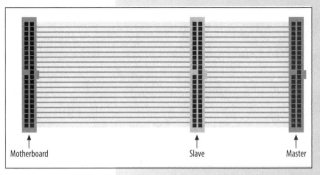

Figure 7-8. A typical IDE cable has three connectors.

6. Install the floppy drive

Installing a floppy drive is an optional step. If you decide to do it, find the floppy disk connector on the motherboard. This will be a 34-pin connector usually labeled FDC1. You'll probably see a small "1" silkscreened next to one end of the connector. Now take a look at the floppy cable. You'll see that one lead is painted red, and this is the side of the cable where pin 1 is located. Align this pin with the pin 1 of the floppy disk connector and insert it fully.

The ability to boot from CDs combined with the affordability of CD burners allow you to break free of floppies forever if you choose, but be careful when making this choice. Some hardware vendors supply BIOS flash utilities that will not work with a CD because of their read-only nature, which means that you may be unable to upgrade your BIOS.

Examine the floppy drive to locate pin 1 on its connector, note its location, and mount the floppy drive in the chassis according to the manufacturer's instructions. Now plug in the floppy drive cable with the red lead aligned with pin 1, and plug the power connector into the power supply harness.

If the data cable connected to the floppy drive is backward, the disk access indicator LED will burn continuously. Just giving the connector a flip should fix the problem.

---

7. Install the TV tuner card

There should be several slot connectors along the back of the motherboard that line up with the expansion slots of the chassis. These are PCI slots, and you're going to insert your TV tuner card into the one closest to the video card. If you're using the PVR-250 card, all you have to do is insert it into the slot and secure it with a screw. Cards that rely on the CPU to encode the video use all the available bandwidth for the video stream, so they require a separate connection to the audio system. This is usually provided by a short

Laying Out Your IDE Channels

A typical motherboard has an integrated IDE controller with two channels, each of which can support up to two IDE devices. Our system will have three devices, so let's take a minute to decide how best to connect them to the available channels. Generally speaking, only one device per channel can have its data on the wire at any given time, but each channel can be operated independently. This means that a device on channel 0 does not need to wait for channel 1 to be available before taking control of its bus, and vice versa. If you place the large volume where your data will be stored all by itself on one of the IDE channels, it should never have to wait before transferring data. Also, when you start burning recorded shows to SVCDs or DVDs, you'll benefit from a continuous stream of data going to your burner.

Choosing a TV Tuner Card

There are basically two kinds of tuner cards: those with hardware MPEG encoders and those without. If you're building your HTPC from a spare system you have lying around, here's some advice on choosing your tuner.

Encoding an MPEG stream is a lot of work for a CPU and if the machine you're using has an outdated CPU, you may end up with less than satisfying results. However, if you choose a tuner card that offers hardware encoding, you transfer the majority of the resource usage to the tuner card. This leaves the remaining resources available for fragging your buddies playing Quake.

However, if the machine you're using has a fairly quick CPU, you can probably get away with a far less expensive tuner card that doesn't have a hardware encoder. (I picked up such a card for $35 at CompUSA; compare that to $150 for the PVR-250.) But even though the machine I designed for this project was more than capable of handling the CPU demands of the cheaper card, I still opted for the PVR-250 because it allows me to use the PC during background recording sessions. Plus, it comes with a remote control; if your card doesn't include one, it's another $40.

Also, think about the kind of encoder you want to use. At the time of this writing, hardware encoders support only MPEG-2. MPEG-4 provides better picture and compression, but you'll have to rely on your computer's processor to do the encoding.

1/8" stereo phono cable. The PVR-250 uses a hardware encoder, which frees up plenty of bandwidth over the PCI bus for the audio stream as well as well as the compressed video stream, so you don't need an additional audio connection. (See the sidebar for more about the different types of TV tuner cards.)

8. Finish up

Almost done! Just close the chassis, pop the Windows XP installation CD into the CD/DVD burner, and start up the machine. Assuming you haven't created any new problems since your last POST, it's now time to install the operating system.

The Software Platform

Believe it or not, building this HTPC on a base of Microsoft Windows XP is accomplished entirely with freely downloadable software (if you don't count the operating system). In fact, in designing this system, I found the Windows-based HTPC software to be far less finicky than comparable Linux software. This project assumes you have Windows installed and some sort of Internet access.

It's probably worth noting that the software we'll be using is community-developed and changing all the time. There's a possibility that versions of applications and drivers mentioned here will no longer be available, although you should be able to get away with using whatever the current versions are. Both the Windows and Linux HTPC software developers have well-populated and frequently updated forums where you can likely find decent help.

---

1. Install all current service packs and security patches

Shockingly, some people don't do this. This PC is going to be connected to the Internet, and the Internet is a scary place to be. Staying on top of updates is the responsibility of everyone who uses it. If you're not the vigilant security type, just enable automatic security. Beyond being just good practice, this project will not work if you haven't installed Windows XP SP1.

2. Install the latest hardware drivers

The successful configuration of this HTPC depends on the reliable interaction of several hardware components. Hardware manufacturers continue to refine their drivers and post these updates on the Web. Download and install any updates according to the manufacturer's recommendations. Exhibit B lists the exact version numbers for each driver I used.

3. Install .NET Framework, Windows Media Player 9, and DirectX 9

Although not absolutely required by the HTPC we're building, you'll want to download a few things from Microsoft. They're all free and are significantly better than the previous versions. You can use Windows Update to make installation easy.

1. Use your web browser and go to *http://windowsupdate.microsoft.com*. Click Yes if you're prompted for permission to install components.

2. Click Scan For Updates. Windows Update will examine your computer for installed updates and report them back to the web site to determine which updates are still required.

3. Select Windows XP from the navigation tree on the left.

You'll find all three of the components you're looking for in this section. Unfortunately, DirectX and Media Player must be installed individually, so you have to do all three separately.

1. Find Microsoft .NET Framework version 1.1 (or a newer version, if available) and click Add.

2. Click "Review and install updates." Any critical updates that you've missed will automatically be added.

3. Click Install Now and then click Accept to accept the license agreement and begin the installation.

When the installation is complete, click Windows XP in the tree on the left to go back in and repeat the process for DirectX 9.0a End-User Runtime. Restart the computer when the installation is finished.

Windows Media Player 9 is not essential to the success to this project; Version 8, which ships with Windows XP, will also work. However, Version 9 is a significant update, and it's free.

When the machine is finished booting, go back to the Windows Update site and add Windows Media Player 9 Series. Go to Review And Install Updates and click Install Now.

The User Interface

In this phase you'll be introducing the user interface to the home theater PC. You'll begin by installing the software that provides the frontend, and configure it to accommodate new components that you'll be adding in the Services Layer.

Enabling Automatic Update for Windows XP

You can configure your PC to check with the Microsoft Windows Update web site and automatically install critical updates at a scheduled time. To enable this behavior:

1. Go to Start → Control Panel.

2. Select Performance and Maintenance.

3. Click the System Control Panel icon.

4. Select the Automatic Updates tab and ensure there is a checkmark next to "Keep my computer up to date."

5. Select "Automatically download the updates, and install them on a schedule I specify" and click OK.

6. Your computer will keep itself well maintained, and you can just keep watching TV.

One more thing: some updates require a reboot. Windows will automatically reboot when necessary. If you want your HTPC to behave like an appliance, then create a user account for using the HTPC and configure it to log on automatically. (See the sidebar on the next page.)

Setting Up Automatic Logon

Before you can establish automatic logons, you need to create a user account for it.

1. Go to Start → Control Panel.

2. Click User Accounts.

3. Click "Create a new account" and name it HTPCUser. Click Next.

4. Select Limited as the account type and click Create Account.

5. Click the newly created user account and then click "Create a password." You can optionally set a phrase to remind you what the password is in case you forget.

6. Close the User Accounts window and the Control Panel.

To enable automatic logons, you also need to make some changes in the Windows Registry:

7. Go to Start → Run.

8. Type `regedit` and click OK.

9. Find the key *HKEY_LOCAL_ MACHINE\SOFTWARE\Microsoft\ Windows NT\CurrentVersion\ Winlogon* and add or edit the following string values:

```
AutoAdminLogon       1
DefaultUserName      HTPCUser
DefaultDomainName    <machine
  name if not part of a domain>
DefaultPassword      <use the
  password you created>
```

Changes to the Registry take effect immediately, so there's no Save command. Just restart your computer, and it should automatically log on with the account you specified.

The software you'll be using to build your HTPC is called myHTPC. It's a free application that provides a highly configurable framework for building an HTPC. Go to *http://www.myhtpc.net* to download the latest version of myHTPC and save it someplace where you can find it easily. Before launching the installer, you need to prepare some folders on the data drive to hold your data files.

1. Open an Explorer window and navigate to the root of your D: drive.

2. Right-click in the file pane and select New | Folder.

3. Type myHTPC and press Enter. You're going to use this as the root of all the media files you create and manage with myHTPC.

4. Repeat the process to create three subfolders in *D:\myHTPC* called Pictures, Music, and Movies. (There will be more folders later as you add modules to myHTPC, but this is enough to get you going.)

All the instructions in this section assume that you're using this folder layout, but of course you can organize your files any way you like. Just keep in mind that file locations in the myHTPC configuration will need to be adjusted for whatever structure you've created.

Now that you've created your folders, it's time to launch the installer. Find the executable you downloaded earlier and run it.

1. When the Welcome screen appears, click Next.

2. Check Yes to agree with the terms of the license and then click Next.

3. Click Next to accept the defaults in the next two dialogs, and Next again to begin the installation.

4. When the installation is complete, uncheck "View the readme file" and check "Launch the configuration wizard." Click OK.

5. When the myHTPC Configuration Wizard appears, click Next.

6. Click Next again to continue past the second page of the wizard.

7. Now you need to define where your pictures should be stored for viewing with myHTPC. Navigate to and select *d:\myHTPC\Pictures* in the tree view and click Next.

8. Repeat Step 7 for both myMusic and myMovies, selecting the Music and Movies folders in *d:\myHTPC*.

9. At the myWeather configuration page click the "Skip this step" button. You'll configure this later from with the configuration utility that comes with myHTPC.

10. Finally, click Finish to complete the Configuration Wizard.

Now launch myHTPC from the Start menu—a screen like Figure 7-9 will appear. The first thing you'll notice is that the interface is clean and simple. The second thing you'll notice is there's no way to watch and record television. The nice thing about myHTPC is that it's really just a shell that you can extend rather easily. Let's begin by getting television integrated.

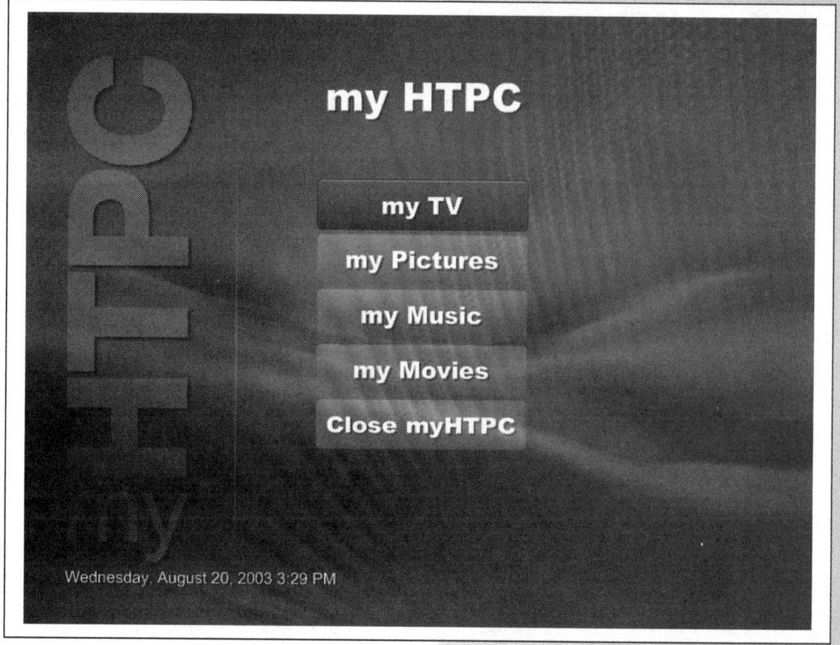

The Services Layer

Now that you've got your user interface in place, you need to establish the underlying services that will be accessed through it. In most cases, each new service will require some configuration changes to the front-

Figure 7-9. myHTPC default user interface.

end, so in some ways the User Interface layer continues to be developed as you add services. We'll be using a program called myHTPC Configure to tie everything together.

1. Add the TV tuning service

We're going to begin with the TV tuner because that's the most exciting part.

Install WinTV-PVR drivers and software

Before you begin, you'll need to download some drivers for the TV tuner card. Go to *http://www.shspvr.com/pvr2_drv-apps.html*, get the Hauppauge WinTV-PVR 250/350 Base CD Install Drivers, and extract the contents to *C:\Windows\temp\pvr-250*.

The instructions here assume that you've purchased and installed the Hauppauge PVR-250 (the PVR-350 will work also). If you've installed a different card, follow the manufacturer's instructions for installing and configuring the device.

---

1. Click the Start menu and right-click My Computer.

2. Select Manage from the context menu that appears. This will open the Computer Management Console.

3. Select Device Manager in the tree view on the left. A new tree view will appear in the right-hand pane that shows all the hardware devices that Windows has identified.

4. Search for the TV tuner card. If this is the first time you've installed the driver, the device may appear as an Unknown Multimedia Controller. Otherwise, expand Sound, Video, and Game Controllers and find Hauppauge WinTV-PVR PCI II (Encoder-16).

5. Once you've found the device, right-click it and select Update Driver.

6. When the Hardware Update Wizard welcome screen appears, select "Install from a list or specific location (advanced)" and click Next.

7. Check "Include this location in the search" on the options screen and enter `C:\Windows\temp\PVR-250` in the combo box.

8. Click Next to begin the search.

9. When the driver is located, click Next to install it.

10. You'll see a warning saying that the driver has not passed the Windows XP Logo testing. Click Continue anyway to install the drivers.

11. When the Hardware Update Wizard completes, click Finish.

You then need to install the software MPEG decoder. Otherwise, you won't be able to watch the video that the tuner card is rendering.

1. Go to Start → Run.

2. Enter `C:\Windows\temp\PVR-250\smd\hcwsmd04.exe` and click OK.

3. Click Next to continue from the welcome screen, and again to install the decoder.

4. When the Installation Complete screen appears, click Finish.

Finally, you'll install the software that enables the infrared remote.

1. Go to Start → Run again and execute `C:\Windows\temp\PVR-250\ir32\ir32.exe`.

2. Select English for the language and click OK.

3. Click Next on the next three screens to accept the defaults and begin the installation.

4. Click Finish when the installation is complete.

Configure the TV module in myHTPC

Before you do anything else, you need to create a folder for the local TV listings that the electronic program guide will be using.

1. Open an Explorer window and navigate to *c:\program files\myHTPC\data*.

2. Create a subfolder called *tv* if the folder does not already contain one.

3. Go into the *tv* folder and create another subfolder called *listings*.

Next, launch Configure myHTPC from the Start menu to add support for the TV module.

1. Select "my HTPC" in the tree view in the left-hand pane (Figure 7-10) and click the New button to drop down a list of available modules.

2. Choose TV from the list, and a new TV module will be created.

The default name of "New TV" doesn't fit our theme, so let's rename

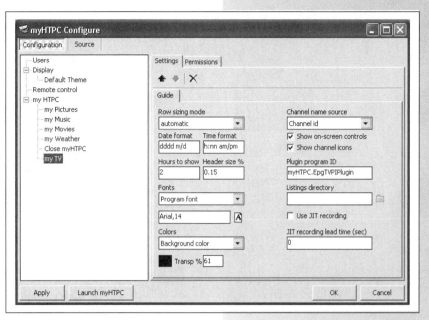

Figure 7-10. Configure the TV/EPG Plugin settings for "my TV".

it. With "New TV" highlighted in the tree view, press F2 to enable editing of the name. I renamed mine "my TV" to be consistent with the rest of the application. Also, since I expect that watching TV is going to be the most used application with myHTPC, I moved the TV module to the top of the list using the arrow buttons on the Settings tab. The remaining settings are acceptable as their defaults for now; you'll fine-tune a few things later.

Now it's time to obtain the plug-in itself. Open up your web browser and point it to *http://www.myhtpc.net/pub/tv plugin/tv plugin.exe*.

There's a space between "tv" and "plugin". If your browser is having trouble, try replacing the space with %20, its hexadecimal equivalent.

This application will download the necessary files to enable television support in myHTPC. Once it's downloaded, launch it to begin the installation process.

1. When the welcome screen appears, click Next.

2. Click Next again to accept the default destination directory.

3. Choose Full Installation from the drop-down list in the Select Components page of the wizard.

4. Accept the default on the Select Start Menu Folder page by clicking Next.

5. Now click Install on the Ready To Install page to begin downloading the required files and installing them in the locations you chose.

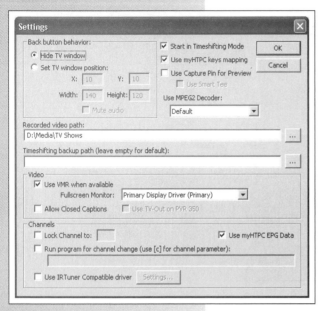

Figure 7-11. Use these settings for the TV plug-in.

6. When the installation is complete, check Start The TV Plugin Setup Screen and click Finish. Modify the configuration to match the one depicted in Figure 7-11.

Click OK to close the Settings window, and launch myHTPC to check your progress. You should see a new button called "my TV" in the list of options, as shown in Figure 7-12. Click on it, and the TV menu will appear. Click on Live TV to test the TV plug-in, and you should see a panel displaying "live" television with a synchronized audio stream, as shown in Figure 7-13. Go ahead and play with the controls on the left—pretty cool, huh? Finally, click Close to exit Live TV. If you tried clicking on TV Guide, you'll know that it doesn't work yet. Let's fix that!

2. Set up the program guide using XMLTV

The electronic program guide (EPG) component of the services layer utilizes XMLTV to create and maintain an XML-based database of your local television schedule. XMLTV is an open source application that uses screen scraping to obtain your local program listings and formats them according to the XMLTV specification. Screen scraping uses regular expressions to extract information from web pages. Nothing will actually appear on the screen, however—everything takes place behind the scenes. As usual, you'll need to grab some files before you can get started. Go to *http://xmltv.sourceforge.net*, and in the Packaged Versions section of the page, follow

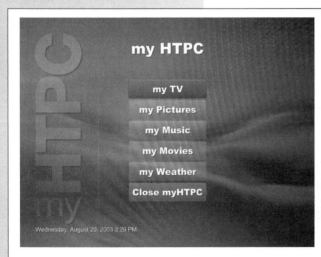

Figure 7-12. The TV module you added shows up in the myHTPC menu.

Figure 7-13. Viewing live TV in myHTPC.

the link for Windows users and download the most recent version, which will be named *xmltv-version-win32.zip*. Inside this archive will be a single folder. Extract this folder to *c:\program files* and rename it *xmltv*.

1. Now open up a command prompt and run:

```
"c:\program files\xmltv\xmltv.exe" tv_grab_na --configure
```

2. Press Enter to accept the default number of retries, and again to accept the default time between attempts.

3. Enter your ZIP code. XMLTV will generate an HTTP request to *http://www.zap2it.com* to determine your channel lineup and present a list of possibilities.

4. Enter the number that corresponds to the most appropriate lineup.

When your channel listing is located, XMLTV will ask you to confirm each channel. If you'd like to accept them all, just type **all** when it asks you if you want to add the first channel. Otherwise, go through the channels one at a time, pressing Enter for each channel you want to add, and typing **no** for each channel you'd like to skip. When you're done, XMLTV will write out a configuration file to use with future grabs.

Now that you've configured XMLTV, you can grab the listings. Enter the following command (including the quotes) at a command prompt:

```
> c:\progra~1\xmltv\xmltv.exe tv_grab_na > c:\progra~1\myhtpc\data\tv\
listings\EPGData.xml
```

Downloading the listing takes a pretty long time. Now would be a good time to multitask.

Install MSXML 4.0 SP2

While you're waiting for the listings to download you can update Windows' XML rendering engine. The architecture of Microsoft's download web site makes it impractical for me to give you a URL to download from, but you should be able to find it by going to *http://www.microsoft.com* and doing a search for msxml. Once you find it, download *msxml.msi* and execute it.

1. When the welcome screen appears, click Next.

2. Check the box next to I Accept The Terms Of The License Agreement on the End-User License Agreement page, then click Next.

3. Enter your information in the Customer Information screen, then click Next.

4. When the Choose Setup Type page is shown, click Install Now.

5. At the end of the installation, click Finish.

Automatic Program Listings

In order to keep the EPG loaded with data, you need to periodically request an update and then fix the listings using the VBScript file. Are you going to remember to do this? I know I can't be trusted, so I set up a Scheduled Task to take care of it for me.

1. Create a file called *EPGUpdate.bat* in *C:\Program Files\myHTPC* that contains the following:

```
@echo off
C:
cd C:\progra~1\xmltv
xmltv tv_grab_na --days 7 > C:\
progra~1\myHTPC\data\tv\listings\
EPGData.xml
C:\progra~1\myHTPC\
FixXMLTVListings.vbs C:\
progra~1\myHTPC\data\tv\listings\
EPGData.xml
```

2. Now go to the Control Panel and select Performance and Maintenance.

3. Select Scheduled Tasks to load the Scheduled Tasks Control Panel.

4. Double-click on Add Scheduled Task to launch the Scheduled Task Wizard. Click Next to continue.

5. Click the Browse button and navigate to *C:\Program Files\ myHTPC*. Select the batch file you just created and click Open.

6. Choose to perform the task Weekly and click Next.

(continued)

Fix the listings file

There's still one last problem to solve. Somewhere along the way, the format that XMLTV creates and the format that myHTPC expects got out of synch. Hopefully this will be corrected in myHTPC by the time you read this, but if not, there's an easy way to fix it. Download *http://myhtpc.net/pub/XMLTV_Fixer/FixXMLTVListings.vbs* and save it to *c:\Program Files\myHTPC*. Then at a command prompt type:

```
> c:\progra~1\myhtpc\FixXMLTVListings.vbs c:\progra~1\myhtpc\data\tv\
listings\EPGData.xml
```

Let's check our progress again. Launch myHTPC, click on "my TV", and then click on TV Guide. You should see a program listing like the one in Figure 7-14. Excellent. So, now that you have the TV working, you're going to want to control it from the couch, no?

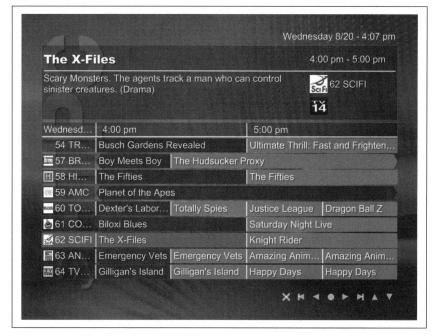

Figure 7-14. The electronic program guide displays the XMLTV data.

3. Configure the IR remote control

No home theater component would be complete without the ability to control it from the couch. This brings us to the IR Remote Control component.

If you're using a TV tuner card other than the Hauppauge and it didn't come with a remote, see Chapter 5, Remotely Control Your Computer, for information about building and programming your own.

Adding support for the infrared remote that comes with the PVR-250 is as simple as editing a text file. Open up *c:\windows\irremote.ini* in Notepad; you'll see that it looks like a standard *.ini* file with section headings in square brackets and key/value pairs. Look for the [Applications] section and add myHTPC= after the last entry in the section.

Then add the following section between two other sections or at the complete end of the file:

```
[myHTPC]
GRNPOWER={alt}{f4}
GO={enter}
0=0
1=1
2=2
3=3
4=4
5=5
6=6
7=7
8=8
9=9
BACK={backspace}
MENU={f12}
RED={app(0x90000)}
GREEN={add}
CHNLUP={up}
CHNLDOWN={down}
VOLUP={right}
VOLDOWN={left}
OK={enter}
YELLOW={app(0xa0000)}
BLUE={subtract}
MUTE={app(0x80000)}
RESERVED=
FULLSCREEN=
REWIND={app(0x320000)}
PLAY={space}
FASTFWD={numpad6}
REC={app(0x300000)}
STOP={numpad5}
PAUSE={app(0x2f0000)}
SKIPREV={ctrl}{shift}b
SKIPFWD={ctrl}{shift}f
```

There's one last thing you need to do to complete the remote control configuration, and then you can move on. When the TV plug-in is running, myHTPC is no longer the application that has focus, and therefore the key mappings associated with it don't work. In fact, the TV plug-in runs with no title at all, so a section cannot be created for it; this forces you to modify the default behavior of the remote. Find the [Default] section and make the following changes to fix that.

```
[Default]
0=0
1=1
```

Automatic Program Listings
(continued)

7. Enter a time you'd like the update to occur. I chose 2:00 A.M. so as not to interfere with the 3:00 A.M. automatic update from Windows Update. Also, select the day of the week you want the update to take place. I chose Sunday. Click Next when you have the schedule set up the way you want it.

8. Enter the username and password you want to use to perform the task and click Next.

9. Finally, click Finish to create the task in the Scheduled Tasks list.

It's a good idea to test your tasks immediately to make sure they work as expected. To test your new task, simply right-click it and choose Run.

```
2=2
3=3
4=4
5=5
6=6
7=7
8=8
9=9
TV={close(radio.exe)}{sleep(750)}{run(wintv2k.exe)}
SOURCE={switch(*task*)}{shift}{tab}
MINIMIZE=
FULLSCREEN={alt}{space}x
RESERVED=
BACK={backspace}

; close current active window; disabled for now
;GRNPOWER={sys(0xF060)}
;GUIDE={run(epgdemo.exe)}
GO={gomenu()}
;GO={run(hcwGo\hcwGo.exe)}
MENU={ctrl}G

;;these 3 buttons are not offical yet
RED={app(0xa0000)}
GREEN={subtract}
YELLOW={app(0x90000)}
BLUE={add}

;;default mappings to drive apps that use APPCOMMANDS on Win2000/XP
MUTE={app(0x80000)}
CHNLUP={up}
CHNLDOWN={down}
VOLUP={right}
VOLDOWN={left}
REC={ctrl}R
STOP={ctrl}S
PAUSE={ctrl}P
PLAY={ctrl}{shift}P
REWIND={ctrl}{shift}B
FASTFWD={ctrl}{shift}F
SKIPFWD={ctrl}L
SKIPREV={app(0xc0000)}
```

Finally, fire up myHTPC and navigate through the selection to verify that the remote is working.

4. Add gaming console support

You could easily stop now and have a very respectable HTPC, but why not add gaming console functionality? myHTPC allows you to add support for MAME, Nintendo, Super NES, Atari, and more. In fact, you can add support for any gaming console for which a Windows- or DOS-based emulator has been developed. In this section we'll be adding support for MAME and Nintendo, but the process is the same for any emulator.

No doubt you've heard of Nintendo and the Nintendo Entertainment System (NES), but perhaps MAME is new to you. MAME stands for

Multiple Arcade Machine Emulator, which allows you to play all the old-school arcade games such as Donkey Kong, Pac Man, Space Invaders, and so on.

A small disclaimer is required here, however. The games themselves are distributed in a form called ROMs, an homage to the fact that these games were originally distributed in Read-Only Memory of arcade consoles. ROMs represent copyrighted materials so I'm not going to show you how to get them, but trust me, you won't have any difficulty tracking them down on the Internet.

The emulators, on the other hand, are perfectly legal. You can download MAME from *http://www.mame.net/downmain.html*; be sure to get the Windows command-line version. The NES emulator is called Nester and can be downloaded from *http://nester.dranalli.com*. Look for the most recent Nester public beta in the Archive section of the page. Both of these files are zip files and simply need to be extracted to a folder; no installer is provided, just like the old days. I extracted both files to *c:\program files* into subfolders named *MAME* and *nester*, and the examples here will assume you did the same.

Create a metafile to list the games

You're now going to configure myHTPC to use a metafile for all the information about the games you will be running. You could write that metafile by hand, but there's a free tool called .My Games that makes it much simpler. Download *MyGames_Full.zip* from *http://myhtpc.net/pub/Tools/MyGames/*, extract it to *C:\Windows\temp\MyGames*, and run *C:\Windows\temp\MyGames\setup.exe* to launch the installer program.

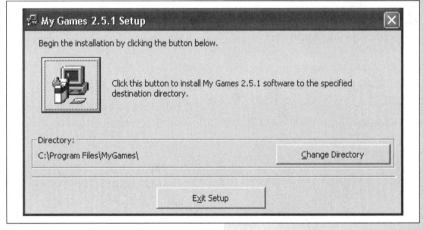

Figure 7-15. Begin the .My Games installation.

1. Click OK to continue from the Welcome screen, and then click the big button to begin the installation (see Figure 7-15).

2. Click Continue to accept the default program group.

3. When the installation is complete, click OK.

Before we launch .My Games we need to prepare some folders for the game files. Create the following folders:

> *d:\MyHTPC\games\console\nes\roms*
> *d:\MyHTPC\games\console\nes\images*
> *d:\MyHTPC\games\arcade\mame\roms*
> *d:\MyHTPC\games\arcade\mame\images*

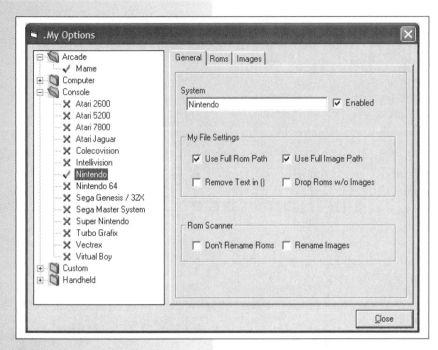

Figure 7-16. Enable Nintendo console emulation on the .My Options page.

For the remainder of this section it is assumed that you have created these folders and you have found some ROMs and copied them to the *roms* folders. Without ROMs, some of these steps will not produce any results.

Now run .My Games from the Start menu. When the program loads, the .My Options screen will automatically appear (see Figure 7-16). You'll notice that Atari Jaguar is enabled by default. We're not using Atari Jaguar for this setup, so you can go ahead and remove it.

1. Uncheck the Enabled box in the right-hand pane of the .My Options page.

2. Click on Nintendo in the tree view and check the Enabled box.

3. Go to the Roms tab and click the + button next to the empty list of Rom Paths.

4. You'll be storing your ROMs in the folder tree you created earlier so we'll add that folder to the paths list. Navigate to *d:\MyHTPC\games\console\nes\roms* in the file selection dialog and click OK.

5. Click on the Images tab. myHTPC can display cover art for media files, and you can take advantage of that to display screenshots from the games you'll be hosting.

6. Click the small button next to the Default Image Path textbox to browse for the folder where the images will be stored. Select *d:\MyHTPC\games\console\nes\images*.

Repeat the above process for MAME, which you'll find enabled in the tree under Arcade. Use *d:\MyHTPC\games\arcade\mame\roms* and *d:\MyHTPC\games\arcade\mame\images* for the file locations. When you're done, click Close.

Now it's time to scan these folders for ROMs.

1. Choose Rom Scan from the Scan menu to begin. You'll see the ROM Scanner screen shown in Figure 7-17.

2. Select All Systems and click Scan Now. .My Games will scan the folders you specified for ROM files and show you the complete list when it's done.

Next, you'll grab some images from the Internet to use with the ROMs found by .My Games. Start by choosing Images | Web | Selected Games W/O Images from the Scan menu. .My Games will go to *http://www.vgmuseum.com* and grab a picture for each of the games. If it encounters multiple possibilities or if the names don't quite match, you will see a window asking you which to use, as shown in Figure 7-18. If the title isn't enough to help you decide, click View to display the pictures directly from vgmuseum.com. When you've picked the right one, click Select to proceed to the next one. This could take a while if you have a lot of games and a slow Internet connection.

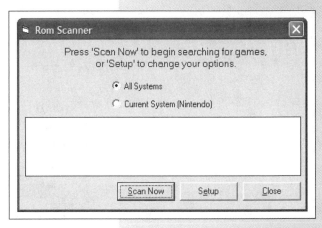

Figure 7-17. Scan for ROMs for all systems.

Figure 7-18. Resolve image scan conflicts by viewing and selecting the appropriate image.

Once you've gathered your list of ROMs and images, it's time to fine-tune them. Many of the games will have downloaded multiple images to choose from. I prefer the in-game images, as the title screens or box cover-art of the games often mean less to me than the screenshots. You can select the alternate images using the Previous and Next buttons below the image. I also like to edit the full name to trim off any unnecessary words, such as revision numbers or country codes.

Next, you're going to create the metadata files for myHTPC, starting with MAME.

1. Click the MAME tab and choose Save As .My from the File menu.

2. Make sure Current System (MAME) is selected and click OK.

3. Save the file as *d:\MyHTPC\games\arcade\mame\mame.my*. Once you click Save, .My Games will create and write the metadata file.

You'll now repeat the process for Nintendo.

1. Click the Nintendo tab and choose Save As .My from the File menu.

2. Click OK on the Options screen.

3. Save the file as *d:\MyHTPC\games\console\NES\Nintendo.my*.

Add the "my Games" module to myHTPC

Now, start up the Configure myHTPC tool from the Start menu. You're going to add another module, just like you did with the TV plug-in, but this time you'll be adding a Group module. Name the new group "my Games" and make sure it's the selected item in the tree. Click the New Item button again and this time add a Media module called MAME to the "my Games" group you just created. Repeat this process to create another Media module called Nintendo.

We'll set up the MAME module first. Click on MAME in the tree to select it, and select Single Metadata File as the Grouping Method. Also set *d:\MyHTPC\games\Arcade\MAME\ MAME.my* as the metadata file.

Now switch to the Display tab and specify Cover Art as the initial display mode. Also, check Square Cells and uncheck all the items in the "Show buttons" list. See Figure 7-19 for a quick view of the correct settings.

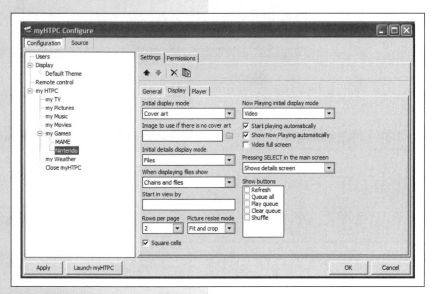

Figure 7-19. MAME display configuration.

Next, switch to the Player tab and click the folder icon next to the Plugin DLL textbox. Open *C:\ Program Files\myHTPC\myHTPC_ ExeMp.dll* as the Plugin DLL, and a list of parameters you can specify will appear. Enter *C:\Program Files\ MAME\mame.exe* as the Executable. If you'd like to enable joystick support enter "-joy " (without the quotes, but including a space after "joy") as the Parameters parameter. All of these settings are shown in Figure 7-20.

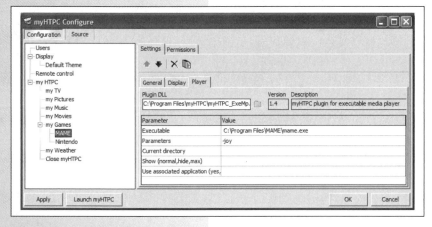

Figure 7-20. MAME player configuration.

Repeat the process to create a new media module for Nintendo, using *d:\MyHTPC\games\console\NES\ Nintendo.my* as the metadata file and specifying *C:\Program Files\Nester\ nester.exe* as the Executable parameter of the Plugin DLL. Nester has built-in support for joysticks, so no further parameters are required.

Now launch myHTPC and see how you're doing. You should see a button called "my Games" now; click it, and you should see the two media modules you just added. If you go into those, a screen resembling Figure 7-21 should appear. Launch some games by selecting the thumbnails. Pretty cool, huh?

Emulators and ROMs abound on the Internet. To add support for other emulators, the process is the same as described above. Simply use .My Games to create a metadata file, and configure the plug-in for each new media module.

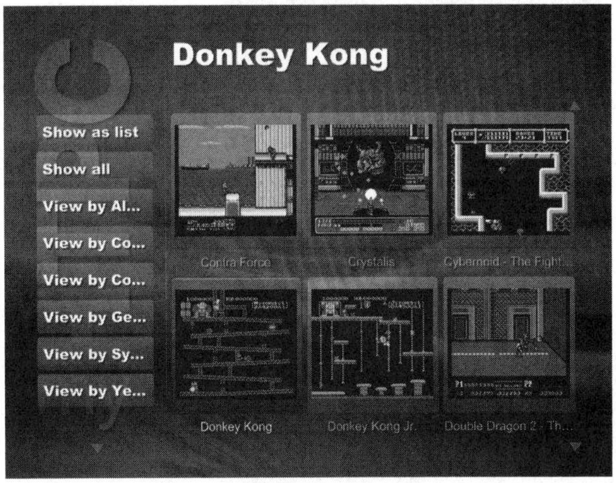

Figure 7-21. The Nintendo games catalog.

5. Configure a weather report

Finally, you're going to configure a weather report. This is a simple task, but requires an Internet connection.

1. Run Configure myHTPC from the Start menu and choose My Weather from the tree.

2. Enter your ZIP code in the Location textbox and click Search.

3. Select your city from the list that appears below. That's it! Click "Launch myHTPC" to check it out.

Wrapping Up

That wasn't too bad, was it? We've gotten a fair amount of functionality with entirely free software, and we can control the whole thing from the couch. Cool!

However, it's important to remember that this is still a computer, and it's always connected to the Internet. Make sure you keep up with all of the critical security patches from Microsoft, or better yet, automate it by enabling automatic updates. Then you can more or less treat your HTPC like a regular appliance.

It's also a good idea to periodically defrag your hard drives. If your files are too fragmented, you might get some blips in the video stream when the drive head has to move a long way to find the next segment, although this isn't very likely.

And that's that. Now it's time to sit back with a remote in one hand and your favorite beverage in the other, and watch some *Golden Girls*. Ahh, bliss.

Setting Up a Radar Image for the Weather Module

Did you happen to notice the textbox in the *my Weather* configuration screen where you can put a Radar Image URL? You can add your own local radar image by using your web browser to go to *http://www.weather.com*.

1. Enter your ZIP code in the Local Forecast area to get to your local weather.

2. When the page loads, scroll down until you can see the Doppler Radar image. Right-click it and choose Properties.

3. Highlight the Address (URL) from the properties sheet and copy it by pressing Ctrl+C.

4. Paste the address in the "my Weather Radar Image URL" textbox, and you're ready to view Doppler radar.

Extensions

There are lots of ways you can build upon what we've done here. Each tuner card can record only one show at a time. If it's in your budget you can add a second tuner, which will resolve single scheduling conflicts. I've found that there's rarely a need for recording more than one show simultaneously.

You can also have the machine running as a server, recording shows that can be rebroadcast to other PCs on your network. You could even create a web interface that allows you to watch your recorded shows from anywhere on the Internet.

The software chosen for this project records video using regular MPEG codecs, which makes it easy to transfer the video to SVCDs or DVDs. You can archive the entire season of your favorite shows without giving up storage on the hard drives.

There are many simple and free MPEG editors available, too. In fact, you can download one from the same page where you got the PVR-250 drivers and software. This makes it easy to remove advertising from the shows you archive.

Lastly, there are some rather expensive but extremely well-designed chassis that are specifically intended for HTPC use. Some great examples are the D.Vine series from Ahanix, Coolor Master's ATC-620, and the HT-200 by Kanam. Some of these even allow you to integrate an LCD display in the face of the chassis where you can display information like MP3 tag info or system status.

Exhibit A: Bill of Materials

Item	Quantity	Part number
Enlight PC case	1	EN-7250
Abit NF7-S motherboard	1	NF7-S
AMD Athlon XP 2400+	1	
Zalman CPU cooler	1	CNPS-5100CU
256MB DDR PC2100 • CL=2.5 • Unbuffered • Non-parity • 2.5V • 32Meg x 64	2	CT3264Z265
IBM 10.1GB 3.5" hard disk drive	1	DTTA-351010
Maxtor 60GB 3.5" hard disk drive	1	96147U8
Panasonic floppy disk	1	JU-257A606P
Sony CD/DVD burner	1	DRU-120A
ELSA GeForce 256 DRR video card	1	Erazor X2
Hauppage TV tuner card	1	PVR-250
Saitek analog/digital games pad	2	P880

Exhibit B: Drivers and Software Versions

Description	Version
Windows XP SP1	5.1.2600 Service Pack 1 Build 2600
Microsoft DirectX 9.0b End-User Runtime	9.0b
MSXML 4.0 SP2 XML Parser	4.0 SP2
Microsoft .NET Framework	1.1
Windows Media Player	9.0
Hauppauge PVR-250 Driver	1.7.21177
Hauppauge Infrared Remote Software	2.35.21052
Hauppauge Software MPEG Decoder	4.0.21154
myHTPC	Alpha Release 24
TV Plugin	1.7.12
XMLTV	0.5.16
.My Games	2.5.1
MAME	0.72
Nester	Public beta 4a

Build a Linux-Based Home Theater PC

8

Cost

$150 - $1000

Time

six hours

Difficulty

4 out of 5

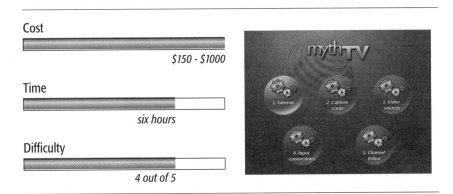

What You Need

- A PC with an available PCI slot (a complete list of components is available in Exhibit A)

- A TV tuner card

- Fedora Core Installation CDs

- An Internet connection (note that downloading these components will take a very long time if your connection is provided by a telephone modem)

For a list of specific parts used in this project, refer to Exhibit A at the end of this chapter.

Well, I promised a Linux-based HTPC, built on Fedora, and I'm here to deliver. Be warned, however, that this project is not for the faint of heart. Figure 8-1 hints at the complexity. Of course, that's not to say that a novice couldn't follow the steps and end up with an HTPC that is easy and fun to use. What makes this project complicated is the frequency with which the many components evolve. During the development of this project, nearly all of the individual components were revised just enough to require changes in the procedure outlined here. This project is based on a fantastic open source program called MythTV that has all the features you'd expect from a PVR, as well as games, weather, and more; however, it also has a long list of dependencies.

This project is based largely on the work of Jarod Wilson. Jarod maintains the definitive guide to installing MythTV on Fedora (see *http://wilsonet. com/mythtv/fcmyth.php*) and has been a valuable ally, always willing to help out. It's very likely that things have changed somewhat by the time you read this, but don't worry—Jarod has you covered.

Fedora was chosen as the platform for several reasons. First, its origin is Red Hat Linux, arguably the most popular Linux distribution in use. Second, for our purposes it's nearly identical to Red Hat Linux with the exception that it's still free and Red Hat isn't. Finally, it supports software installation via RPMs, which, when combined with the Debian Advanced Package Tool

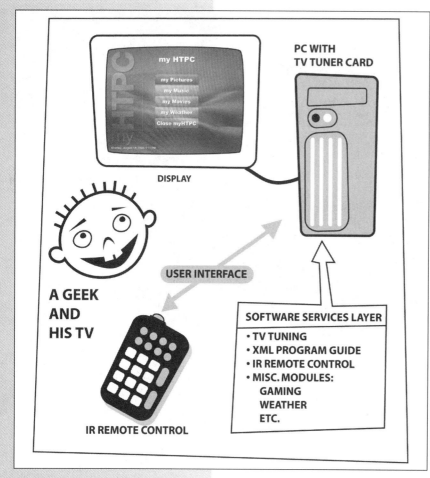

my HTPC

my Pictures
my Music
my Movies
my Weather
Close myHTPC

DISPLAY

PC WITH
TV TUNER CARD

A GEEK
AND
HIS TV

USER INTERFACE

IR REMOTE CONTROL

SOFTWARE SERVICES LAYER

• TV TUNING
• XML PROGRAM GUIDE
• IR REMOTE CONTROL
• MISC. MODULES:
  GAMING
  WEATHER
  ETC.

Figure 8-1. Conceptual diagram illustrating the components of the Linux-based HTPC.

(APT), greatly simplifies the process of installing applications including all dependencies. A gentleman named Axel Thimm has simplified the process even further by building packages that are patched or otherwise optimized for building this HTPC. Try this even once without capitalizing on his efforts, and you'll realize he's possibly worthy of sainthood.

If you already have a PC that you intend to use as a starting-point to build your HTPC, be warned that you may encounter difficulties beyond those I've already pointed out. This project assumes you're building your HTPC on the hardware specified in Chapter 7, Build a Windows-Based Home Theater PC.

The Platform

A reliable system calls for a stable platform. In this first phase of the project you'll be building that foundation.

1. Install software prerequisites

As you know, you'll be building this project from a base of Fedora Core 1. Whether you've already installed it or you are just planning your installation now, ensure that these packages are included:

> KDE Desktop Environment
> MySQL (hidden during installation under SQL Database Server)
> Development Tools
> Kernel Development
> X Software Development
> KDE Software Development

The system this project is based upon has a 60GB second hard disk drive. I mounted this entire volume as */var* and formatted it as ext3 because MythTV creates the folders it uses under */var* and I wanted to chunk out most of my storage for MythTV. You're entitled to create whatever configuration you choose, but be warned that MythTV is going to burn through your storage if you intend to use it fully.

Setting up automatic login

Before you can establish automatic login, you need to create a user account for it. There are many ways to do this—if you already know what you're doing, feel free to use your favorite. The account name you're going to create is htpcuser. Here's one way to accomplish this:

1. From the Red Hat menu, choose Users and Groups from the System Settings submenu.

2. Enter the root password when prompted to do so. (You do know the root password, don't you?) This opens the Red Hat User Manager.

3. Click the Add User button and enter the following values:

```
User Name: htpcuser
Full Name: HTPC User
Password: <must be greater than 6 characters>
Confirm Password: <same as above>
```

4. Accept the defaults for the remaining values, and any missing values will automatically be generated for you. Go ahead and close the User Manager.

5. Now that you have your user account, you can configure Fedora to automatically load this account when the system boots up.

6. Open the Red Hat menu and select Login Screen from the System Settings submenu; you may be asked to enter the root password again. This will launch GDM Setup.

7. To enable automatic login, just click Login A User Automatically On First Bootup (make sure a checkmark appears in the box to the left) and select htpcuser from the drop-down box labeled Automatic Login Username.

8. Click Close and you're done!

Now whenever the machine reboots, it will automatically log in using the account you created.

2. Install the Debian Advanced Package Tool (APT)

As previously mentioned, this project has a large number of software dependencies. While it's technically simple to manage them all, in reality it's a real pain-in-the-aero-chair. APT really streamlines this by gathering all the requirements and installing them if necessary, so we'll be using that instead of manually managing all the dependencies.

A Graphical APT Tool

You might also want to install the GUI frontend to APT, called *synaptic*. It's pretty straightforward to use, and one of its nicest features is the ability to perform queries against all the APT repositories to find the packages you're looking for. This is especially useful if you're having trouble finding the current version of any of the packages referred to in this project. To install *synaptic*, run:

```
#apt-get install synaptic
```

To find the current ATrpms kernel, for instance, type **kernel#** in the Find Package box and then look in the list for the kernel that ends with *.rh9.at*.

Axel Thimm has also made it simple to get and install APT with a pre-configured set of APT repositories. Install his *atrpms-kickstart* package by opening a terminal window and running:

```
$ su
# rpm –ivh http://atrpms.physik.fu-berlin.de/dist/fc1/atrpms-kickstart/
atrpms-kickstart-20-1.rhfc1.at.i386.rpm
```

Axel never sleeps, so by the time you read this he may have updated *atrpms-kickstart*. If so, you'll have to either adjust the URL to correspond to the current version or download the current version to install it from a local source. Using your web browser and navigating to *http://atrpms.physik.fu-berlin.de/dist/fc1/ atrpms-kickstart/* will help you figure out what the current version is.

Once the installation is complete, you're ready to get the complete APT package and upgrade all the RPMs you already have installed. This can take a while, especially if you don't have a broadband connection to the Internet:

```
# apt-get update && apt-get dist-upgrade
```

Reboot when APT returns control to the terminal:

```
# reboot
```

Once you're back up, start a terminal session and use APT to install qt-MySQL:

```
$ su
# apt-get install qt-MySQL
```

3. Install the ATrpms kernel

Although not absolutely required, we're going to download and install Axel Thimm's customized version of Fedora Core's stock kernel that has been patched for v4l2 (Video for Linux), as well as a few other things (a complete list is posted at *http://atrpms.net/dist/fc1/kernel/*). To install the kernel and its source, execute the following command:

```
# apt-get install kernel#2.4.22-1.2179.nptl_47.rhfc1.at kernel-
source#2.4.22-1.2179.nptl_47.rhfc1.at
```

This package receives a lot of attention from Axel and is virtually guaranteed to be a newer version by the time you read this. Check *http://atrpms.physik.fu-berlin. de/dist/fc1/kernel* to see what the current version is.

Now it's just a matter of editing GRUB's configuration file to load the new kernel as the default. Go to */boot/grub/grub.conf*, change default=n to default=0, and reboot.

Once you're up and running again, open a terminal session. (From now on, I'm going to assume that if a line starts with $ or # you'll know to open a terminal session and type whatever follows the $ or #.) Axel has also created a bunch of kernel modules we'll take advantage of during this project. These packages include the name of the kernel they're matched to in their name. To make things easier, create an environment variable with the name of the kernel:

```
$ su
# export KERNEL=`uname -r`
```

Those are back quotes around uname -r, not regular single quotes. The distinction is not trivial. If you use single quotes, $KERNEL will hold the string uname -r. What you want is to trap the kernel version in the string, which will be something like 2.4.20-30_37.rh9.at.

If you're not running the plain old uniprocessor version of the kernel, then uname -r will return a string that is formatted as <version>-<release><flavor>. Unfortunately, the kernel modules are named using <flavor>-<release>-<version>. For example, if you're running the smp version of the kernel, uname -r will return 2.4.20-30_37.rh9.atsmp (version=2.4.20, release=30_37.rh9. at, and flavor=smp). The corresponding kernel module will be named something-kmdl-smp-2.4.20-30_37.rh9.at. Do the following to correctly format the KERNEL variable for your kernel:

```
# uname -r
2.4.20-30_37.rh9.atsmp
# export KERNEL=smp-2.4.20-30_37.rh9.at
```

4. Install the video card drivers

This project includes an nVidia video card. Although Fedora does a reasonable job of getting you started with a default driver, it's not the most appropriate driver for the hardware in this project. Let's install the latest binary release of the nVidia kernel driver:

```
# apt-get install nvidia-graphics4363-kmdl-$KERNEL
# apt-get install nvidia-graphics4363
```

Next, edit */etc/X11/XF86Config* and make these changes:

1. If present, comment out the line that reads Load "dri" by adding a # to the beginning of the line.

2. Immediately following the last line in Section "Module", add Load "v4l" to optimize v4l to X video transfers.

3. Find the line that reads Driver "drivername" and make sure it reads Driver "nvidia".

4. Add TV Out options if required (see sidebar).

To load the new driver, simply log out and log back in. You should see an nVidia splash screen to let you know the installation was successful.

Adding TV Out Options for nVidia Video Cards

My nVidia card automatically detects that I've connected it to a television using an S-Video cable. If yours doesn't, and you'd like to output to a TV, you can add options to the "Device" section for the video card that specify how the card should treat the television. The following options should get you started on most nVidia-based cards:

```
Option "SecondMonitorHorizSync"
       "30-50"
Option "SecondMonitorVertRefresh"
       "60"
Option "TVStandard"       "NTSC-M"
Option "TVOutFormat"      "SVIDEO"
```

For more information about configuring your card for use with a television, including how to enable display on two monitors simultaneously (not supported on all cards), see *http://www.nvidia.com/object/linux*.

The Services Layer

The services layer can almost be thought of as a second foundation. Taken together, these services form the source of all the information displayed in the user interface.

1. Install the Advanced Linux Sound Architecture (ALSA)

Installing the Advanced Linux Sound Architecture is optional, but I recommend it. Also, if you happen to be interested in using the digital outputs to connect to a receiver, Fedora's default OSS drivers will not work. ALSA makes up the audio system module of the services layer.

To install ALSA, execute:

```
$ su
# apt-get update
# apt-get install alsa-kmdl-$KERNEL
# apt-get install alsa-driver alsa-utils
```

You need to edit *etc/modules.conf* to enable the kernel modules. Again, if you've built your PC using the specified hardware, you'll need to configure ALSA to use the nVidia nForce2 driver. Begin by commenting out the existing OSS modules. For this system, add a # to the beginning of the lines that read:

```
alias sound-slot-0 i810_audio
post-install sound-slot-0 /bin/aumix-minimal -f /etc/.aumix -L > /dev/
null 2>&1 || :
pre-remove install sound-slot-0 /bin/aumix-minimal -f /etc/.aumix -S >
/dev/null 2>&1 || :
```

(Your system might have slightly different lines, but they should be close enough to identify them.) Then add these lines at the top of the file:

```
# ALSA portion
alias char-major-116 snd
alias snd-card-0 snd-intel8x0
# module options should go here

# OSS/Free portion
alias char-major-14 soundcore
alias sound-slot-0 snd-card-0

# card #1
alias sound-service-0-0 snd-mixer-oss
alias sound-service-0-1 snd-seq-oss
alias sound-service-0-3 snd-pcm-oss
alias sound-service-0-8 snd-seq-oss
alias sound-service-0-12 snd-pcm-oss

# Save & restore settings
post-install snd-card-0 /usr/sbin/alsactl restore >/dev/null 2>&1 || :
pre-remove snd-card-0 /usr/sbin/alsactl store >/dev/null 2>&1 || :
```

Save the file. Then create a new file called *ethome/htpcuser/.asoundrc* and fill it with the following text:

```
pcm.emu10k1 {
type hw
card 0
}

ctl.emu10k1 {
type hw
card 0
}
```

Now it's time to reboot again. When the rebooting process completes, you'll need to adjust the volume because the ALSA installation sets all levels to zero. There are a few tools that can correct this, but we'll use the Gnome Volume Control applet. On the Red Hat menu, choose Volume Control from the Sound & Video submenu. Raise the sliders labeled Vol and PCM. Now test the new ALSA configuration by playing a sample sound:

```
$ /usr/bin/aplay /usr/share/sounds/KDE_Startup.wav
```

You should hear the KDE startup sound. If you don't, verify the values in */etc/modules.conf*. If you are using a different sound card, you can determine the appropriate settings by visiting the ALSA project's sound card matrix page at *http://www.alsa-project.org/alsa-doc*. You should also verify your *.asoundrc* file while you're there.

2. Install MythTV

As mentioned in the overview, we're going to use MythTV as the user interface to our HTPC. MythTV is a fantastic open-source project that provides a cohesive frontend out of what would otherwise be a bunch of disconnected parts. This is where using APT really pays off. Without it you'd be forced to build MythTV from scratch, accounting for a vast amount of dependencies and sub-components. Not only is that time-consuming, it's also error-prone. With APT you can install a smorgasbord of applications using a single command, like so:

```
$ su
# apt-get install mythtv-suite
```

You'll see all the work Axel has saved you flash before your eyes.

3. Install tuner card drivers

It's now time to install the TV tuner card drivers. We've chosen the Hauppauge WinTV PVR-250 because it has a hardware MPEG encoder. Using a hardware encoder dramatically reduces the burden on the CPU during the recording process. (The installation process will be the same for WinTV PVR-350/Freestyle cards as well.) Run the following command:

```
# apt-get install ivtv-firmware
# apt-get install ivtv-kmdl-$KERNEL
# apt-get install ivtv
```

Next you need to add configuration information for the *ivtv* kernel module to the top of */etc/modules.conf*. (Again, those are backquotes, not single quotes.)

```
# For ivtv
path[toplevel]=/lib/modules/`uname -r`/drivers/media/video
# For bttv and saa7134
path[toplevel]=/lib/modules/`uname -r`/v4l2
# default path
path[toplevel]=/lib/modules/`uname -r`
# ivtv modules setup
alias char-major-81 videodev
alias char-major-81-0 ivtv
options ivtv debug=1
options tuner type=2
options msp3400 once=1 simple=1
add below ivtv msp3400 saa7115 tuner
```

Exit and save the file. Check that the modules load properly:

```
# /sbin/depmod -a
# /sbin/modprobe ivtv
# exit
```

Next, check to see if the kernel sees the card:

```
$ /sbin/lspci -v
```

This will spit out information about all the devices your kernel recognized. Scroll through to verify that there's an entry that says something like:

```
01:0a.0 Multimedia video controller: Internext Compression Inc: Unknown
device 0016 (rev 01)
        Subsystem: Hauppauge computer works Inc.: Unknown device 4009
        Flags: bus master, medium devsel, latency 32, IRQ 10
        Memory at d8000000 (32-bit, prefetchable) [size=64M]
        Capabilities: [44] Power Management version 2
```

Finally, you want to confirm that the card can capture video, but first you need to set up the card's parameters:

```
$ su
# /usr/lib/ivtv/test_ioctl -u 0x3000
# /usr/lib/ivtv/test_ioctl -p 4
# /usr/lib/ivtv/test_ioctl -f width=720,height=480
# /usr/lib/ivtv/test_ioctl -v input=3,output=1
```

The second of the four settings specifies that the input should be set to the tuner. It's possible that your card will have its tuner input at a different number. To determine which number to specify for your card, run:

```
/usr/lib/ivtv/test_ioctl -n
```

This will enumerate all the inputs for your card. Count down the Name fields from the top starting with 0 to find the number for your tuner input (it should be called Tuner 0).

What to Do If the Drivers Fail

If you see this error when you try to capture video:

```
cat: /dev/video0: Input/output
error
```

then reload *ivtv* by issuing the following command:

```
# /sbin/rmmod ivtv
# /sbin/modprobe ivtv
```

and try the capture again.

If the video turned out okay but there was no sound, the *msp3400* module may not have loaded correctly. To fix that enter:

```
# /sbin/rmmod ivtv
# cd /lib/modules/$KERNEL/
kernel/drivers/media/video
# mv msp3400.o msp3400.o.orig
# /sbin/depmod -a
# /sbin/modprobe ivtv
```

and try the capture again.

Now perform the test:

```
# cat /dev/video0 > /tmp/test_capture.mpg
(ctrl-c to stop the capture)
# mplayer /tmp/test_capture.mpg
```

If the captured video looks and sounds like what you'd expect from your television, you've completed the driver setup successfully.

4. Install LIRC

When you installed *mythtv-suite* back in Step 2, a version of LIRC was installed that didn't have proper support of the Hauppauge remote. However, support is included in Version 0.7.0, which at the time of this writing was not ready to be released. Unfortunately, LIRC doesn't compile correctly against the custom kernel due to the updated *i2c* support. Once again, it's Axel to the rescue! He's created a package that's installable via APT.

To complete the installation of LIRC, perform these commands:

```
# apt-get install lirc-kmdl-$KERNEL
# apt-get install lirc
```

When the installation completes, you need to put a configuration file that corresponds to the Hauppauge remote in place.

If your remote is gray, execute the following:

```
# cp /usr/share/doc/ivtv-*/lircd-g.conf /etc/lircd.conf
```

If it's black:

```
# cp /usr/share/doc/ivtv-*/lircd.conf /etc/lircd.conf
```

Now you need to add information to */etc/modules.conf* for LIRC. Find the line that says:

```
add below ivtv msp3400 saa7115 tuner
```

And add this line immediately below it:

```
add above ivtv lirc_dev lirc_i2c
```

Then add one line near the top, after this section:

```
# For ivtv
path[toplevel]=/lib/modules/`uname -r`/drivers/media/video
# For bttv and saa7134
path[toplevel]=/lib/modules/`uname -r`/v4l2
# default path
path[toplevel]=/lib/modules/`uname -r`
```

that reads:

```
alias char-major-61 lirc_i2c
```

Exit and save the file and load the modules manually:

```
# /sbin/depmod -a
# /sbin/modprobe lirc_dev
# /sbin/modprobe lirc_i2c
```

If you don't receive any errors, configure the daemon to load at boot:

```
# /sbin/chkconfig lircd on
```

Now go ahead and start the daemon manually by executing:

```
# /sbin/service lircd start
# exit
```

To test LIRC now, launch irw:

```
# /usr/bin/irw
```

Press some buttons on the remote, and you should see the raw IR codes scroll by.

The final step is to create a resource file that tells *lircd* what to do when you press a button on the remote. Create a new file in */home/htpcuser/.lircrc* and copy the contents from Exhibit B into it. (Note that this code is case sensitive.) If you'd rather not type it all in, you can download it from *http://www. homehacking.com*.

5. Set up MySQL

MythTV uses MySQL to store all its configuration information, as well as the complete television schedule for its electronic program guide (EPG). The first thing you need to do is ensure that MySQL loads at startup:

```
# /sbin/chkconfig mysqld on
# /sbin/service mysqld start
```

Then, set a password for *mysql*:

```
# mysql -u root mysql
mysql> UPDATE user SET password=PASSWORD('yourpassword') WHERE
user='root';
mysql> FLUSH PRIVILEGES;
mysql> quit
```

Now we can create the tables for MythTV in preparation for populating the database. For each of the following lines you'll be prompted for the password you created in the previous step:

```
$ mysql -u root < /usr/share/doc/mythtv-0.14/database/mc.sql
$ mysql -u root < /usr/share/doc/mythmusic-0.14/musicdb/metadata.sql
$ cd /usr/share/doc/mythgame-0.14
$ mysql -u root < metadata.sql
$ mysql -u root < nesdb.sql
$ mysql -u root < snesdata.sql
$ mysql -u root < /usr/share/doc/mythvideo-0.14/videodb/metadata.sql
$ mysql -u root < /usr/share/doc/mythgallery-0.14/database/gallery.sql
```

One last thing we need to do before we reboot. Fedora Core contains a *mysqladmin ping* check in its *mysqld* init script, which fails after a password is set for the root account. The check will hang for 10 seconds, and then falsely report a failed *mysqld* startup. To remedy this, edit */etc/init.d/mysqld* as root, changing the two lines that read:

```
"`/usr/bin/mysqladmin ping 2> /dev/null`"
```

To something like this:

```
"`/usr/bin/mysqladmin -umysql ping 2> /dev/null`"
```

The User Interface

Although there was no real fanfare, you installed the user interface when you installed MythTV. However, you still need to tailor it for your machine's configuration.

1. Configure MythTV

MythTV comes with a graphical setup program that you can use to complete the configuration. To launch it, run:

```
$ mythtvsetup
```

If this is the first time you've run *mythtvsetup*, answer Yes to the two questions about clearing settings before starting configuration. The Main setup screen, which you can see in Figure 8-2, has five configuration choices—General, Capture Cards, Video Sources, Input Connections, and Channel Editor—which are described in the following sections.

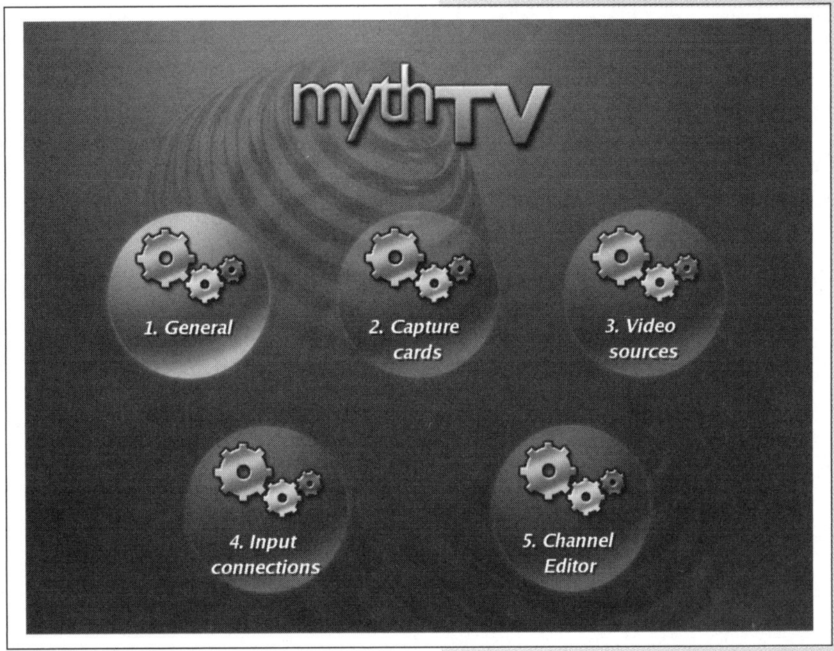

General

You're not actually going to change

Figure 8-2. MythTV's Main setup screen.

any of the defaults in this section, but you need to go through the motions to push the data into the database. Just keep clicking Next until you return to the Main setup screen.

Capture cards

There shouldn't be any capture cards configured if this is the first time you've run the setup tool. Select "(New Capture Card)" and press the spacebar to begin. Choose Tuner 0 as the Default Input and Hardware MPEG Encoder Card as the Card Type. Then click Finish. You'll be returned to the Capture Cards list, where your newly configured card should now appear. Press Esc to return to the Main screen.

Video sources

Just as with the Capture Cards, this list should be empty. Select "(New Video Source)" and press the spacebar to continue. Type a name that's meaningful to you as the Video Source Name (I called mine "Comcast Cable"); this is the name that will appear in the sources list. You then need to enter your ZIP code. When you reach the fifth digit of your ZIP code, it will briefly appear that your computer has hung. This is not the case—rather, MythTV has secretly run *xmltv* in the background to obtain a list of providers in your ZIP code. When it completes its query and populates the Provider list, select your provider from the list and click Finish.

MythTV will start downloading the channel list for your location. When it's done it will return you to the Input Sources list. When that happens you should see your new video creation source in the list. Press Esc to return to the Main screen.

Input connections

The last thing you need to do is assign an input source to your tuner input. Select Input Connections and you'll see a list of all the inputs your card has to offer and the sources they're connected to. By default they should all be connected to "(None)". Use the arrow keys to select "/dev/video0 (Tuner 0) -> (None)" and press the spacebar to continue. Select the video source you created and click Finish. Now press Esc to return to the Main screen, and again to exit the setup program altogether.

Channel editor

The channel editor is used to globally alter channel information, including items like hue, contrast, fine-tuning and others. Skip this section in the configuration for now. You may want to go back to it later if some of your channels are out of tune. If so, wait until after you run the *mythfilldatabase* utility, which we'll be doing now.

The Program Guide database

You might have noticed that *mythtvsetup* asked you to run *mythfilldatabase* when it returned you to the terminal window. *mythfilldatabase* downloads all the programming information for your area and inserts it into the MythTV Program guide database. To start, execute:

```
$ mythfilldatabase
```

This can take quite a while. Now may be a good time to prepare some yerba mate and watch some TechTV.

Automatic Program Listings

In order to keep the EPG loaded with data, you need to periodically request an update. This is pretty simple using crontab.

```
$ crontab -e
```

Add the following to the file and save it.

```
### Run mythfilldatabase every
night at 4:30 am
30 04 * * * /usr/bin/
mythfilldatabase
```

Let's see if it works! Run the MythTV backend server, which you'll configure to load automatically in just a bit:

```
$ mythbackend &
```

And also the program that converts *lircd* input into commands for MythTV:

```
$ irxevent &
```

If you haven't received any errors, load the frontend:

```
$ mythfrontend
```

You should see something like the screen shown in Figure 8-3.

You now need to set up a way to get out of here. MythTV pretty much takes over your computer if you let it. Use the arrow keys to navigate to

Figure 8-3. Main MythTV frontend.

Setup (it's beyond the bottom of the initial screen) and press the spacebar to continue. Select General and press the spacebar to access the General Settings page. Click Next to move to the second screen of the general settings and choose ESC as the System Shutdown key. Next, enter poweroff as the Halt Command. Click Finish.

Now, if you press Esc enough times, you'll be given the option of exiting MythTV or exiting and shutting down the computer. Choose Yes, Exit Now.

Finally, configure the backend to load at startup:

```
$ su
# /sbin/chkconfig mythbackend on
```

2. Finishing touches

If you plan on using your MythTV as a dedicated HTPC, you're going to want to make it more appliance-like. This means having all the required daemons and applications running automatically whenever the system boots up. It would also be nice to reduce the amount of text that scrolls by during the boot process. Luckily, there's a cure for what ails you.

First off, you're going to want to configure automatic login as described at the beginning of this chapter in "Setting up automatic login."

Next, you'll want `irxevent` and the MythTV frontend to load automatically, too. This can be done using the Gnome Session Properties tool. You'll find it on the Red Hat menu under Preferences/More Preferences/Sessions. Select the Startup Programs tab and click Add. In the Startup Command textbox, enter */usr/local/irxevent* and accept the default order of 50. Click OK. Repeat this process for */usr/bin/mythfrontend* using an order of 60. Both of these programs will now load at startup.

3. Configure MythTV's optional components

As you may have noticed, when you installed `mythtv-suite` using APT, you installed every available add-on along with it. You've already configured the database for each of the additional modules, but some additional setup is required to get all the modules working properly.

MythMusic

All the required software should already be configured for MythMusic. If you already have a music collection on your PC and you'd like to have Myth be aware of it, you can either move the entire repository to the default location that MythMusic uses or reconfigure MythMusic to look in your current location.

MythGames

MythGames requires some additional applications to be installed before you can use it. Luckily, these are also available using APT.

```
# apt-get install xmame fceultra zsnes
```

In addition to installing the emulators, you need to tell MythTV where to find them.

1. Select Setup from the main MythTV screen.

2. Choose Game Settings.

3. Select General Settings.

4. You can change the Game Display Order if you'd like. This setting controls the nesting of the categories under MythGame. The default is System Year Genre Gamename, but I find that I'm less interested in the year and the genre than I am in the name. So I changed mine to System Gamename.

5. Click Next.

6. Change the MAME Binary Location to */usr/bin/smame.SDL* (case sensitive).

7. Click Next.

8. Accept the defaults on all the remaining screens by clicking Next and then Finish.

9. Select Scan For Games.

One last thing: you'll need to obtain ROMs for the emulators. I won't tell you how, but a little birdie named Google might be able to help.

MythGallery

Here you simply need to specify the location of the pictures you want to view through MythGallery and click Finish. There are some other settings you can play with while you're here—they're fairly self-explanatory, so I'll leave you to it.

MythVideo

Here again, the only thing you have to do is configure the file location under General Settings if you'd prefer something other than the default.

MythWeather

Setting up the weather plug-in is pretty simple. From the main MythTV screen choose Settings and then Weather Settings. Select the units you prefer (Fahrenheit or Celsius), your location, and the aggressiveness with which you want to obtain data. Then press "I" to save your settings. It's that easy.

If you navigate back to the main screen and choose Weather you should see the current weather conditions. Use the arrows to switch to different screens showing various forecasts and a radar image.

MythDVD

There's not much to configure here either. All the defaults will work well, but you won't be able to rip DVDs unless the transcode daemon is running. The simplest way to get it running and ensure that it's always running when necessary is to launch mythtvsetup.

1. Select General Settings.

2. Click Next to proceed to the Host-Specific Backend Setup screen.

3. Enable "Auto-run The Transcoder After Each Recording."

4. Click Next and then Finish to return to the main screen.

5. Press Esc to exit.

Wrapping Up

That wasn't too bad, was it? We've gotten a fair amount of functionality with entirely free software, and we can control the whole thing from the couch.

However, it's important to remember that this is a computer and it's always connected to the Internet. Make sure you keep up with all of the security patches from Red Hat. Better yet, automate it using the Red Hat Network.

Now you can schedule your HTPC to capture every episode of *Good Eats* so they'll be readily available every time you forget why eggs are so amazing.

Extensions

While we've created a machine that can really do a lot, there are still some ways we can improve it. If there's room in your budget why not add a second tuner? This resolves single scheduling conflicts and there's rarely a need for recording more than two shows simultaneously.

MythTV also makes is possible to have the machine running as a server, recording shows that can be rebroadcast to other PCs on your network. You could even create a web interface that allows you to watch your recorded shows from anywhere on the Internet.

The software we've chosen records video using regular MPEG codecs, which makes it easy to transfer the video to SVCDs or DVDs. You can archive the entire season of your favorite shows for viewing whenever you want without giving up storage on the hard drives.

MythTV also includes a simple MPEG editor that makes removing commercials from your recording as simple as pressing a single key (assuming you've enabled automatic commercial skip).

There are a handful of additional plug-ins for MythTV, too. You can find them at *http://www.mythtv.org*.

Lastly, there are some rather expensive but extremely well-designed chassis that are specifically intended for HTPC use. Some great examples are the D.Vine series from Ahanix, Coolor Master's ATC-620 and the HT-200 by Kanam. Some of these even allow you to integrate an LCD display in the face of the chassis where you can display information like MP3 tag info or system status.

Exhibit A: Bill of Materials

The components used in this HTPC are listed here. For a guide to putting them all together, as well as tips on how to select your own components, see Chapter 7.

Item	Quantity	Part number
Enlight PC case	1	EN-7250
Abit NF7-S motherboard	1	NF7-S
AMD Athlon XP 2400+	1	
Zalman CPU cooler	1	CNPS-5100CU
256 MB DDR PC2100 • CL=2.5 • Unbuffered • Non-parity • 2.5V • 32Meg x 64	2	CT3264Z265
IBM 10.1GB 3.5" hard disk drive	1	DTTA-351010
Maxtor 60GB 3.5" hard disk drive	1	96147U8
Panasonic floppy disk	1	JU-257A606P
Sony CD/DVD burner	1	DRU-120A
ELSA GeForce 256 DRR video card	1	Erazor X2
Hauppage TV tuner card	1	PVR-250
Saitek analog/digital games pad	2	P880

Exhibit B: Remote Configuration (.lircrc)

```
# .lircrc key bindings
#
# Suggested remote key bindings for MythTV Version .8 and up
#
# This is for the newer, light grey remote with red/yellow/blue/green
# keys that comes with the Hauppauge WinPVR 250 and 350(?) cards
#
# This file is case sensitive - so keep that in mind.

# Channel Up
begin
prog = irxevent
button = CH+
repeat = 3
config = Key Up CurrentWindow
end

# Channel Down
begin
prog = irxevent
button = CH-
repeat = 3
config = Key Down CurrentWindow
end
```

```
# OK/Select
begin
prog = irxevent
button = OK
repeat = 3
config = Key space CurrentWindow
end

# Play key for selecting recordings
begin
prog = irxevent
button = PLAY
repeat = 3
config = Key space CurrentWindow
end

# Record key for identifying recordings in EPG
begin
prog = irxevent
button = RECORD
repeat = 3
config = Key space CurrentWindow
end

# Pause playback
begin
prog = irxevent
button = MUTE
config = Key P CurrentWindow
end

begin
prog = irxevent
button = PAUSE
config = Key P CurrentWindow
end

# Escape/Exit/Back
begin
prog = irxevent
button = BACK/EXIT
config = Key Escape CurrentWindow
end

# Also "Power off" key
begin
prog = irxevent
button = OFF
config = Key Escape CurrentWindow
end

# Also "Stop" for movie playback
begin
prog = irxevent
button = STOP
config = Key Escape CurrentWindow
end
```

```
# Also "RED", for instinct ;)
begin
prog = irxevent
button = RED
config = Key Escape CurrentWindow
end

# BLANK on VCR key for deleting recordings from playback screen
begin
prog = irxevent
button = BLANK
config = Key D CurrentWindow
end

# Turns on 'Browse' mode to allow scrolling OSD data while staying on
current channel (use arrows)
# Use any ESC key to exit browse mode
begin
prog = irxevent
button = GREEN
config = Key O CurrentWindow
end

# Blue to record a show seen in browseable OSD
begin
prog = irxevent
button = BLUE
config = Key R CurrentWindow
end

# Displays EPG when watching Live TV
begin
prog = irxevent
button = MENU
config = Key M CurrentWindow
end

# Yellow to select and change to the highlighted channel from active
EPG (because OK records)
begin
prog = irxevent
button = YELLOW
config = Key M CurrentWindow
end

# Toggles Full Screen Mode
begin
prog = irxevent
button = FULL
config = Key F CurrentWindow
end

# Fast forward (default in Myth is 10 minute segment)
begin
prog = irxevent
button = SKIP
config = Key Page_Up CurrentWindow
end
```

```
# Rewind (default in Muth is 10 minute segment)
begin
prog = irxevent
button = REPLAY
config = Key Page_Down CurrentWindow
end

# Scroll Down
begin
prog = irxevent
button = VOL-
repeat = 3
config = Key Left CurrentWindow
end

# Scroll Up
begin
prog = irxevent
button = VOL+
repeat = 3
config = Key Right CurrentWindow
end

# Rewind (default in Myth is 30 seconds)
begin
prog = irxevent
button = REW
repeat = 3
config = Key Left CurrentWindow
end

# Fast Forward (default in Myth is 30 seconds)
begin
prog = irxevent
button = FFW
repeat = 3
config = Key Right CurrentWindow
end

# Bring up OSD (this will auto-fade after a few seconds unlike GREEN
which reqs ESC to exit)
begin
prog = irxevent
button = GO
config = Key I CurrentWindow
end

# Numeric key definitions
begin
prog = irxevent
button = 0
config = Key 0 CurrentWindow
end

begin
prog = irxevent
button = 1
config = Key 1 CurrentWindow
end
```

```
begin
prog = irxevent
button = 2
config = Key 2 CurrentWindow
end

begin
prog = irxevent
button = 3
config = Key 3 CurrentWindow
end

begin
prog = irxevent
button = 4
config = Key 4 CurrentWindow
end

begin
prog = irxevent
button = 5
config = Key 5 CurrentWindow
end

begin
prog = irxevent
button = 6
config = Key 6 CurrentWindow
end

begin
prog = irxevent
button = 7
config = Key 7 CurrentWindow
end

begin
prog = irxevent
button = 8
config = Key 8 CurrentWindow
end

begin
prog = irxevent
button = 9
config = Key 9 CurrentWindow
end
```

Chapter 8, Build a Linux-Based Home Theater PC

Exhibit C

Exhibit C: Drivers and Software Versions

Description	Version
Fedora Project Linux	Core 1
Custom ATrpms Kernel	2.4.22-1.2179.nptl_47.rhfc1.at
atrpms-kickstart	20-1.fhfc1.at
atrpms	54-1.rhfc1.at
qt-MySQL	1:3.3.1-0.fdr.3.1
nvidia-graphics-kmdl-2.4.22-1.2179.nptl_47.rhfc1.at	1.0_4363-50.rhfc1.at
nvidia-graphics-glx	1.0_4363-50.rhfc1.at
alsa-kmdl-2.4.22-1.2179.nptl_47.rhfc1.at	1.0.4-7.rhfc1.at
alsa-driver	1.0.4-22.rhfc1.at
alsa-utils	1.0.4-7.rhfc1
mythtv-suite	0.14-37.at
ivtv-kmdl-2.4.22-1.2179.nptl_47.rhfc1.at	0.1.9-25.rhfc1.at
ivtv	0.1.9-25.rhfc1.at
lirc-kmdl-2.4.22-1.2179.nptl_47.rhfc1.at	0.7.0-20_cvs20040208.rhfc1.at
lirc	0.7.0-20_cvs20040208.rhfc1.at
xmame	0.74.1-1.fr
fceultra	094r3-1
zsnes	1.36-3

Create Time-Shifted FM Radio

9

Cost

$150 - $300

Time

eight hours

Difficulty

4 out of 5

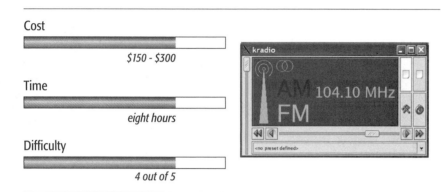

What You Need

- An FM radio transmitter

- An FM broadcast antenna

- Tools to assemble your transmitter (optional)

- Audio cables and adapter to connect your stereo or computer to your transmitter

- Wireless IR receivers (one for each room you'll listen from)

- FM radios (one for each room you'll listen from)

- Wireless IR transmitter

- An FM radio card

- A computer running Linux, with a sound card

- A wireless IR keyboard with batteries, or other remote control solution (optional)

- An MP3 of "Guerrilla Radio" by Rage Against The Machine (mandatory)

For a list of specific parts used in this project, refer to Exhibit A at the end of this chapter.

I wake up at about 6:30 A.M., but Howard Stern starts at 6:00. I'd like to listen to his whole radio show every day, but not so much that I'm willing to give up half an hour of sleep. There are also times when I'd like to back it up a few seconds to replay some funny thing someone said. My TiVo has a button to rewind eight seconds—if I could add that to all the radios in my house, it would be perfect.

If it were a TV show, I'd just set up TiVo to tape it every day, and then start watching the show from the beginning at 6:30. Radio is better than TV in the morning, though, because it doesn't require as much attention. I move around the house while I'm getting ready, and I have radios in every room, and even in the shower. So whatever hack I build to time-shift radio needs to work with whole-house audio.

Whole-house audio is a great idea: you can listen to your television, radio, CD player, or Oggs/MP3s anywhere in your house. Unfortunately, most of the whole-house audio solutions available today are intended for serious audiophiles. I appreciate sound quality as much as the next guy, but it's not worth it to me to spend thousands of dollars to listen to a perfect reproduction of the Howard Stern show while I'm in the shower.

So in a nutshell, I want to time-shift live FM radio, and control and listen to it from anywhere in my house. Figure 9-1 shows how the components of this project fit together. We'll make some custom scripts (called Frank) for

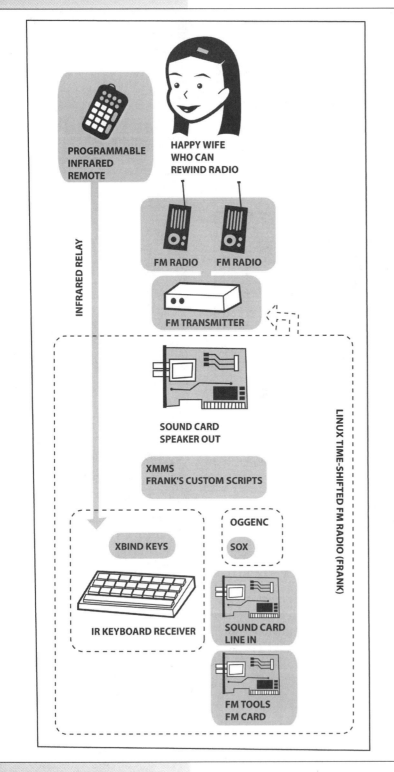

Figure 9-1. Conceptual diagram for whole-house time-shifted FM radio.

scheduling and buffering to record audio from an FM tuner card. Frank will start recording the audio using Sox and OggEnc, and then play it back with a few seconds of buffer using XMMS, a Linux media player. During playback, audio will be played through the sound card, which is connected to an FM transmitter. The FM transmitter allows us to listen to buffered audio from any radio in the house. You'll control the system to pause, rewind, and fast-forward the radio broadcast with a programmable IR (infrared) remote across a whole-house IR distribution system.

Project Overview

This project will be built in six phases, which correspond to the six layers of the project architecture:

1. FM Receiver

2. Audio Recorder

3. Audio Playback

4. Whole-House Audio

5. Whole-House Control Distribution

6. Scheduling and Buffering

Each of these components is modular, so you can complete them in a different order if you're waiting for a part to arrive or if you're particularly interested in a certain aspect of the project. You can even pick and choose the components you want to do: if all you want is a whole-house audio system, work through Phase 4 and Phase 5. If you want to record

FM radio to listen to on your portable audio player, work through Phase 1, Phase 2, and Phase 6. If you think the way I implemented whole-house control distribution is stupid, and you probably will, you can do it your own way—as long as it interacts with the layers above and below it in a similar way.

Shortcut: Just listening to radio on the go? Grab a Radio YourWay from PoGo! Products.

This project needs a better name than "Whole-House Time-Shifted FM Radio," so we'll call the project Frank. Why Frank? It's a nice name. Richard Nixon had a hedgehog called Frank.

FM Receiver

There are a couple of different ways to capture FM transmissions. The first is to connect your stereo to your sound card's line-in port. This doesn't require the purchase of a radio card, and can be used with FM, AM, or satellite radio, or with any other kind of audio that your stereo can output. You'll get the best sound quality possible, as standalone stereo equipment is optimized for sound quality. On the downside, this method is very complex because you have to create a way for the computer to control the stereo. Unless you want to leave the stereo turned on and set to the same station at all times, the computer will need to be able to turn the radio on and tune it to a particular station. You could accomplish this with an IR blaster, but that would add another layer of complexity and some additional cost.

Adding an IR blaster is described in Chapter 6. You can use the software and scripts in this project with an external stereo by replacing the lines in the script that call the *fm* tool with commands that send IR signals to set your radio station.

I decided to use a different method instead: installing an internal FM radio card that can be controlled by software. While this limits me to FM-only broadcasts and requires me to set up another FM antenna, I felt that the benefits of this design outweigh the disadvantages. I can tune the station using software, without the need for an external IR controller, and I can record one FM station while using my stereo for other things. This is particularly important to me because my TV and DVD player also pipe audio through the stereo.

1. Choose and install an FM card

A few years ago, I bought the Hauppauge WinTV-Go-FM card because I needed to import video from my camera, and that happened to be the only model of video capture card that Circuit City had in stock.

This spontaneous purchase worked great for me, but you might not have the same luck with an off-the-shelf FM card. Several phases in this project depend on Linux software. Because this project uses Linux, your life will be much easier if you choose a card that can be tuned by Linux. My Hauppauge card worked perfectly with Linux, but other cards might not.

If you're branching out on your own and using Windows for this project, you don't need to worry about driver availability. One of the nice things about Windows is that consumer hardware vendors always release Windows drivers. You do have to make sure you can tune the card from a command line, though, so that you can change stations using a script.

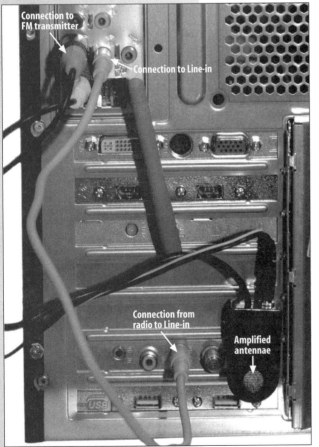

Figure 9-2. An FM card doesn't send sound over the PCI bus, so you need to connect it externally to your sound card.

If at all possible, choose an FM tuner card that's supported by Video for Linux (see *http://www.exploits.org/v4l/* for more information). The FMIO tools (a popular set of Linux tools for working with FM cards) support a handful of cards that aren't supported by Video for Linux; a list of supported cards is at *http://www.jumbo.narod.ru/fmio.html*. Though this project doesn't use the FMIO tools, there's no reason you can't modify the script to use FMIO instead of FM Tools (covered in the next step).

Most FM radio cards connect to your computer using the PCI bus, so you'll need to open up the case to connect it. Some cards, including the well-supported D-Link DSB-R100 USB FM Radio, can connect externally. If you use an externally connected card, you may be able to get away with not using an external antenna, which may save you a few dollars.

Unless your FM card is built into a sound card, you'll need to connect the line-out from the FM card to your sound card's line-in port, as illustrated in Figure 9-2. This may seem odd, but the audio captured by the FM card doesn't traverse the PCI or USB connection—it must go through your sound card.

Figure 9-2 shows a couple of connections that you haven't made yet. For now, just get the sound card and the radio card connected.

2. Install FM Tools

Your Linux distribution probably came with a graphical tool for listening to the radio, but you can't call graphical tools from scripts. The appropriately named FM Tools are designed to be used by other programs, and they work with all Video for Linux–supported cards. Download FM Tools from *http://www.exploits.org/v4l/fmtools/* to your home directory, open a console, and use the traditional install procedure:

```
tar -xvzf fmtools*
cd fmtools*
make
make install
```

After installation, allow the *fm* tool to be executed by any user by linking it to the */usr/bin* directory. Execute the following command from the FM Tools installation directory:

```
ln fm /usr/bin/fm
```

You can use the *fm* tool to tune in a radio station and mute the radio. For example, the following commands tune in WBCN 104.1 in Boston, set the card to a moderate volume (48,000 out of a possible 64,000), and then turn the radio off:

```
fm 104.1 48000
fm off
```

This is exactly what Frank's custom scripts will do to tune in stations. My card doesn't seem to support controlling volume, so I haven't been able to experiment with that parameter. Frank's custom scripts set the volume to a moderate level, about 75%. Experiment with your card and see if it makes a difference.

To confirm that you've connected everything correctly and that all the necessary software is working, open a console and issue the command fm *station*. You should see a message similar to the following:

```
Radio tuned to 104.12 MHz at 12.50% volume
```

At this point, you'll probably hear the radio through your speakers. Congrats! You've just turned hundreds of dollars' worth of computer hardware into a $10 radio. The fact that you can hear the radio is encouraging, but you don't actually want to listen to live radio.

3. Connect the antenna

Every FM radio needs an antenna, though this isn't always obvious. Many FM radios use an internal antenna, or use the power or headphone cord as the antenna. Unless you purchased an external FM radio device, your FM radio card can't use an internal antenna because it's buried inside your computer's case—a less than ideal place to receive radio signals.

Figure 9-3. KRadio's simple interface, hosted on a Windows XP-based X Server.

You'll need to listen to live radio through your computer in order to tune your antenna effectively. I did this using Kradio; you can grab the latest version from *http://www.kawo1.rwth-aachen.de/~witte/kradio.html*. You'll also need the *libsndfile* library, which you can find at *http://www.mega-nerd.com/libsndfile/*. The screenshot in Figure 9-3 shows what may be the most bloated remote control ever: the KRadio X interface running on my Windows XP laptop using Cygwin (across a wireless network, of course). Tune KRadio to the radio station that you listen to most frequently. You'll probably just hear static right now, because you haven't connected your antenna yet.

If your FM radio card included an antenna, start by connecting that antenna to the correct port on your FM radio card. The port is probably a female coaxial port, and it may also require connecting two separate wires with screws. Adjust the antenna until you hear a clear signal. Then, tune in a few more stations and find the antenna position that has the clearest signal across the stations you plan to record.

If you can't get a clear signal, the antenna doesn't have enough signal-grabbing ability to compensate for your particular environmental conditions and the interference from your computer. Hardcore electronics stores carry FM antennas, but the large franchise stores do not. Ramsey Electronics (*http://ramseyelectronics.com/*) is a great source. As a rule of thumb, the higher you can get your antenna, the better your reception. For detailed information about improving your reception, visit *http://www.wnku.org/reception/fmtips.html*.

In my case, the computer was located in my basement with my other A/V equipment. Apparently, traveling through several feet of concrete and earth negatively impacts FM signals. I probably should have run an antenna above ground for this project; however, an amplified antenna from Radio Shack, shown in Figure 9-4, did the trick without requiring me to drill any holes.

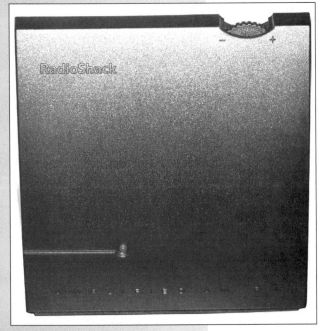

Figure 9-4. An amplified antenna was the only way to get decent reception in my basement.

The amplified antenna needs power, but doesn't turn itself on or off automatically. To avoid running up your probably-already-outrageous electricity bill, hook it up to an X10 switch, and turn it on or off with your radio by modifying Frank's scripts. For more information on X10, refer to one of the many X10 projects in this book.

Audio Recorder

The only decision you have to make during this phase of the project is which compressed audio format you're going to use. The major contenders, in my mind, are MP3 (MPEG-1/2 audio layer 3) and Ogg Vorbis. In a nutshell, Ogg is free and higher quality, while MP3 is compatible with more portable devices.

For a comparison of MP3/MP3 Pro, Ogg, WMA (Windows Media Audio), and RA (Real Audio), check out *http://ekei.com/audio/*.

MP3 is currently the most popular audio format, and it was my original choice when I created the first version of Frank. It has serious drawbacks, though. First, it's not free—software companies need to pay for a license to use the format. Visit *http://www.mp3licensing.com/royalty/software.html* for a list of prices. Second, the original MP3 format is a bit outdated. There are several other formats available today that provide higher compression and/or better sound quality than MP3. There's even a direct replacement for MP3, called MP3Pro. MP3Pro improves quality, but it costs even more than MP3.

Nonetheless, MP3 is attractive because of the wide variety of software that it is compatible with. For example, I have owned half a dozen different portable audio players—everything from an iPod to a car stereo. Some of them support newer formats, but *all* of them support MP3s.

However, Red Hat has decided not to include support for MP3s. While this is an annoyance, I can't blame them for the decision. After all, Red Hat distributes their software for free, and paying licensing fees for free software would break their business model. In order to play back MP3s using Red Hat's audio player (XMMS), you'll need to upgrade it. The easiest way to do this is to install the RPM from *http://havardk.xmms.org/dist/xmms-1.2.7-rh8-rh9-rpm/*. Notice that you don't pay for this software. At the time of this writing, lots of free software to encode, decode, and play back MP3 files is still available; however, this may not always be the case.

Ogg Vorbis, the free format of choice, provides better quality and/or smaller file sizes. However, only one of my portable audio players supports it: my PalmOS device, with help from POggPl (available at *http://poggpl.sourceforge.net/*). Even with this huge drawback, Ogg is the format for me. You're welcome to choose another format, of course; if you do, just replace OggEnc with LAME in the recording script.

This project uses two tools to pull audio from the line-in of the sound card and save it as an Ogg Vorbis file: SoX (Sound eXchange) and OggEnc. SoX pulls the audio from the line-in, and then sends it to standard out in an uncompressed WAV format. Even if you decide to use MP3 instead of Ogg, you'll still need to use SoX.

OggEnc, as the name indicates, encodes the audio from SoX and saves it as a compressed Ogg file. If you use the MP3 format, just replace OggEnc with LAME. The audio recorder is initiated by the scheduling and buffering component, and it receives audio input from the FM receiver.

Both SoX and OggEnc are included with Red Hat, but if your distribution doesn't include it, you can download them from *http://sox.sourceforge.net/* and *http://freshmeat.net/projects/oggenc/*.

Test SoX and OggEnc now to verify that everything is connected and working properly. Open a terminal and switch to your home directory if necessary. Then execute the following command to encode audio from your line-in and save it to the file *radio.ogg*:

```
sox -t ossdsp -c 2 -w -s -r 44100 /dev/dsp -t wav - | oggenc - -o
radio.ogg
```

If you're using MP3, you can use the command:

```
sox -t ossdsp -c 2 -w -s -r 44100 /dev/dsp -t wav - | lame -h -k
- radio.mp3
```

Your output should resemble the following:

```
sox: Length in output .wav header will be wrong since can't seek to fix
it
Opening with wav module: WAV file reader
Encoding standard input to
        "radio.ogg"
at quality 3.00
        [  0.1%] [201m42s remaining] |
```

OggEnc is processor intensive, but you don't need a high-powered system to keep up with it. Encoding a stream from the radio uses 8-9% of my AMD Athlon XP 2800+ processor.

Wait a few minutes, then open a second terminal. Use the su command to become root, and kill the recording process with the command killall sox. Your output should resemble the following:

```
Done encoding file "radio.ogg"

        File length:  1m.0s
        Elapsed time: 1m.2s
        Rate:         1.0006
        Average bitrate: 120.1 kb/s
```

You can also press Ctrl+C to stop recording, but that doesn't provide you the summary information. In the next phase, you'll set up the playback mechanism so you can listen to it.

Audio Playback

In this phase, you'll configure your computer to log in automatically, and verify that your audio player of choice can play your recorded files. Choose an audio player that meets these requirements:

- Fits your budget. (Ideally, it's free.)

- Can play your chosen audio format.

- Can be controlled from a script.

- Can play back files that are being actively recorded.

- Optionally, provides a graphical interface for easy control when you're sitting at a computer.

I chose XMMS because it *almost* meets all of these requirements. XMMS is an extremely popular player and is included with most Linux distributions, so it's well supported. It's also very extensible, and you can find many different plug-ins and skins. This makes it easy to customize.

The one requirement XMMS didn't fully meet is the ability to play back files that are being actively recorded. XMMS can do this, but it has some significant limitations. XMMS seems to only check the length of an audio file when it first opens it. As a result, XMMS cannot rewind or fast-forward live radio recordings. It will play back and pause, but it ignores all requests to rewind or fast-forward within the newly recorded portion of an audio file. This is a significant drawback; however, every other player I experimented with refused to play the newly recorded portion of the audio file at all.

Fortunately, XMMS exposes a set of APIs called xmms_remote. These APIs enable scripts and other programs to remotely control XMMS. Frank's custom scripts, located in the "Scheduling and Buffering" component of the architecture, can use these APIs and therefore force XMMS to close and reopen the live audio file when necessary. It's a hack, but that's okay.

XMMS is open source, so I could theoretically create my own fork of XMMS designed specifically to work with live audio files. The necessary changes wouldn't be useful to most of XMMS's audience, though. They would also cause a performance impact, because XMMS would need to constantly re-check the current state of an audio file that was being actively recorded. Therefore, hacking a custom script that doesn't require changing XMMS's code seems to be a better choice for the initial version of Frank. The Audio Playback component is initiated by the Scheduling and Buffering component, and it plays audio to the user through the Whole-House Audio component.

Developers create a "fork" of an application when they make edits to an application's source code that are not integrated back into the original application.

---

1. Configure automatic login

When Frank starts playing my radio show every morning, I want it to launch XMMS on the desktop and allow me to control it either from a remote or with a mouse and keyboard. This requires a user to be logged in with an active X session, however. If I reboot my computer and don't log in, or if I lose power, Red Hat would be waiting for me to provide a username and password to log in again. To ensure that a desktop environment is always available, configure your computer to log in automatically.

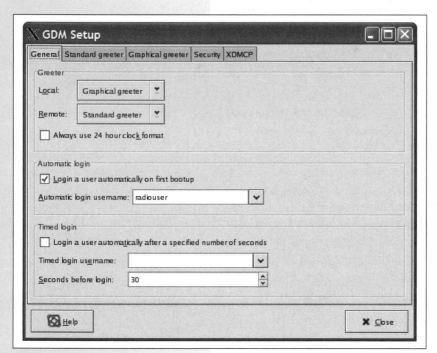

Figure 9-5. Automatic login allows you to schedule XMMS to start playback.

If you're using the system as a desktop, then configure your normal user account for automatic login. Or, if you prefer, you can create a dedicated user account for this purpose named radiouser. To create a user, click the Red Hat menu, click System Settings, then click Users and Groups.

If you're using Red Hat, launch gdmsetup to automatically log in this user account when the system boots up. To enable automatic login, just select "Login a user automatically on first bootup" and select the radiouser account, as shown in Figure 9-5. Click Close. Now, radiouser will automatically log in when the system starts up.

2. Install and test XMMS

To determine whether XMMS is installed on your system, open a terminal and issue the command which xmms. If you don't have XMMS installed, head over to *http://www.xmms.org/* and download and install the latest version.

Assuming you created an audio file in the previous phase, open a terminal and switch to your home directory. Then, play that audio file with the command xmms radio.ogg. XMMS should launch and start playing the file. Figure 9-6 shows XMMS, with a custom skin, playing the *radio.ogg* file.

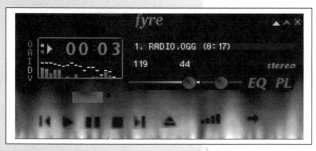

Figure 9-6. XMMS playing the radio.ogg file.

If XMMS seems too small to you, press Ctrl+D to double (or actually, quadruple) the size.

Whole-House Audio

In this phase, you'll create a system for distributing audio from your computer throughout your house. If you're lucky enough to already have such a system in place, or if you only plan to listen to the time-shifted radio through a single pair of speakers, you can skip this phase.

Sound quality, cost, ease of installation, and portability are the most significant factors when choosing a whole-house audio system. At the high end, you can install whole-house audio that provides home theater–quality sound to multiple speakers in every room of your house. These systems typically provide controls built into the wall of each room that allow you to control the volume and other aspects of the audio equipment. You can find an excellent description of such systems at *http://www.hometech.com/learn/audio.html*.

Quality is not the most important factor to me, though. Cost is important, because honestly now, there are much more important things to spend money on than whole-house audio. Plus, I dread the idea of running wires all around my 1950s house, and it would take me so long that I'd probably never complete the project anyway. Portability is important, too. If I move, I wouldn't want to leave a wired whole-house system behind. Chances are good that it wouldn't improve the value of my house much, so I'd be taking a loss.

For this project, I found a whole-house audio solution with acceptable quality that was less than $100, installed in about an hour, and that I can easily take with me anywhere I move. This system uses a wireless protocol, similar to 802.11x, but significantly easier to install (although less secure). And as if that weren't perfect enough, it turns out that I already had compatible wireless clients spread around my house. Basically, I'm going to install a pirate radio station.

You don't need to be a rebellious DJ-with-a-cause to set up your own pirate radio station. In fact, you don't even need to be a pirate, or to break any laws. You can legally set up an FM radio transmitter that can broadcast a short distance, as illustrated in Figure 9-7. I've done this in the past to connect my MP3 player to my car stereo. For about $30, I bought a radio transmitter from the neighborhood electronics store. That transmitter worked only for a few feet, though, so it's not good enough to broadcast around an entire home.

This project will provide some background information about FM transmitters and the laws that regulate broadcasting in public frequencies. I'll walk you through the process of choosing from the many FM transmitters

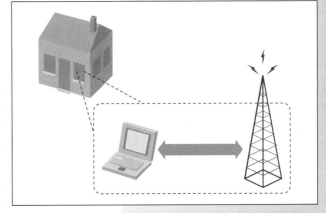

Figure 9-7. Want your MP3s in a different room? Build a tiny radio station!

available, and then we'll go live by hooking it up to your computer and tuning in your radios.

1. Choose a transmitter

There are quite a few different types of radio transmitters available. You can find FM transmitters at your local electronics store, but they're not the kind you want. The $30 battery-powered transmitters are intended to broadcast from an MP3 player to your car or home stereo. The problem is, they only broadcast a few feet. Also, the frequency they broadcast on tends to drift over time, so you may need to tune the radio each time you use it.

I'm not quite sure why higher-power FM transmitters are not more commonly available. I did an extensive search of nearby hardcore-geek–oriented electronics shops, and wasn't able to find a single transmitter capable of broadcasting throughout my house. My first thought was that the FM transmitters were legally questionable, and that any company large enough to have a lawyer knew better than to sell them. However, the Federal Communications Commission (FCC) Part 15 rules specifically allow for low-power wireless stereo extension FM transmitters of the type needed to broadcast audio around your house.

Part 15 rules also allow for the 802.11x networks we've all come to rely on. You can read the Part 15 rules at *http://www.fcc.gov/oet/info/rules/PART15_8-26-03.pdf*. You won't read them all, of course, because the document is 122 pages long and you've got a project to finish. Skip to Section 15.239, which among other rules specifies that you can use transmitters in the range of 88–108 MHz (you know, like the numbers on your FM radio dial) as long as the field strength is less than 250 microvolts/meter.

> Don't believe the FCC enforces this? Head over to Google and search for "site: www.fcc.gov 15.239".

Thanks to the Internet, you can find a wide variety of both legal and potentially illegal FM transmitters. Most are sold as kits, because the target audience tends to be electronics enthusiasts, and because the vendors feel that selling it disassembled reduces their liability. These kits take between 4 and 10 hours to assemble, depending on your skill with a soldering iron. Some places will sell you an assembled kit, but they'll charge you an extra $40–$50, and you'll need to fax them a form to reduce the company's liability if the FCC tracks you down for misusing the equipment.

Ramsey Electronics (*http://www.ramseyelectronics.com*) is a great source for FM radio kits. The two models that you'll find most interesting are the FM10A and the FM25B. The FM10A will run you about $60, including the case and the power supply. It's more than powerful enough to broadcast stereo FM signals all around your home, but you'll find yourself fiddling

Pirate radio seems like a silly way to communicate in the Internet age, but yeah, people really do misuse radio transmitters. For some well-thought-out insight into the pirate radio subculture, check out the Pirate Radio Survival Guide at *http://www.frn.net/special/prsg/*.

with it on a regular basis because the exact frequency it transmits on tends to drift. The FM25B doesn't have this problem, but it'll cost you about $120.

> Ramsey doesn't seem to sell the transmitters assembled. However, if you search around, you'll find many places that resell the same kits assembled.

For my purposes, I decided on the C. Crane Digital FM Transmitter (*http://www.ccrane.com*), shown in Figure 9-8. This transmitter comes completely assembled and has a digital tuner that doesn't drift. It costs about $80, which puts it solidly below the FM25B. The C. Crane transmitter isn't nearly as powerful as the Ramsey transmitters. In fact, it wasn't even powerful enough to broadcast around my modest house—until I hacked it.

> Another advantage of the Crane transmitter is that it turns itself off automatically. If you're using another transmitter, you'll need to rig an X10 switch to allow you to turn it off when not in use (unless you're broadcasting 24/7).

To summarize, the things to consider when choosing an FM transmitter are:

- **Whether the transmitter is a kit or prebuilt.** If you know how to use a soldering iron, you can save yourself a few dollars and buy a kit. Most places that sell kits will also sell them assembled for you.

- **Broadcast range.** Many transmitters are intended for use over larger areas, such as school campuses. I don't need that kind of power; to cover my house, I just need to be able to broadcast about 50 feet. You also definitely need the ability to control the power output. You should use the least amount of power possible to avoid interfering with your neighbors.

- **Sound quality.** At the lowest end of the scale, an AM radio transmitter will cost you about $30. AM doesn't have stereo, though, and sound quality is comparatively poor. That's why talk radio dominates AM, and most music stations use FM. FM radio transmitters come in many different flavors, including mono and stereo.

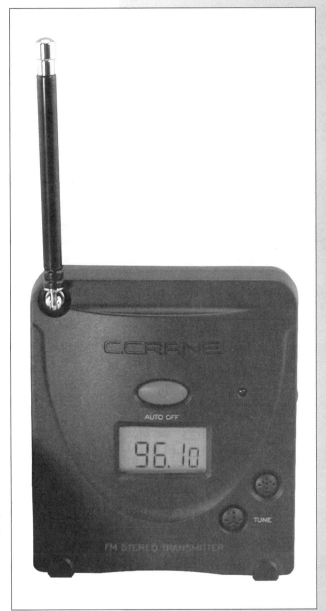

Figure 9-8. The C.Crane transmitter is cheap, and you can crack the case to get more power out of it.

- **Analog or digital tuning.** I hate radios with analog tuners. For some reason, they always shift away from the station I tune in, even if I never adjust them. Transmitters have similar problems. Analog tuners are cheaper, but digital tuners are more precise.

- **Stability.** Cheap transmitters will change their frequency of operation with time, temperature, battery levels, and proximity to other objects. For example, the FM10A from Ramsey Electronics will fluctuate if exposed to temperature changes, while FM25B (at about three times the price) will remain stable. Your family won't be too excited about your new radio's tricks if it keeps falling out of tune!

- **Price.** You can spend as little as $35 on a stereo FM transmitter kit, but after you factor in a power supply and case, you'll be spending about $60. High-quality transmitters can approach $1000. Cost is more important to me than sound quality, though, so I chose one of the least expensive models.

Power decreases by the square of distance. So, for every doubling in distance, the signal power is quartered. Table 9-1 shows how far you can reach with radios with power outputs in the FCC-allowed range. These distances are very rough approximations, based on a clear signal with typical antennas, and line-of-sight between the transmitter and your radio. You'll get less distance within a house, though exactly how much less will vary. In a typical wood and drywall American house, you might have as much as half the outdoor range; in a concrete and metal office building, you may get far less.

Table 9-1. The more power, the farther your reach

Microvolts per meter	Range
5	100 feet
20	200 feet
60	600 feet
250	1260 feet

2. Build or hack your transmitter

If you decided to buy an FM transmitter kit, break out your soldering iron and assemble it according to the provided instructions. If you decided to go with the Crane or other prebuilt unit, all you need is a screwdriver.

> Try the Crane transmitter before you modify it to make sure it works; if it doesn't, you can return it knowing you weren't responsible for the damage. And it might even have enough power for you without modification.

1. Use a flat-head screwdriver to remove the two round rubber feet from the back of the case. Only remove the feet that have arrows pointing at them; the ones at the bottom of the case do not need to be removed. This reveals the two top screws shown in Figure 9-9. Use a small Phillips-head screwdriver to remove the these screws.

2. Remove the cover to the battery compartment and remove the small silver screw inside it.

3. With the screws removed, there are only two things preventing you from removing the back cover: a wire that connects the right side of the battery compartment to the transmitter's internals, and the Input Level dial that is connected to the front portion of the case and protrudes through a hole in the back. Gently push in the Input Level dial while slowly pulling the back cover away. Pull the top of the case away, but keep the bottom together so as to not break the wires connecting to the battery compartment.

Figure 9-9. Three screws hold the transmitter's case together.

Thanks to Wireman of xmfan.com for documenting the Crane hack described here so clearly.

---

4. Locate the VR2 control at the top of the circuit board, near the center, and use your small Phillips-head screwdriver to rotate it clockwise until it faces left, at about 9 o'clock (Figure 9-10). Do not apply force.

5. Push the cover back into place and replace the three screws. Verify that the power plug and the Input Level dial are aligned with the openings in the case.

3. Connect and tune the transmitter

In this final step, you'll connect the FM transmitter to the audio source, tune it to an unused frequency, and tune your FM radios to this new station.

Figure 9-10. The Crane transmitter's power controller's default setting makes it underpowered.

FM transmitters generally include either stereo RCA connections or a headphone jack. If your audio source has a different type of connector, head down to an electronics store and pick up an adapter, such as the one shown in Figure 9-11.

Once you get the transmitter connected to your audio source, you need to tune both the transmitter and your radio to an empty station. Grab the radio with the best reception and tune it to a frequency with nothing but static, as far from licensed radio stations as possible. For example, if you find radio stations at 94.5, 98.1, 101.9, and 104.1, your best choice would be a frequency in the 88-89 MHz range. You don't want to choose a frequency within .5 MHz of another station, because you will cause interference.

After you find a station, go to each of the radios in your house and listen for other stations. I checked five radios around my house, and each received slightly different signals. In fact, I couldn't find a single station that didn't have an audible signal on at least one radio. I chose the frequency with the lowest cumulative interference: 88.5 MHz. Because of the way the FCC distributes licenses, you'll probably end up with a frequency at the bottom of the scale.

Once you find an empty station, turn up the volume and listen to the static for a moment. Then, start up your computer and play the *radio.ogg* file you recorded earlier. If your transmitter is working correctly, you should be able to hear your recording play through your radio.

If you're using the Crane transmitter, adjust the Input Level dial all the way down, and then gradually turn it up until the red light begins to blink. This signals that the incoming signal (from your computer) is too loud, and the loudest part of the signals are being clipped. Adjust the Input Level dial down until the light occasionally blinks faintly.

Have someone else go to the radio farthest from your transmitter, and listen to the quality of the signal. If it seems weak, turn up the power on your transmitter. If it comes through clearly, turn down the power on your transmitter until the quality degrades, and then turn it back up again until the signal is acceptable. Remember, you want to use as little power as possible to reduce the likelihood that you'll cause interference with your neighbors.

And when you're done with all that, congrats! You've got your very own radio station!

Figure 9-11. You may need an adapter to connect your transmitter to your computer or stereo.

Whole-House Control Distribution

Broadcasting audio around your home is only half the battle—the other half is controlling your music. For that, you'll need to find a way to make your IR remote work anywhere in your house. In this project, you'll be hooking up a system to translate IR signals into radio frequency (RF) transmissions that can pass through walls, and then convert them back into IR.

After completing the previous phase, you can listen to your music collection or your TV from anywhere in your house using any FM radio. You lose something, though: the ability to pause the music, change tracks, or change stations. With conventional stereo equipment, you can control this with an IR remote, but those only work when you are standing in the same room as the system. Now that you're piping sound from your computer to anywhere in your home, you also need a way to pipe IR signals back to the computer, and a way for your computer to interpret these signals.

1. Choose an IR relay system

Wireless IR relay systems consist of two components: the IR receiver and the IR transmitter. These components work by translating IR signals into radio signals that can travel through walls. Therefore, the IR receiver is also a radio transmitter, and the IR transmitter is a radio receiver. For simplicity, I'll use the term *receiver* to mean the IR receiver, and *transmitter* to refer to the IR transmitter positioned beside your A/V equipment.

There are three main ways to control your IR systems from around your house without any additional wiring. All three methods use RF signals to wirelessly relay commands from your remote control to an IR transmitter located next to your equipment. They all work well and are priced similarly. Your choice should be based on how you will use your new system.

The first method is to strap the IR receiver directly to your existing remote control; then, you can use your remote from anywhere in your house without having to point it at the audio equipment. The advantage of this design is that you don't need to purchase any additional remotes. The downside is that you'll need to carry that remote with you wherever you roam around the house. Also, you may need to use a separate remote to control the radio you use to listen to your broadcast. But if you want to control your equipment from many different places around your house and you don't mind carrying the remote around, this design is right for you.

The second method is to purchase an RF remote with an IR transmitter. This works similarly to the previous method, but instead of strapping an IR receiver onto your existing remote, you'll purchase a new, programmable remote with an RF transmitter built in. This *would* be the ideal method, except for the lack of flexibility offered by nonprogrammable universal remotes. If you're like me, you have fairly unique or new electronic equipment that isn't compatible with typical universal remotes. Learning remotes work great, but remotes that combine both RF and learning capability tend to be large and heavy—too big, in my opinion, for the constant use that a typical remote control gets. The RF transmitter tends to be underpowered, as well, and might transmit reliably through the door on an entertainment center, but they don't work consistently from one side of my house to the other (after all, a couple of AA batteries isn't enough for a powerful radio transmitter).

The third method is the one I used for this project: place one IR receiver in each room where you'll use the remote. This doesn't give you the same flexibility as the first system, but it also doesn't require you to buy a new remote or strap an IR receiver onto your current one. If you're going to be controlling your private radio broadcasts in only two or three rooms besides the one where your computer is located, this is the best model to choose.

You can find these IR receiver/transmitter pairs (known as remote extenders) at many electronics stores, at a cost anywhere between $40 and $80. If you do a search for "Remote Extender," you'll turn up several vendors who will sell you such a device. I wasn't able to identify any particular advantages or disadvantages when I compared models; they all seem to work just fine. So pick one based on cost and appearance.

2. Configure the transmitter and receivers

Place the IR transmitter/RF receiver (the one with the external antenna) in the room with your audio/video equipment. The IR signals sent from the transmitter need to be able to reach all of the A/V equipment that you plan to control. If your equipment is located in different rooms, you'll need to purchase additional transmitters, and possibly an extension emitter than can be wired inside a closed entertainment center. Plug in the IR transmitter and extend the antenna.

If you're using stationary IR receivers, place them in the rooms where you want to be able to control your equipment. Generally, you want to place the receiver on top of or as close as possible to the radio you'll be using to listen to your FM transmissions, as shown in Figure 9-12.

Figure 9-12. The Powermid IR receiver uses RF signals to transfer IR signals back to my computer.

If you're using an IR receiver that connects to your remote, verify that it works properly by holding it in front of the remote. If it works, go ahead and adhere it. (You may find that the tape included doesn't hold for very long, and in a week or two you'll be digging out the duct tape.)

3. Install the IR keyboard

There are two ways you can allow remote control over your PC. Most people build or purchase an IR receiver and install LIRC or WinLIRC. Chapter 5, Remotely Control Your Computer, provides instructions on how to do that.

For this project, I provide for remote control a bit differently. My home theater PC is located in my media room, and the display is connected to a TV located in a different room. To allow myself to use a keyboard and mouse from another room using the IR relay system, I bought an infrared keyboard, as shown in Figure 9-13. The IR keyboard's receiver plugs into your computer's PS2 port, and acts like a real keyboard in every way. It works with any operating system, and doesn't require any extra software. In order to use a remote control with this system, all I needed to do was purchase a learning remote and teach it some keypresses.

You won't find an IR keyboard at an electronics store—trust me, I looked. Instead, you'll just find RF wireless keyboards that use radio signals. This makes sense, because radio signals provide a much greater range than IR signals, and can be pointed in any direction. IR signals are pretty limiting for the purposes most people use keyboards for. However, since you'll be using the keyboard to program a learning remote, an IR keyboard is a must. You can find one online by searching for "infrared PS2 keyboard" on Google.

Figure 9-13. The IR keyboard works like any other keyboard.

WARNING

Overall, IR keyboards stink. Keys often repeat for no particular reason, so you need to edit your preferences to disable repeating keys. Also, the Caps Lock key tends to get stuck even when you haven't pressed it. I don't suggest relying on an IR keyboard as your primary way of controlling the computer. I did most of my work using SSH and remote X sessions from my Windows system. Thanks again, Cygwin.

Once you've got your IR keyboard, plug the IR receiver portion of it into your computer's PS2 mouse and keyboard ports. Position the IR transmitter portion of your IR relay system as close to the keyboard's receiver as possible, and ensure that nothing is blocking the signals between the two. Then, open a terminal and go into another room with an IR receiver. Point the keyboard at the IR receiver (you may need to be fairly close) and test it out. If the IR relay system is working correctly, the keypresses should appear in your terminal window.

4. Program the remote

Before you actually program the remote, you must determine which keys from the IR keyboard you're going to remap to the five playback scripts. You need to identify keys for the following functions:

- Rewind

- Pause

- Fast-forward

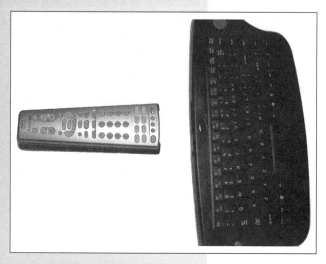

Figure 9-14. Program your learning remote with your IR keyboard.

- Play
- Radio station presets for buffered playback of live radio (one per station)

This was easy for me because my wireless keyboard already had rewind, stop, pause, and fast-forward labels on keys F5 through F8. I borrowed the F9 key to use as the play button, and I used F10 and F11 to start buffered playback of live radio on my two favorite stations.

Once you've decided which keys you're going to use, place both the keyboard and remote on a flat surface. Point the keyboard's IR transmitter directly at the remote's IR receiver, as shown in Figure 9-14. Follow your remote's instructions for learning a new IR signal. Once the remote is in learning mode for one of the buttons you plan to program, press the corresponding key on your keyboard.

My remote, the Sony RM-VL900, allows me to program each of the keys for eight different devices. I used the tape-player device for Frank. Who uses a tape player these days anyway? This isn't 1988 anymore, folks. Get those tapes encoded into Ogg files before they break down.

5. Install XBindKeys

If you're not using an IR keyboard to control your radio, you should skip this step.

Programming a learning remote using an IR keyboard allows you to simulate actual keys being pressed on the keyboard when remote buttons are pushed. If you just wanted to turn your remote into a really uncomfortable and limited keyboard, this would be fine. However, our goal is to launch Frank's custom script with the simulated keypresses, so we'll need to add some software that starts a new process when a keypress is detected.

KDE (K Desktop Environment) includes some limited support for shortcut keys. Specifically, you can use the *kmenuedit* tool to launch an application when a shortcut key, such as Ctrl+Shift+T, is pressed. This would work, but it would require us to set up a menu item for each of the scripts we need to call, and it would limit us to using KDE.

The XBindKeys tool is a better way to accomplish our goal. Download and install the latest version from *http://hocwp.free.fr/xbindkeys*. Then, while logged in as the user account that automatically logs in (not su'd to root or another user), execute the following command:

```
xbindkeys --defaults > ~/.xbindkeysrc
```

Because the *.xbindkeysrc* file starts with a dot, it'll be hidden in a standard directory listing. To view this and other hidden files, use `ls -a`.

Later, you'll edit the *.xbindkeysrc* file so that special keys will launch Frank's custom script that controls playback and recording of your radio. We won't edit that file until the last phase of this project, though, because the script hasn't been created yet.

In the meantime, configure *xbindkeys* to automatically run when the user logs in. To do this, launch the Sessions tool by opening the Red Hat menu, clicking Preferences, clicking More Preferences, and then clicking Sessions. After the Session tool starts, follow this procedure to cause *xbindkeys* to automatically start:

1. Click the Startup Programs tab.

2. Click the Add button.

3. Enter **xbindkeys** and click OK.

4. Close the Sessions tool.

Scheduling and Buffering

All this project is missing now is something to tie all the different components together. You need a script that *xbindkeys* can trigger and that will pass commands such as rewind, fast-forward, and pause on to XMMS. This script must be able to tune in radio stations, record them, and play the recording back. And because these recordings will quickly fill up your disk space, the script should also be able to clean up every few days.

You also need a way to schedule these recordings, although unlike TiVo, you don't really need to browse listings. In my case, there's only one show I want to record anyway, so I don't mind scheduling manually from the command line. The crontab program (Step 4) is perfect for the job.

I did my best to build a time-shifted FM radio without having to write my own code, and thanks to the open source community, I managed to find just about everything I needed. I only needed to write a script to glue the different components together, and modify XMMS's behavior a bit.

1. Install the Perl modules

Even though it's primarily a graphical tool, XMMS provides some useful command-line functionality. You can issue commands such as `xmms pause` or `xmms play`, although unfortunately you can't rewind or fast-forward using command-line parameters. However, XMMS provides a C API, xmms_remote, that enables more complete control over playback.

I decided to create a Perl script to control XMMS using the Xmms::Remote Perl module, which in turn uses the xmms_remote interface. This may seem like one layer too many—after all, why use Perl to interface between the command line and a C API? The answer is that Perl is easy to hack and tweak. It enabled me to change minor aspects of the script's behavior without recompiling, which shortened the development time. You'll probably end up doing some tweaking as well.

Theoretically, I could also fork XMMS and edit the source code to better support playback of actively growing files. However, I'm not an XMMS developer and I'm not at all familiar with its inner workings, so there's a good chance I would introduce a bug in my fork. Also, you wouldn't be able to use the latest version of XMMS, because you'd always have to use my forked version.

It's possible that the XMMS developers will eventually update the application to support playback of audio files that are actively being recorded; check *http://www.homehacking.com* for an update. If they do fix it, Frank's custom script will detect that things are working properly and avoid using the rewind and fast-forward hacks.

Assuming that you've decided to use Perl, you'll need to install a couple of freely available Perl modules:

1. Download the Xmms::Remote module to your home directory. The module is available at *http://search.cpan.org/author/DOUGM/*, and will be named *Xmms-Perl-*.tar.gz*.

2. Download the Ogg::Vorbis::Header module to your home directory. The module is available at *http://search.cpan.org/author/DBP/*, and will be named *Ogg-Vorbis-Header-*.tar.gz*.

3. Open a terminal, switch to the directory you saved the files in, and then execute the following commands:

   ```
   su
   tar -xvzf Xmms-Perl*
   tar -xvzf Ogg-Vorbis-Header*
   ```

4. Install the Xmms::Remote module. Use the same terminal and execute the following commands:

```
cd Xmms-Perl*
perl Makefile.PL
make
make install
```

5. Install the Ogg::Vorbis::Header module. Use the same terminal and execute the following commands:

```
cd Ogg-Vorbis-Header*
perl Makefile.PL
make
make install
```

Special thanks to Robin Smidsrød, the developer of CtrlXMMS. Before Frank grew into its own Perl script, it relied on CtrlXMMS. Even though Robin hadn't touched CtrlXMMS in years, he was very prompt and helpful.

2. Create the script

If it's not already installed on your system, install *aumix* from *http://www.jpj. net/~trevor/aumix.html*.

Save the following script as *frank* in the */usr/bin/* directory. You can also download it, along with any updates I've made, from *http://www. homehacking.com*.

```perl
#!/usr/bin/perl
#
# Frank 0.1
# (C) Tony Northrup (tony@northrup.org), 2003

use Xmms::Remote;
use Ogg::Vorbis::Header;

$buffer = 5;              # Minimum seconds of delay behind live
recording
$frankdir = "/var/frank";     # Directory to store recordings
$audioext = "ogg";          # File extension of audio files

# This may take several seconds to run, so it's possible
# for multiple occurences to be called simultaneously
# while the user pushes buttons on the remote.
# Check and see if more than one instance is running. If
# so, die.
die if ((`ps -A|grep frank|wc -l`) > 1);
```

```
$_=$ARGV[0];
SWITCH: {
    if (/^help$/) { help(); last SWITCH; }
    if (/^play\-last$/) { play_last(); last SWITCH; }
    if (/^play\-live$/) { play_live($ARGV[1], $ARGV[2] || "1h",
$ARGV[3] || "radio"); last SWITCH; }
    if (/^pause$/) { pause(); last SWITCH; }
    if (/^stop\-play$/) { stop_play(); last SWITCH; }
    if (/^ff$/) {jump($ARGV[1] || 30); last SWITCH; }
    if (/^rw$/) {jump(-(abs $ARGV[1]) || -8); last SWITCH; }
    if (/^stop\-record$/) {stop_record(); last SWITCH; }
    if (/^record$/) {record($ARGV[1], $ARGV[2] || "1h", $ARGV[3] ||
"radio"); last SWITCH; }
    if (/^off$/) {off(); last SWITCH; }
    if (/^clean$/) {clean($ARGV[1] || 7); last SWITCH; }
    $nothing=1;
}

help() if ($nothing eq 1);

sub help {
    print <<EOM;
Usage: frank <command> [parameter(s)]

Parameters:
help                    - Show this help
play-last                  - Plays the active or most recent
recording
play-live <station> [time] [label]    - Records and plays live radio.
                        Default = 1 hour.
pause                   - Pause or unpause
stop-play                  - Stops playback
ff [seconds]              - Jump forward.
                        Default = 30.
rw [seconds]              - Jump backward.
                        Default = 8.
record <station> [time] [label]       - Starts recording for specified
time.
                        Default = 1 hour.
stop-record               - Stops recording
off                       - Stop everything
clean <days>               - Delete files older than <days>.
                        Default = 7.

Note:
<station> is an FM frequency.
<time> can be anything the unix sleep command accepts:
1m = 1 minute, 1h = 1 hour.

EOM
}

sub pause {
    system "xmms --play-pause";
}

sub stop_play {
    system "xmms --stop";
}
```

```perl
sub stop_record {
    system "killall sox";
    system "fm off";
    system "killall sleep";
}

sub play_last {
    # If the file is already playing, just pause/unpause it.
    # Otherwise, mute the line in (attached to the radio) and start
    # playing the last (and possibly active) file.
    my $remote=Xmms::Remote->new;
    if ($remote->is_playing eq 1)
    {
        print "Pausing.\n";
        pause();
    }
    else
    {
        print "Starting XMMS\n";
        # Start XMMS, mute the line-in (live radio) and set the system
        # and XMMS volume moderately.
        system "aumix -l 0 -v 70";
        system "xmms \`cat $frankdir/active\` &";
        my $remote=Xmms::Remote->new;
        $remote->set_volume(70);
    }
}

sub play_live {
    # Start recording the radio, wait a few seconds to provide
    # XMMS with the buffer it needs, and then start playing.
    record ($_[0],$_[1]);
    sleep $buffer;
    play_last();
}

sub record {
    # Stop any previous recordings and turn the radio on
    system "killall sox";
    system "fm $_[0] 48000";

    # Initiate the recording. Change these lines to use a file type
    # other than ogg
    system "echo $frankdir/$_[2]-\`date +%Y%m%d-%H%M\`.$audioext >
$frankdir/active";
    system "(sox -t ossdsp -c 2 -w -s -r 44100 /dev/dsp -t wav - |
oggenc -Q - -o \`cat $frankdir/active\`) &";

    # Start a process that will sleep for the length of the recording,
    # and then kill sox and turn the radio off.
    system "sleep $_[1] && frank stop-record &";
}

sub off {
    system "killall xmms";
    stop_record();
}
```

```perl
sub clean {
    system "find $frankdir/*.$audioext -mtime +$_[0] -exec rm -rf {}
\\;"
}

sub jump {
    # Calculate new position in audio file relative to current
    my $remote=Xmms::Remote->new;
    my $previoustime = $remote->get_output_time;
    my $absolutetime = $previoustime+(1000*$_[0]);

    # Check the current length of the audio file. If we're jumping
    # beyond the end, request XMMS jump only to the end (minus the
buffer)
    my $active = `cat $frankdir/active\n`;
    chomp $active;

    # Try to check the length of the file. If it's not an OGG file,
that's okay.
    my $oggfile = Ogg::Vorbis::Header->new($active);
    if ( $oggfile )
    {
        my $length = ($oggfile->info('length') - $buffer) * 1000;
        if ( $absolutetime > $length ) { $absolutetime = $length; }
    }
    $remote->jump_to_time($absolutetime);
    sleep 1;

    # Ask XMMS for the current time to verify that the jump
    # was successful. If it wasn't, stop and restart XMMS
    # and try again.
    my $actualtime = $remote->get_output_time;
    if (($actualtime < ($absolutetime-1000)) || ($actualtime >
($absolutetime+1000)))
    {
        # We have to stop and restart XMMS, which causes XMMS to
        # play a bit of the beginning of the file. To prevent the user
        # from hearing this, temporarily mute XMMS.
        my $currentvolume = $remote->get_volume;
        $remote->set_volume(0) if ($currentvolume > 0);

        $remote->stop;
        $remote->play;
        sleep 1;

        $remote->jump_to_time($absolutetime);
        $remote->set_volume($currentvolume) if ($currentvolume > 0);

        sleep 2;

        # Check to see if this second attempt to jump was successful.
        # If not, we're probably past the end of the file.
        # Return to previous position. This should never happen with
OGG files.
        if ($remote->get_output_time < $absolutetime)
        {
            $remote->jump_to_time($previoustime);
        }
    }
}
```

For information on how to use Frank directly, execute `frank help` from a terminal window.

3. Understand and hack the script

First, let me apologize for the overuse of the system command in the script. Frank evolved from a set of shell scripts, so I was therefore looking for command-line tools to accomplish what I needed, rather than looking for ways to get the job done natively in Perl. Also, you may have noticed from the style that I'm more of a C programmer than a Perl programmer. Well, it's just a hack, right?

Most of Frank's logic exists in the `jump` subroutine. This subroutine takes a single parameter: the relative distance to jump, in seconds. So the script can call `jump(-8)` to rewind 8 seconds, `jump(30)` to fast-forward 30 seconds, and so on. When playing back prerecorded files, the script only needs to calculate the position within the audio file, and make a call to Xmms::Remote's jump_to_time subroutine.

If you were listening to prerecorded songs and using XMMS interactively, you wouldn't even attempt to fast-forward past the end of the file. However, when using my TiVo to watch buffered live TV, it's common to fast-forward to the end of the file to catch up (as closely as possible) to live TV. To allow this, Frank checks the length of the file using the Ogg::Vorbis::Header module. If the user attempts to fast-forward past the end, Frank instead jumps to a point `$buffer` seconds behind the end of the file. The buffer (five seconds by default) is required by XMMS when playing actively recorded files, unfortunately.

```
    # Try to check the length of the file. If it's not an OGG file,
    that's okay.
    my $oggfile = Ogg::Vorbis::Header->new($active);
    if ( $oggfile )
    {
        my $length = ($oggfile->info('length') - $buffer) * 1000;
        if ( $absolutetime > $length ) { $absolutetime = $length; }
    }
```

I discovered while creating Frank that XMMS is capable of playing files that are being actively recorded, but can only jump within the portion of the audio file that existed at the time XMMS began playing it. In other words, XMMS does not notice that the audio file has gotten longer since it first opened the file, and therefore ignores requests to jump within the newly recorded audio.

The ability to rewind and fast-forward within the newly recorded audio is critical for time-shifting FM radio or other broadcasts being played back in XMMS. Frank doesn't know whether XMMS will be able to successfully jump to a particular portion of the file, so it attempts the jump, waits one second, and then checks to see if the current position is within one second of the requested position.

XMMS measures time in milliseconds, which is why I multiple the requested jump time by 1000.

```
$remote->jump_to_time($absolutetime);
sleep 1;

# Ask XMMS for the current time to verify that the jump
# was successful. If it wasn't, stop and restart XMMS
# and try again.
my $actualtime = $remote->get_output_time;
if (($actualtime < ($absolutetime-1000)) || ($actualtime >
($absolutetime+1000)))
    {
```

As shown below, if the jump wasn't successful, Frank stops and restarts XMMS, forcing XMMS to notice that the audio file has gotten longer. The sleep 1 seems necessary, or else XMMS will ignore the jump request. All this jumping around causes XMMS to make some confusing sounds, so Frank mutes XMMS during the operation.

```
my $currentvolume = $remote->get_volume;
$remote->set_volume(0) if ($currentvolume > 0);

$remote->stop;
$remote->play;
sleep 1;
```

If you're not playing back Ogg files, Frank can't detect when a requested jump would go beyond the end of the file. Therefore, the script requests that XMMS make the jump, and afterward checks that XMMS's current position is not lower than the position it was asked to jump to. If it is, the script asks XMMS to return to the original position in the audio file.

```
# Check to see if this second attempt to jump was successful.
# If not, we're probably past the end of the file.
# Return to previous position. This should never happen with OGG files.
if ($remote->get_output_time < $absolutetime)
{
    $remote->jump_to_time($previoustime);
}
```

The rest of the script should be fairly easy to understand based on the comments within the code. If you're hacking the script yourself and you're using MP3 instead of Ogg, you can set the $audioext variable to mp3 by replacing the definition near the beginning of the script with this definition:

```
$audioext = "mp3";
```

Then, replace the line that calls oggenc in the record subroutine with this line:

```
system "(sox -t ossdsp -c 2 -w -s -r 44100 /dev/dsp -t wav - |lame -h
-k - \`cat $frankdir/active\`) &";
```

If you want to conserve processing time, remove the -h from the LAME command line, or better yet replace it with -f. Quality will suffer, but the processing time required by the encoder will decrease.

4. Schedule the recordings

With TiVo, you schedule recordings by using your remote to navigate its graphical menus. Frank isn't so friendly. To schedule your recordings with Frank, you'll use crontab, Linux's scheduler. crontab is capable of starting programs on a recurring basis, including daily, weekly, and monthly.

I've listened to the same morning show, on the same station, at the same time, for years and years, so crontab's repetitive nature is perfect for me. On the other hand, if you listen to a radio show that changes schedule regularly, crontab won't be the best way to schedule your recordings; instead, you can use the at command to manually schedule each upcoming episode. (For more information, execute man at from within a terminal.)

Frank was designed to be used by non-technical people. Unfortunately, scheduling cron jobs is a bit too technical for non-geeks, so your non-nerd family members will just have to ask you to schedule their recordings. Alternatively, you can map the frank play-record *station duration* command to a button on the remote, and they can take advantage of buffering when listening to live radio, without scheduling a recording ahead of time. For example, I've mapped different stations to the 1, 2, and 3 buttons on the remote, which allows Frank to be used just like any radio with presets. My wife can press the 1 button, and her favorite radio station starts up with all of Frank's buffering capabilities.

To schedule a recording, open a terminal and su to the user you configured to automatically log in at startup. Then, execute the command crontab -e. This allows you to edit the user-specific crontab file in vi. If you're not familiar with vi, it's not terribly intuitive. You can read all about it using the man vi command, But if you don't want to bother learning vi just to schedule your recordings, just press i when vi first appears and type your crontab parameters and commands. When you're done, press Esc, and then type ZZ to save the file.

If you'd rather use another editing tool, just edit the */var/spool/cron/*username file.

The user's crontab file will contain a set of parameters and a set of commands. For the purposes of this project, you only need to provide a single parameter: DISPLAY=:0. This will cause XMMS to use the locally connected monitor and the automatically logged-in user's session. If you do not provide this parameter, XMMS won't be able to find an X session to display its GUI, and will simply shut down.

After the parameter, list your commands. crontab commands contain the minute, hour, day of month, month, day of week, and command to be executed. The fields are separated by tabs. If you don't want to use one of crontab's values when scheduling your recording, just place an asterisk in that field.

After you've entered your schedule, you can review it with the crontab -l command. My crontab file, edited for brevity, follows. The first line sets the default display parameter for all scheduled jobs to the local display. The second line records the FM station 104.1 for five hours starting at 6:00 A.M. every day from Monday through Friday. The third line starts playing that broadcast at 6:30. In addition to letting me sleep in, this 30-minute buffer also gives me a chance to fast-forward through commercials as I listen to my morning radio show. The last line asks Frank to delete recordings older than three days.

---

crontab -l displays the current user's tasks. So, if you're not logged in as the same user you used to edit crontab, you won't see your jobs.

```
[radiouser@redhat tnorthru]$ crontab -l
DISPLAY=:0

00    06    *    *    1-5    frank record 104.1 5h stern &
30    06    *    *    1-5    frank play-last &
13    02    *    *    *      frank clean 3 &
```

5. Configure .xbindkeysrc

You may recall that when you installed *xbindkeysrc*, you created a default *.xbindkeysrc* file. This default file has a couple of settings, but you need to edit it to map the function keys to your XMMS control scripts. I used F5 through F9 to program the rewind, stop, pause, fast-forward, and play buttons, and the F10 and F11 keys to program preset buttons for my two favorite stations. So my *.xbindkeysrc* file looks like this:

```
"frank rw&"
  F5

"frank stop-play&"
  F6

"frank pause&"
  F7

"frank ff&"
  F8

"frank play-last&"
  F9
```

```
"frank play-live 104.1 1h&"
  F10

"frank play-live 94.5 1h&"
  F11
```

If you're using the function keys, you can specify them as I did in my file: F1, F2, F3, etc. If you're using another special key that you don't know how to specify, you can use XEV to determine the ASCII code associated with that key. Within an X terminal, issue the command xev to bring up an X window. XEV outputs a great deal of information to the terminal as you move the mouse or press keys. Simply press the key you're remapping, and XEV will reward you with the associated ASCII code.

Reading the comments within the default *.xbindkeysrc* file is the best way to understand how it should be formatted. After you edit the file and save it, execute xbindkeys as your user account to cause the changes to take effect immediately.

Test this out by pressing the button you mapped to the start-playback script. You should see XMMS launch and begin playing the most recently recorded file. Play with the other buttons you programmed to ensure that they're all working correctly.

Once you've verified that *xbindkeys* is working properly, copy the *.xbindkeysrc* file to the home directory of every user that will be logging into your computer's desktop environment. If a user logs in and doesn't have the script mappings, your remote control won't work.

Wrapping Up

Your system shouldn't require any maintenance other than changing the batteries in your remote. There are a few things that might cause problems, however:

- Your inexpensive FM transmitter may drift to a different frequency.

- A new radio station may appear and conflict with the station you've chosen.

- You may get a bit overzealous when hacking your transmitter, and the FCC could show up at your door.

As a general note, when backing up your system, make sure the *.xbindkeysrc* file (located in each home directory) and the */usr/bin/frank* script are backed up.

You'll know the project is a success if your family starts wanting to listen to their own favorite radio station. Yep, it might be time to buy another transmitter, and set up a second station in your house.

Chapter 9, Create Time-Shifted FM Radio

Extensions

This was a big project. But if you're *still* not yet satisfied, there are several ways you can take it a bit further:

- Add additional transmitters to allow different family members to listen to their own audio sources simultaneously.

- You might want additional feedback when rewinding and fast-forwarding. TiVo provides "bing" and "bong" sounds when buttons are pressed; adding similar sounds to Frank would make it much more fun.

- Use speech synthesis to read news and weather at the press of a button. Check out the Festival Speech Synthesis System at *http://www.cstr. ed.ac.uk/projects/festival/* and the Speech::Rsynth Perl module at *http:// ftp.linux.cz/pub/perl/modules/by-module/Speech/*.

- Use the same system to play back your entire digital audio collection. This is actually much easier than time-shifting live radio. Search around at Sourceforge, and you'll find many projects that can help you do this.

- Set up your own radio station for everyone at the dorm, office, or apartment complex to listen to.

FCC rule 15.215(a) says, "Unless otherwise stated, there are no restrictions as to the types of operations permitted under these sections." So you can play your music for your neighbors or coworkers, and you don't have to worry about getting a note from the RIAA.

- Most people do most of their radio listening in the car. Normally, when you get in your car in the morning, you can pick up your morning radio show at the same point it was at when you walked out the door. Frank might break that, though. If you haven't caught up to live radio by the time you leave for work, you'll miss a few minutes. You can fix this, though. Stick a computer in your car with a wireless network, and have it either start recording before you get in the car, or download the radio show from Frank. You can also grab the current position in the radio show, and pick up where you left off—the Xmms::Perl module knows how to report the current position.

- Record audio from your digital cable TV system.

- Automatically download your favorite NPR shows from the Internet.

- Record audio from XM Radio.

- Download schedules of radio programs that will be broadcast, and allow scheduling by browsing the schedule.

Exhibit A: Bill of Materials

This list shows the parts that I used, though of course you can substitute parts from other manufacturers. All parts are available from large hardware stores or home-automation web sites.

Item	Quantity	Approximate cost
Infrared PS2 keyboard	1	$30
Hauppauge WinTV-Go-FM card (Model 191)	1	$50
Crane Digital FM Transmitter	1	$80
Powermid set (transmitter and receiver)	1	$53
Extra Powermid IR transmitter	1	$34
Sony RM-VL900 learning remote	1	$40

Exhibit B: Software Versions

This list shows the versions of software components originally used to create this project, for your reference. You can, and should, use updated versions whenever possible.

Description	Version
Red Hat Linux personal edition	9.1
Frank	0.1
XMMS	1.2.8
Aumix	2.7
SoX	12.17.3
OggEnc	1.0
FM Tools	0.99.1
KRadio	0.3.0-alpha2
Perl	5.8.0
XBindKeys	1.6.4
Xmms::Remote	0.12
Ogg::Vorbis::Header	0.03

Access Your Entire Media Collection Over the Internet

Cost

$0

Time

less than an hour

Difficulty

3 out of 5

What You Need

- Web server running IIS (or Apache with ChiliASP!)
- Media player that supports WinAMP-style playlist and URLs
- Broadband Internet connection

Do you remember when music was distributed on vinyl? Record albums were prone to damage and dust, and they were too large to be truly portable. Plus, you couldn't possibly listen to them in the car. The first major improvement to that format to gain wide acceptance was the cassette tape, but those had their limitations as well. They were susceptible to environmental hazards, like heat, and eventually wore out through continued use. They also eliminated the random-access feature that vinyl provided. Then along came compact discs. CDs were still in danger of damage from scratches, but to a much lesser degree than vinyl. The format took off because of the convenient form factor and random-access features. But of course it would be only a matter of time before improvements in distribution formats made CDs inconvenient or unnecessary, if not obsolete.

These days, few true geeks are listening to music that hasn't been digitized for use with a computer or portable device. You've probably already ripped your entire CD collection. Perhaps you've been downloading music from the Internet, either using a peer-to-peer system like Kazaa (Gnutella, Napster, WinMX, etc.) or one of the legal online music outlets like iTunes or eMusic (or again, to our surprise, Napster). You've probably enjoyed the benefits of having an entire music collection accessible from a computer-based player like MediaPlayer, WinAMP, or many others that are too numerous to list.

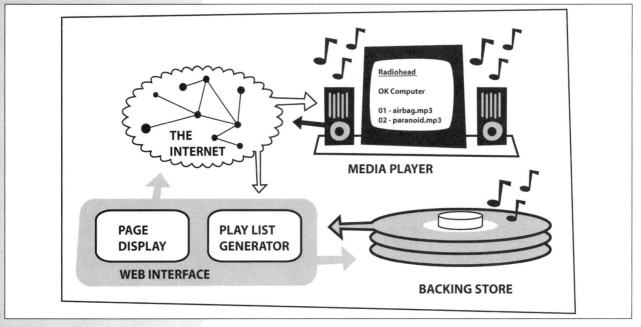

Figure 10-1. Conceptual diagram of a web-accessible media library.

So how would you like to be able to access your collection from anywhere, using nothing but a web browser? This project, conceptualized in Figure 10-1, makes it possible. You can even use the architecture of this project to create web sites that allow you to access other media formats such as images or video. In fact, anything represented as a file on your computer can be accessed similarly.

Project Overview

In order to expose your media collection to the Internet, you'll be creating Active Server Pages (ASP) to access a backing store of media files and format it for viewing as a web page.

This project basically consists of three layers, as shown in Figure 10-1. There's a backing store that contains all the media files; you'll be accessing this information and reformatting it for presentation through a web browser by the web interface. Then we have the web interface layer. Although you'll be using ASP to generate the pages, they could just as easily be written in Perl, JSP, or any other language that supports dynamic page generation. In addition to presenting the files in a manner that allows for easy navigation, the scripts will also dynamically generate WinAMP-style playlists that automatically download to the Media Player layer.

The Media Player

Any media player that can play files specified as a URL and read WinAMP-style playlists will be fine for this project. Naturally, WinAMP will work, as will XMMS and Windows MediaPlayer. I created this project about three years ago and have been using Windows MediaPlayer to access it all along; Recently, I started using XMMS with equal success.

The Backing Store

You could get into some very complex stuff with the backing store using a database management system like MySQL or Microsoft SQL Server Desktop Engine (MSDE). Doing so would allow you to associate all kinds of information with your files; for example, you could add information that would allow you to view songs by genre or decade. However, we're going to keep things simple in this project and use a "database" that will be easy to access and understand—your filesystem. Using your filesystem as your backing store offers the advantage of simplicity at the expense of imposing some restrictions on how you view your library.

To start off, you'll need to have storage that is both large enough to accommodate your music collection and that is accessible to your web server. Chances are that both the web server and the media library are on the same machine, but they don't need to be.

If you don't already have a web server running, see Chapter 12, Watch Your House Across the Network, for a detailed guide to setting up Internet Information Server (IIS).

---

1. Create the filesystem for your media library

You'll be relying on the structure of your filesystem to impose order on your media library. To accomplish this, you'll begin by creating a folder in which the entire library will be nested. Inside this folder you'll create individual folders for each artist in your collection; within each artist's folder will reside subfolders for each album. It's in these album folders that you'll store your actual MP3 files. Figure 10-2 should give you the basic idea.

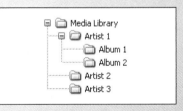

Figure 10-2. The filesystem structure provides order to your media library.

You can group the songs any way you like. Grouping by album makes sense to me, but perhaps you don't have complete albums in your collection. The scripts that build the web pages don't actually care if the songs are truly related by album, only that the songs are contained in subfolders of the artist's folder. You could just as easily create a folder called "all songs" and load it up, or you could group by genre instead of artist. In fact, as long as your MP3 files are nested two layers beneath the root of the library, you can create any structure you desire without modifying the scripts at all.

2. Create a virtual directory to access your media library

Although the scripts for this project have direct access to the filesystem, web browsers will not be able to retrieve the audio files unless a path to them is provided. With IIS you can create links to portions of the filesystem outside the web site itself (or even on a completely different machine) using *virtual directories*, and have them appear to be part of the web site.

1. Open the Internet Service Manager for your web server.

2. Right-click on your web site, select New → Virtual Directory, and then click Next.

3. Enter an alias for the directory; this need not be the same as the actual directory name. If you'd like to be consistent with the scripts that follow, call it *mp3*. Click Next.

4. Enter the complete path to the directory, including the drive letter, or click Browse and navigate to the directory to avoid typing it in. Click Next.

5. Make sure that Read is the only selected option on the Access Permissions page. Click Next.

6. Click Finish.

Now you can access your MP3s—assuming they're already stored in the directory you pointed the alias to—using your web browser and the URL:

http://mywebserver/mp3/artist/album/song.mp3

This is exactly how the filenames will be formatted in the playlists that the scripts generate.

The Web Interface

This project relies on ASP, which is built into IIS. ASP can dynamically generate web pages using any ActiveX compliant language. You'll be using VBScript here, but you could just as easily use JavaScript or Perl. I'll get into the details of the scripts later, but the basic idea is that the filesystem is parsed and represented in HTML and then sent to the browser. For simplicity's sake I've kept the format of the generated pages rather sparse in order to focus on the mechanics of the parsing process. Adding style is simple if you know HTML; if you don't, these pages are still functional even if they're not pretty.

1. Create the default page script

When you specify a URL in your web browser without providing a page name, IIS will automatically serve up the default page. This page can have any of several names (*index.htm*, *default.htm*, or *default.asp*) without any further configuration of IIS. We'll be using the name *default.asp* as the name of our default page. You can create this file using any text editor and save it in the root directory of your web server.

Let's now look at the *default.asp* script.

```
<%@ LANGUAGE=VBScript %>
<% Option Explicit %>
```

These first two lines are not necessary, but are good practice. The first line specifies that VBScript is the language used in this script. VBScript is the default language for IIS, but since this is configurable (and could therefore change), it's always a good idea to specify up front. The second line forces you to declare all your variables, a convention that is not otherwise required by the language. However, it eliminates one very common and extremely frustrating source of code errors: misspelled variable names.

The complete code listing without inline discussion can be found in Exhibit A.

```
<!-- #INCLUDE FILE="playlist.asp" -->
<!-- #INCLUDE FILE="display.asp" -->
```

The major work of the script will be broken out into two modules, which are really nothing more than additional ASP files. They must be included in this page in order to provide access to the methods defined in them.

```
Const MEDIA_LIBRARY_URL    = "mp3"
Const MEDIA_LIBRARY_PATH   = "c:\media_library"
Const TEMP_URL             = "temp"
Const TEMP_PATH            = "f:\Web sites\music\temp"
```

Another good programming practice is to *virtualize* names that frequently appear in your scripts but that are subject to change. Not doing so will force you to scour your code whenever a change occurs. The above code provides aliases to two folders in two forms, URLs and paths. Your browser needs the URLs, but the scripts have access to the filesystem, which requires physical paths instead. MEDIA_LIBRARY is the root location where your MP3s are stored, and TEMP is a regular folder on the web site where playlists will be placed once they're generated.

Now, on to where the action is.

```
If Request.QueryString.Count = 0 Then
    DisplayArtists
```

When you go to the default page for the first time, you want to see a list of all the artists in your collection (see Figure 10-3). Unless you manually type a query string in the URL—something you shouldn't do unless you prefer typing to clicking—the Request.Query.Count will equal 0 and the DisplayArtists subroutine will be called. We'll discuss this subroutine later; for now, you just need to know that DisplayArtists will display a list of all the artists.

```
Else
    Select Case Request.QueryString("action")
    Case "artist"
        DisplayAlbums Request.QueryString("artist")
    Case "play"
```

What Is a Query String?

Query strings are a mechanism to pass information to a web server as part of the URL. In this project, they tell the default page what action you'd like to perform and pass any additional information that might be required to perform that action. For example, if there's a folder in the root of your media library called *Radiohead*, the DisplayArtist() subroutine will create a link will that points to *http://mywebserver/default.asp?action=artist&artist=radiohead.* Everything following the question mark in the URL is considered the query string. The string can be further broken down into key/value pairs, separated by ampersands, which define a variable name and the value assigned to it in the string. In this example, there's a variable called artist whose value is radiohead.

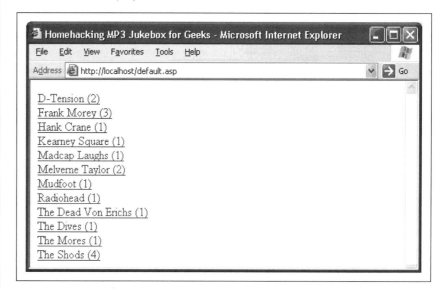

Figure 10-3. The default view for the Jukebox shows all the artists.

Our application defines an action variable with two possible values: artist and play. If a user clicks on an artist in the list, the page is called back with the query string specifying artist as the action. This in turn calls the DisplayAlbums subroutine with the selected artist as an argument, which displays all the albums and songs by the artist (see Figure 10-4). From this page, a user can click on anything and the script will be called again, this time with action set to play. Exactly what happens next depends on the nature of the item that was clicked. Clicking the artist's name will play everything by that artist; clicking an album title will play the album; and clicking a song will play that song.

```
Select Case Request.QueryString("type")
Case "artist"
```

```
                Response.Redirect GenerateArtistPlaylist(Request.
QueryString("artist"))
            Case "album"
                Response.Redirect GenerateAlbumPlaylist(Request.
QueryString("artist"), Request.QueryString("album"))
            Case "song"
                Response.Redirect GenerateSongPlaylist(Request.
QueryString("artist"), Request.QueryString("album"), Request.
QueryString("song"))
```

The type of playlist that is generated is controlled by the addition of another variable to the query string. The variable type directs the script to call the appropriate playlist generator function and has three possible values: artist, album, and song. The arguments for each function are also included in the query string, which may include artist, album, and song.

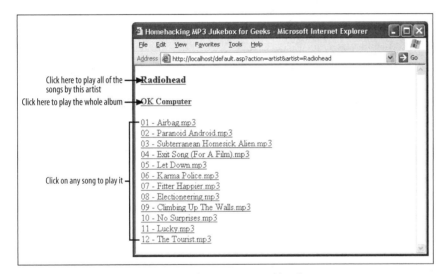

Figure 10-4. Each artist's page shows all the songs grouped by album.

2. Create the page display script

Encapsulating the display-related subroutines in a separate file is not necessary; they could just as well be defined in *default.asp*, but I wanted to prevent the default page script from getting overcrowded with code. Keeping the subroutines in a separate file also has the advantage of allowing you to easily replace display-related subroutines without tampering with the rest of the code.

Page generation is handled by the script *display.asp*, which defines only two subroutines, DisplayArtists() and DisplayAlbums(strArtist). The first subroutine basically creates a list of hyperlinks, one for each artist, that link back to the default page with action set to artist and artist set to the artist named in the link.

The complete code listing without inline discussion can be found in Exhibit B.

Let's now look at the *display.asp* script.

```
Sub DisplayArtists()
    Dim objFSO           ' File system object
    Dim objArtist         ' Artist folder object
    Dim strScriptName     ' Name of parent script
    Dim intAlbumCount     ' Number of album subfolders for each artist
```

Even though you haven't set `Option Explicit` in this file as you did in *default.asp*, you still must declare all the variables that you'll be using in this subroutine because the option is called in *default.asp*, which is including this file. Once that's out of the way, create a `FileSystemObject` object to begin parsing the root folder of your media library.

Separating functionally related code into individual script files allows for much neater code. However, page directives in a parent page (like `Option Explicit` in *default.asp*) will cascade into any included pages. In other words, child pages included in an ASP page are beholden to the rules defined in the parent page.

```
Set objFSO = Server.CreateObject("Scripting.FileSystemObject")
```

Then you store the name of your script, currently called *default.asp*, to prevent looking it up repeatedly in the `for` loop. Doing this as shown below instead of hardcoding it to "default.asp" allows you to change the name of the file without breaking anything.

```
strScriptName = Request.ServerVariables("SCRIPT_NAME")
```

You now enter the loop, creating a temporary file object (`objArtist`) for each subfolder in the root of the media library. You also store the number of subfolders in each folder to display next to the artist's name as an indicator of the number of albums you have from each artist.

```
For Each objArtist in objFSO.GetFolder(MEDIA_LIBRARY_PATH).
Subfolders
        intAlbumCount = objArtist.SubFolders.Count %>
```

Next, you create the actual link using inline HTML. I could have used the `Response.Write` method to write the necessary HTML tags, but I chose this style because I find it's easier to distinguish the HTML elements from the procedural code. The downside is that HTML and ASP code are intertwined, which can make debugging a greater challenge. Fortunately, geeks write perfect code the first time, every time.

```
<a href='<%= strScriptName %>?action=artist&artist=<%=
objArtist.Name %>'
```

Spaghetti Code

HTML is nothing but a formatting language. We use it to define the layout and some simple behavior for web pages. But even for a simple task like displaying today's date on a page, HTML alone will not suffice. For this we need a real programming language like Perl or VBScript.

Unfortunately, this nearly always results in formatting code (HTML) being intertwined (like spaghetti) with procedural code. For simple pages this isn't really too much of an issue but for more complex web applications, spaghetti code can have a severe impact on readability and make debugging nearly impossible.

Looking towards the future, expect tools that make it much easier to maintain clear separations between formatting and procedural code. Microsoft's ASP.NET is an example of this programming.

It's nice to do a little branching on the number of albums to add a tool tip that's intelligent. The script shouldn't say, "Click here to listen to all 1 albums."

```
<% If intAlbumCount = 1 Then %>
    title='Click to see the <%= intAlbumCount %> album.'>
<% Else %>
    title='Click to see all <%= intAlbumCount %> albums.'>
<% End If %>
    <%= objArtist.Name %> (<%= intAlbumCount %>)<br>
</a>
<% Next
```

Finally, you destroy the objects you created, since you're done with them.

```
'Clean up
Set objFSO = Nothing
Set objArtist = Nothing
End Sub
```

The `DisplayAlbums(strArtist)` subroutine is mechanically similar to `DisplayArtists()`, but has a different purpose. You'll use it to display all the albums and the songs on each album for whichever artist is passed as the argument.

The first thing to do in this script is create a heading for the page with the name of the specified artist and link it to a function that creates a playlist for all the songs by that artist.

```
<a href='<%= strScriptName %>?action=play&type=artist&artist=<%=
strArtist %>'
    title='Click here to play all songs by this artist.'>
    <%= strArtist %>
```

Here you can see that the `action` is `play`, the `type` is `artist`, and the `artist` is the artist whose albums you're looking at.

Next, you loop through the subfolders in the artist's folder and create a link to the function that generates playlists for individual complete albums.

```
For Each objAlbum in objFSO.GetFolder(MEDIA_LIBRARY_PATH & "\" &
strArtist).Subfolders %>
    <a href='<%= strScriptName %>?action=play&type=album&artist=<%=
strArtist %>&album=<%= objAlbum.Name %>'
        title='Click here to play the whole album.'>
        <%= objAlbum.Name %>
    </a>
```

You also create links for each song (as long as it's an MP3 file) in an inner loop; this loop calls a function that generates a playlist containing only that single file. You could have linked directly to the file instead, but we do it this way to make it too much trouble to simply download the MP3 files.

Copyrights and the Internet

Sharing copyrighted material on the Internet is illegal. Fair use states, more or less, that you can copy copyrighted materials for archiving or for transferring to another media type, as long as you've paid for it and it's for your own use. It's also okay to stream your audio files so that a handful of your friends can listen to your music. However, these scripts aren't doing streaming—they simply allow the client to download the original files. Don't allow unfettered access to your collection. Use password protection as a minimum and don't advertise that you're running a site like this. Leaving the door wide open is arguably intent to distribute.

```
For Each objSong in objAlbum.Files
    If objFSO.GetExtensionName(objSong) = "mp3" then %>
        <a href='<%= strScriptName %>?action=play&type=song&artist=<%=
strArtist %>&album=<%= objAlbum.Name %>&song=<%= objSong.Name %>'
            title='Click here to play this song.'>
            <%= objSong.Name %>
        </a>
```

And that's all there is to displaying the files. Now you need to generate the playlists.

3. Create the playlist generator script

In its most basic form, a WinAMP playlist is nothing but a text file with the location of each file represented as a path or a URL. The *playlist.asp* script will generate basic playlists dynamically for all of a chosen artist's songs, for individual albums, or for a single song. Three separate functions create the three different types of playlists, making it easy to add new playlist generators if you need to. For example, if you wanted a generator that randomly grabbed 10 songs from the whole collection, you could write a function to do that, and then just add another case to the Select statement in *default.asp* that branches to the various playlist generators.

The complete code listing without inline discussion can be found in Exhibit C.

Let's take a look at the functions used in the *playlist.asp* script. The first function creates a playlist from all the songs by a given artist. Again, all your variables need to be declared before first use.

```
Function GenerateArtistPlaylist(strArtist)
    Dim objFSO          ' File system object
    Dim strPlaylist     ' Playlist filename
    Dim objPlaylist     ' Playlist file object
    Dim strArtistURL    ' Base URL to album
    Dim objAlbum        ' ALbum folder object
    Dim objSong         ' Song file object
```

After the declarations you instantiate a FileSystemObject object that you'll be using for a number of file-related tasks.

```
Set objFSO = CreateObject("Scripting.FileSystemObject")
```

The first task for the FileSystemObject is to create a temporary filename. The GetTempName method randomly generates a temporary file name to which you append the extension *.m3u*, the standard extension for a WinAMP playlist.

```
strPlaylist = objFSO.GetBaseName(objFSO.GetTempName) & ".m3u"
```

After that, you create a new text file with the name you generated, overwriting any file that may already exist with that name.

```
Set objPlaylist = objFSO.CreateTextFile(TEMP_PATH & "\" &
strPlayList, True)
```

To avoid repeatedly looking up the server name from the `ServerVariables` collection of the `Request` object in your loop, you build a string and store it in a variable for easy reference.

```
strArtistURL = "http://" & Request.ServerVariables("SERVER_NAME") &
"/" & MEDIA_LIBRARY_URL & "/" & strArtist
```

Now it's just a matter of looping through each album folder and adding the URL for each song to the text file. Notice the use of the `Replace()` method. Some MP3 players that can otherwise read WinAMP playlists and play files from URLs sometimes choke on spaces in URLs. To avoid that, replace any spaces with the ASCII code equivalent, %20.

```
For Each objAlbum In objFSO.GetFolder(MEDIA_LIBRARY_PATH & "\" &
strArtist).Subfolders
    For Each objSong in objAlbum.Files
        If objFSO.GetExtensionName(objSong) = "mp3" Then
            objPlaylist.WriteLine Replace(strArtistURL & "/" &
objAlbum.Name & "/" & objSong.Name, " ", "%20")
        End If
    Next
Next
```

This function returns a complete URL for the temporary playlist file that was created so that it can be downloaded. In VBScript this is accomplished by assigning the return value to the function's name.

```
GenerateArtistPlaylist = "http://" & Request.
ServerVariables("SERVER_NAME") & "/" & TEMP_URL & "/" & strPlaylist
```

Finally, you dispose of the objects you created and no longer need.

```
objPlaylist.Close
Set objPlaylist = Nothing
Set objFSO = Nothing
End Function
```

The next function, `GenerateAlbumPlaylist(strArtist, strAlbum)`, returns a URL referring to a playlist that includes all the songs for a specified album. It's mostly the same as the previous function, with the exception that instead of looping through all the albums, only the specified album is parsed.

The last function differs from the previous one only by specifying the song instead of looping to grab them all. `GenerateSongPlaylist(strArtist, strAlbum, strSongFilespec)` wraps a single song in a playlist and returns a URL to the location of the generated file. The complete listing for all three functions can be found in Exhibit C.

Wrapping Up

That's all there is to it! You might find that expanding your collection is easier if the tool you use to rip your CD collection can read data from CDDB, an online database with album and track data for just about every CD in the world. You can then automatically save the files into folders in compliance with the system you've defined for your library.

If you have a PC integrated with your home audio system, you might find yourself using this application in place of your CD collection. I find this to be especially nice when I have parties and don't want to play DJ. My guests can have fun without mixing up all my CDs in their drunken stupor.

If you've never played with dynamic page creation tools like ASP, I hope this simple project has given you a sense of how powerful they can be. I also encourage you to add your own personal flair to the look and feel of the pages.

Extensions

For the sake of being concise, this project provides only essential functionality, but some very simple additions can make your new system a pleasure to use.

- You could add cover art to each album and modify the display functions to insert the images in the page. You could even get fancy and use screen-scraping techniques to automatically grab cover art from a web site like Amazon.com or Buy.com.

- One limitation of this project is that you can't mix and match songs from several artists or a specific subset of songs from one artist. For example, you can't create a playlist of your three favorite songs from three different artists. This can be corrected in various ways. Perhaps you could modify the single song function so that it appends to the playlist rather than creating a new one each time. Or maybe you could keep track of the songs you're selecting using session variables.

- Wouldn't it also be nice to be able to upload MP3s from anywhere on the Web to your collection? You could add a form that allows you to browse your local filesystem and transfer selected files to the correct location on your web server.

- MP3 files generally contain a lot of meta-information in ID3 tags. You could add functionality to parse that data and include it in the display routines to provide richer information about the music you collect. You could even create tools that allow you to modify or insert tags.

- Another idea would be to keep track of usage data. Would you like to know your own personal top ten? It wouldn't take much to coax the playlist generator functions to keep track of stuff like that.

- You could also place a real database between the files and the application, allowing you to keep track of all kinds of things. Doing so makes it easy to create playlists based on anything from genre to "songs that start with Q."

- Lastly, because I wanted to make it as generic as possible, this project only plays MP3 files. But because your site is for your own personal use, you get to call the shots and can easily add other media formats. For example, you could modify the display and playlist routines to allow files with an .OGG extension; if you prefer Windows Media Audio files, add those. This is your site; make it do whatever you want it to.

Exhibit A: default.asp

```
<%@ LANGUAGE=VBScript %>
<% Option Explicit %>
<!-- #INCLUDE FILE="playlist.asp" -->
<!-- #INCLUDE FILE="display.asp" -->
<%


    'Constants
    Const MEDIA_LIBRARY_URL      = "mp3"
    Const MEDIA_LIBRARY_PATH      = "c:\media_library"
    Const TEMP_URL            = "temp"
    Const TEMP_PATH              = "c:\inetpub\wwwroot\temp"
%>

<html>
<head>
<title>Homehacking MP3 Jukebox for Geeks</title>
</head>

<body>
<%
    If Request.QueryString.Count = 0 Then
        DisplayArtists
    Else
        Select Case Request.QueryString("action")
        Case "artist"
            DisplayAlbums Request.QueryString("artist")
        Case "play"
            Select Case Request.QueryString("type")
            Case "artist"
                Response.Redirect GenerateArtistPlaylist(Request.
QueryString("artist"))
            Case "album"
                Response.Redirect GenerateAlbumPlaylist(Request.
QueryString("artist"), Request.QueryString("album"))
            Case "song"
                Response.Redirect GenerateSongPlaylist(Request.
QueryString("artist"), Request.QueryString("album"), Request.
```

```
QueryString("song"))
            End Select
        End Select
    End If
%>
</body>

</html>
```

Exhibit B: display.asp

```asp
<%
    Sub DisplayArtists()
        Dim objFSO          ' File system object
        Dim objArtist        ' Artist folder object
        Dim strScriptName    ' Name of parent script
        Dim intAlbumCount    ' Placeholder for number of album
subfolders for each artist

        Set objFSO = Server.CreateObject("Scripting.FileSystemObject")

        strScriptName = Request.ServerVariables("SCRIPT_NAME")

        For Each objArtist in objFSO.GetFolder(MEDIA_LIBRARY_PATH).
Subfolders
            intAlbumCount = objArtist.SubFolders.Count %>

            <a href='<%= strScriptName %>?action=artist&artist=<%=
objArtist.Name %>'
            <% If intAlbumCount = 1 Then %>
               title='Click to see the <%= intAlbumCount %> album.'>
            <% Else %>
               title='Click to see all <%= intAlbumCount %> albums.'>
            <% End If %>
                <%= objArtist.Name %> (<%= intAlbumCount %>)<br>
            </a>

        <% Next

        'Clean up
        Set objFSO = Nothing
        Set objArtist = Nothing
    End Sub

    Sub DisplayAlbums(strArtist)
        Dim objFSO          ' File system object
        Dim objAlbum         ' Artist folder object
        Dim objSong          ' Song file object
        Dim strScriptName    ' Name of parent script

        Set objFSO = Server.CreateObject("Scripting.FileSystemObject")

        strScriptName = Request.ServerVariables("SCRIPT_NAME")
%>
        <h3>
            <a href='<%= strScriptName %>?action=play&type=artist&artis
t=<%= strArtist %>'
```

Exhibit C

```
                    title='Click here to play all the songs by this
artist.'>
                <%= strArtist %>
            </a>
        </h3>
<%
        For Each objAlbum in objFSO.GetFolder(MEDIA_LIBRARY_PATH & "\"
& strArtist).SubFOlders %>
            <h4>
                <a href='<%=strScriptName %>?action=play&type=album&art
ist=<%= strArtist %>&album=<%= objAlbum.Name %>'
                    title='Click here to play whole album.'>
                    <%= objAlbum.Name %>
                </a>
            </h4>
<%          For Each objSong in objAlbum.Files
                If objFSO.GetExtensionName(objSong) = "mp3" then %>
                    <a href='<%= strScriptName %>?action=play&type=son
g&artist=<%= strArtist %>&album=<%= objAlbum.Name %>&song=<%= objSong.
Name %>'
                        title='Click here to play this song.'>
                        <%= objSong.Name %>
                    </a><br>
<%              End If
            Next
        Next

        'Clean up
        set objFSO = Nothing
        Set objAlbum = Nothing
        Set objSong = Nothing
    End Sub
%>
```

Exhibit C: playlist.asp

```
<%
    Function GenerateArtistPlaylist(strArtist)
    ' This function creates a playlist of all the songs by a given
artist and
    ' returns the playtlists filename for download.

        Dim objFSO          ' File system object
        Dim strPlaylist     ' Playlist filename
        Dim objPlaylist     ' Playlist file object
        Dim strArtistURL    ' Base URL to album
        Dim objAlbum        ' ALbum folder object
        Dim objSong         ' Song file object

        ' Create new empty playlist in temp folder
        Set objFSO = CreateObject("Scripting.FileSystemObject")
        strPlaylist = objFSO.GetBaseName(objFSO.GetTempName) & ".m3u"
        Set objPlaylist = objFSO.CreateTextFile(TEMP_PATH & "\" &
strPlayList, True)

        ' Build base path to album string to avoid redundant server
variable lookup
```

Exhibit C

```
                        strArtistURL = "http://" & Request.ServerVariables("SERVER_
        NAME") & "/" & MEDIA_LIBRARY_URL & "/" & strArtist

                Response.Write "playing" & strArtist
                ' Create playlist from all of artist's albums
                For Each objAlbum In objFSO.GetFolder(MEDIA_LIBRARY_PATH & "\"
        & strArtist).Subfolders
                    For Each objSong in objAlbum.Files
                        If objFSO.GetExtensionName(objSong) = "mp3" Then
                            objPlaylist.WriteLine Replace(strArtistURL & "/" &
        objAlbum.Name & "/" & objSong.Name, " ", "%20")
                        End If
                    Next
                Next

                ' Return playlist filename
                GenerateArtistPlaylist = "http://" & Request.
        ServerVariables("SERVER_NAME") & "/" & TEMP_URL & "/" & strPlaylist

                'Clean up
                objPlaylist.Close
                Set objPlaylist = Nothing
                Set objFSO = Nothing

        End Function

        Function GenerateAlbumPlaylist(strArtist, strAlbum)
            ' This function creates a playlist from all the audio files in an
        album
            ' folder and returns the name of the playlist for download

                Dim objFSO          ' File system object
                Dim strPlaylist      ' Playlist filename
                Dim objPlaylist      ' Playlist file object
                Dim strAlbumURL      ' Base URL to album
                Dim objAlbum        ' ALbum folder object
                Dim objSong         ' Song file object

                ' Create new empty playlist in temp folder
                Set objFSO = CreateObject("Scripting.FileSystemObject")
                strPlaylist = objFSO.GetBaseName(objFSO.GetTempName) & ".m3u"
                Set objPlaylist = objFSO.CreateTextFile(TEMP_PATH & "\" &
        strPlayList, True)

                ' Build base path to album string to avoid redundant server
        variable lookup
                strAlbumURL = "http://" & Request.ServerVariables("SERVER_
        NAME") & "/" & MEDIA_LIBRARY_URL & "/" & strArtist & "/" & strAlbum

                ' Create playlist from complete album
                Set objAlbum = objFSO.GetFolder(MEDIA_LIBRARY_PATH & "\" &
        strArtist & "\" & strAlbum)
                For Each objSong in objAlbum.Files
                    If objFSO.GetExtensionName(objSong) = "mp3" Then
                        objPlaylist.WriteLine Replace(strAlbumURL & "/" &
        objSong.Name, " ", "%20")
                    End If
                Next
```

Exhibit C

```
        ' Return playlist filename
        GenerateAlbumPlaylist = "http://" & Request.
ServerVariables("SERVER_NAME") & "/" & TEMP_URL & "/" & strPlaylist

        'Clean up
        objPlaylist.Close
        Set objPlaylist = Nothing
        Set objFSO = Nothing
    End Function

    Function GenerateSongPlaylist(strArtist, strAlbum, strSongFilespec)
    ' This function takes a single song file and adds it to a playlist.
Then it returns
    ' the playlist filename for download

        Dim objFSO          'file system object
        Dim strPlaylist     'playlist filename
        Dim objPlaylist     'playlist file object
        Dim strAlbumURL     'Base URL to album

        ' Create new empty playlist in temp folder
        Set objFSO = CreateObject("Scripting.FileSystemObject")
        strPlaylist = objFSO.GetBaseName(objFSO.GetTempName) & ".m3u"
        Set objPlaylist = objFSO.CreateTextFile(TEMP_PATH & "\" &
strPlayList, True)

        ' Build base path to album string to avoid redundant server
variable lookup
        strAlbumURL = "http://" & Request.ServerVariables("SERVER_
NAME") & "/" & MEDIA_LIBRARY_URL & "/" & strArtist & "/" & strAlbum

        ' Create playlist for single song
        objPlaylist.WriteLine Replace(strAlbumURL & "/" &
strSongFilespec, " ", "%20")

        ' Return playlist filename
        GenerateSongPlaylist = "http://" & Request.
ServerVariables("SERVER_NAME") & "/" & TEMP_URL & "/" & strPlaylist

        'Clean up
        objPlaylist.Close
        Set objPlaylist = Nothing
        Set objFSO = Nothing
    End Function

    Function GenerateSelectionPlaylist(strArtist, strAlbum,
arrSongFilespecs)
    ' This function takes a selection of song files and adds it to a
playlist. Then it returns
    ' the playlist filename for download

        Dim objFSO          'file system object
        Dim strPlaylist     'playlist filename
        Dim objPlaylist     'playlist file object
        Dim strAlbumURL     'Base URL to album

        ' Create new empty playlist in temp folder
        Set objFSO = CreateObject("Scripting.FileSystemObject")
        strPlaylist = objFSO.GetBaseName(objFSO.GetTempName) & ".m3u"
```

Exhibit C

```
            Set objPlaylist = objFSO.CreateTextFile(TEMP_PATH & "\" &
    strPlayList, True)

            ' Build base path to album string to avoid redundant server
    variable lookup
            strAlbumURL = "http://" & Request.ServerVariables("SERVER_
    NAME") & "/" & MEDIA_LIBRARY_URL & "/" & strArtist & "/" & strAlbum

            ' Create playlist from selected songs
            For Each objFile in arrSongFilespecs
                If objFSO.GetExtensionName(objFile) = "mp3" Then
                    objPlaylist.WriteLine Replace(strAlbumURL & "/" &
    objFile.Name, " ", "%20")
                End If
            Next

            ' Return playlist filename
            GenerateSongPlaylist = objPlaylist.Size

            'Clean up
            objPlaylist.Close
            Set objPlaylist = Nothing
            Set objFSO = Nothing
        End Function
    %>
```

Home Security

Part III of this book covers home security–related topics. Chapter 11 solves a problem I've always struggled with—why can I unlock my car remotely, but not my house? You'll get the opportunity to break apart some expensive electronic equipment and do some soldering in order to unlock your door with a keychain remote. Your computer will know when you get home and can turn on some lights, or even start playing your favorite music. In Chapter 12, you'll use inexpensive wireless cameras to monitor multiple locations around your home from across the Internet. In Chapter 13, you'll build your own completely customizable home security system, with motion detectors, video cameras, off-site backups (in case a thief steals your computer), and alarm notifications sent to your mobile phone or email.

Keyless Entry Welcome Home

Cost

$170 - $250

Time

three hours

Difficulty

5 out of 5

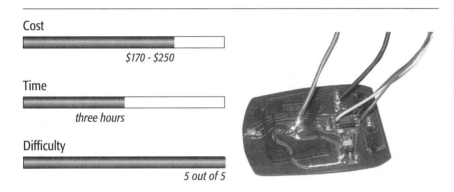

What You Need

- Kwikset TitanOne keyless remote deadbolt

- X10 SlimLine keychain remote

- X10 plug-in RF base

- X10 lamp modules or wall switches (optional, and as many as you need)

- X10 CM11A PC interface (optional)

- Soldering iron with solder

- 2 solid-state relays

- 2 electro-mechanical micro relays

For a list of specific parts used in this project, refer to Exhibit A at the end of this chapter.

For quite some time people have been able to unlock their cars without the use of a key. At first, it was a keypad embedded in the door that you would use to enter a numeric secret code. Later on, cars began to come equipped with an RF receiver that responded to a small keychain remote to unlock the doors. That feature is nearly ubiquitous these days—just about every new car comes with keyless remote entry as a standard feature.

And unlocking the door is usually only part of the story. Cars with these systems also typically offer a host of other convenience features. Some cars beep the horn to let you know that they're locked; some flash the headlights to help you find them in a parking lot; and most turn on the interior light so you can easily find the ignition.

So why hasn't this technology hit home—literally? Why do I still need to use a key to get into my house? There are some keyless remote entry systems available on the market, but getting any special features requires you to purchase expensive proprietary systems. It would be nice if I could extend an existing system to send X10 signals. Take a look at Figure 11-1 and you'll see that that's just what I did.

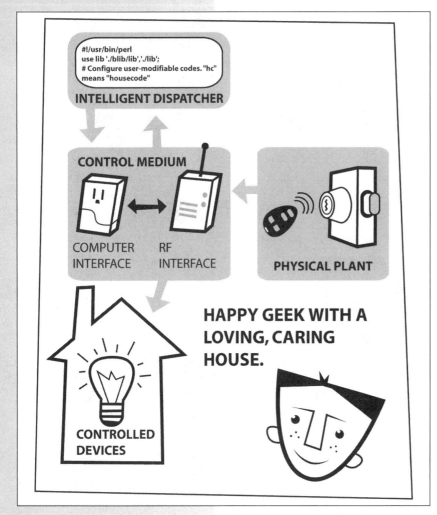

```
#!/usr/bin/perl
use lib './blib/lib','./lib';
# Configure user-modifiable codes. "hc"
means "housecode"
```
INTELLIGENT DISPATCHER

CONTROL MEDIUM

COMPUTER INTERFACE   **RF INTERFACE**

PHYSICAL PLANT

HAPPY GEEK WITH A LOVING, CARING HOUSE.

CONTROLLED DEVICES

Figure 11-1. Conceptual diagram of the keyless remote access system with convenience features.

Project Overview

To be honest, the Kwikset lock is pretty darn cool all by itself. If you're just interested in keyless entry, you'll probably be happy just buying this lock and installing it according to the manufacturer's instructions. But how geeky is *that*? We can go much further. For example, I like how the interior light in my car goes on when I unlock the car with my keychain remote. With a little ingenuity I can make my house do the same thing. I have the following three goals for this project:

- I want visual confirmation that the house is locked. The deadbolt already supplies this as a small LED on the lock bezel, but I want more. I'd like some lights to flash, like the parking lights on my car, to tell me that the house is locked. After all, I could be halfway down the driveway when I remember to lock the door.

- I want lights to come on when I unlock the door. Moreover, I want the choice of which lights to illuminate to be somewhat intelligent. For example, if I unlock the house in broad daylight, there's obviously no need to illuminate the outside of the house. But very late at night I'd like a path to my bedroom illuminated, not just the entry area.

- If I lock the house manually using the knob, I don't want to trigger the other events.

To make all this possible, the lock needs a way of communicating its state to some other device that can provide such services.

Like many of the other projects in this book, this project consists of modular parts. If there are aspects of the project that you don't care about, you can omit them, usually with no side effects. I'll explain how throughout the process.

Let's now examine the conceptual diagram in Figure 11-1 in detail. The actual, physical lock is referred to as the *physical plant*. You'll make some small modifications to provide a means to transmit events from the physical plant onto a *control medium*. The devices that can transmit over the control medium can either directly trigger the controlled devices to turn on or off, or relay those events to an *intelligent dispatcher*. The dispatcher can process the events and place commands back on the control medium to be received by the controlled devices. It's possible to eliminate the dispatcher and have events managed by the interface alone, but this will severely limit the flexibility of the system; this is explained in the section "The Control Medium." Once the modifications to the lock are complete, you can install it according to the manufacturer's instructions.

> Control medium? Intelligent dispatcher? What the heck is this stuff? In English: the control medium is nothing more than the electrical wires in your house's walls, and the intelligent dispatcher is your computer.

Linking the Physical Plant to the Control Medium

The first thing you need is a means to relay the state of the lock to the other parts of the system. In other words, when the door is locked, you want the lock to be able to announce that it's locked; you want a similar announcement when it's unlocked. These announcements will be used as triggers to indicate to the system that an event has occurred.

In order to create a communication link between the lock and the control medium, you're going to embed a tiny RF transmitter in the lock. This transmitter started its life as a compact X10 keychain remote; when stripped of all its outer trappings, it fits neatly into the lock. You'll use it to send one X10 signal for a locking event, and another for an unlocking event.

The keychain also requires a power source. Until now it simply had a compact 3V battery, but you won't want to deal with changing that battery when it dies. Instead, you'll be tapping into the lock's power supply: four AA batteries.

The house code and unit code for the keychain remote are configured by pressing specific buttons for three seconds to enable setup mode, and then pressing repeatedly to assign the desired code. Without the buttons, this is not very easy to do. So to prevent the code from being lost and having to reconfigure the remote, I'm just going to leave it in its default configuration. This means that it will be able to send ON and OFF commands to devices A1 and A2.

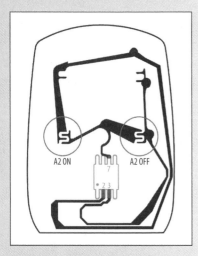

Figure 11-2. Determine where the traces from your buttons go so you can reproduce their effect by other means.

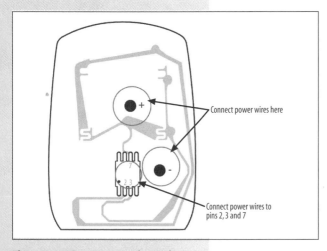

Figure 11-3. Connect your wire to pins 2, 3, and 7 on the chip.

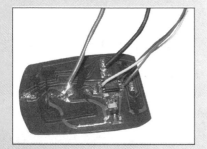

Figure 11-4. The three leads are soldered to the pins of the IC chip, and wires draw power from the lock's batteries.

But first you need to hack into the keychain remote itself. This is where the difficulty in this project lies. In other projects, I've emphasized that excellent soldering skills are not required; unfortunately, the same cannot be said for this project. Here, you'll be attempting to solder wires to the leads of a surface-mount microcontroller. If you create a bridge between leads, the device will likely not function. I created two such bridges while building a prototype, and ended up having to enlist the help of a friend with better skills. (Better tools might have helped as well.)

1. Determine how the remote functions

The principle behind any switch—and the buttons on the keychain remote are indeed switches—is that they allow you to toggle between an open and closed circuit. The buttons on the remote can be considered *normally open momentary switches*. This means that if you were to place that switch in a circuit, under normal circumstances that circuit would not be closed; that is, there would be a break in the circuit at the switch itself. Pressing the button closes the circuit, but only as long as you hold the button. Releasing the button returns it to the normal position.

Figure 11-2 shows the circuit board that resides inside the keychain remote. (Note that the figure disregards many of the traces and most of the components to highlight the ones that are important to us.) The two circles are the pads of the middle two buttons. Pressing the buttons bridges the gap between the two poles of the switch. Notice how the two buttons share a common pole that can be traced back to pin 7 on the chip; the remaining poles can be traced to other pins. Connecting pin 2 to pin 7 will send the X10 signal A2 ON; similarly, connecting pin 3 to pin 7 will send the A2 OFF signal. Manually bridging these pins with a piece of wire will cause the remote to operate just as if you were pressing the buttons. This is our goal in this step.

You'll start by soldering signal wires to the three pins whose locations are shown in Figure 11-3. This will allow you to easily accommodate your switching components. Be warned that soldering these wires is not easy to do. A magnifying glass will help you see better, and a precision tip on your soldering iron can be very helpful. If you find you can't do it, ask a friend to help. (Every geek has at least one friend who can solder.) Figure 11-4 shows a finished product.

The connections to the microcontroller are pretty fragile; a dab of hot glue will help prevent the wires from pulling loose. Considering how much trouble it was to get them on there in the first place, you probably won't want to do it repeatedly.

---

2. Embed the remote control circuit

All you need to do to make your lock send X10 signals is to transfer the function of the remote's buttons to some part of the lock. There is more than one way to do this kind of thing. You could replace the buttons on the remote with your own normally open momentary push button switches, and then figure out a way to have the mechanical motion of the lock press the buttons. This is a fairly simple solution, but it would be difficult to implement this in a way that would allow the device to discern between manual and remote actuation. Therefore, it fails to meet our needs.

A better solution for this project is to find places on the lock's circuit board that have power only when the lock is in specific states (locked, locking, unlocked, etc.), and use that power to drive micro relays that close the same circuit that used to be closed by the buttons on the remote. Observing the lock's behavior is the best way to track down such things.

You might think that the first, obvious place to look is at the terminals that provide power to the motor. After all, these are clearly powered only when the lock is locking and unlocking. Unfortunately, this fails to distinguish between locking and unlocking, and therefore won't work for this project.

A better idea is to take advantage of the visual feedback that the lock provides when you operate it via the motor. There is an LED on the bezel of the portion of the lock that mounts on the outside of the door. When the door locks, the LED blinks red a few times and stops; when the door is unlocked, it blinks green. You can use the power that drives this behavior to drive a small circuit that will "push" the buttons for you.

You might be wondering why we chose to use the second set of buttons on the keychain remote rather than the first. The choice has to do with the way the remote is configured. Earlier I mentioned that the lock is programmed by holding down certain buttons to switch the remote into setup mode. Specifically, you hold down the top ON button for three seconds to enable changing the house code, and you do the same thing with the top OFF button to select a unit code. Rather than risk placing the remote into setup mode by using the A1 buttons, this project will use the A2 buttons.

You might also be wondering why we're using house code A. In the first project in this book, we recommended staying clear of house code A simply because you might have a neighbor who is also running X10, and you don't want RF signals from his house bleeding into yours and controlling things on your system. In this project, we chose house code A, as well as unit codes 1 and 2, because those are the default settings for the keychain remote. This is important, because it's possible that the remote's settings could be lost every time you change the batteries. Once you get this thing embedded in your lock, you certainly won't want to have to reconfigure it if it loses its settings.

Once you've got everything soldered together, test that you've successfully bypassed the switches by touching the other ends of your trace wires to see if the remote is operating properly. If the LED on the remote flashes when you touch either of the wires connected to pins 2 and 3 of the remote's microcontroller to the wire connected to pin 7, you can be fairly confident that you've done it correctly. If all is well, you just need to make connections occur whenever the door lock is operated via the remote control. We'll use a small relay to do this when we build the button-pressing circuit.

Finally, you'll connect the two wires you attached to the remote for power to the top two terminals in the battery compartment, as shown in Figure 11-4. (Normally, the remote is operated by a 3V compact battery.)

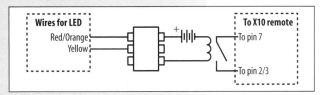

Figure 11-5. The control circuit for the X10 remote.

Figure 11-6. You'll use two circuits to control the buttons on the X10 remote.

3. Build the button-pressing circuit

Now that you've determined roughly how you're going to cause the lock to influence the X10 remote, you need to devise a mechanism to make it happen. Take a look at the diagram in Figure 11-5. The LED on the outside lock can light up in either red or green and is controlled by three wires. A yellow wire connects to the common cathode; the red light is controlled by the red wire; and the green light is controlled by the orange wire. The amount of current delivered to the LED is not enough to drive the coil of the electro-mechanical relay, but it is sufficient to drive a small optically coupled relay. You'll use one of those relays to control the flow of power from the batteries in the lock; this will drive the coil that will close the loop for the X10 remote's buttons.

You'll need two of these circuits, one for locking and the other for unlocking. Figure 11-6 shows one of these circuits. Both circuits will share the yellow wire from the LED harness as well as the wire connected to pin 7 of the remote's microcontroller.

There's not a whole lot of room inside this lock for your components, and you'll have to do some genuine hacking—I'm talking about the machete kind—to make more. Look inside the battery compartment cover, and you'll see a couple of ribs that strengthen the cover itself and hold the batteries in place. These can be easily removed with a pair of pliers: just grab hold of one of the ribs at either end and twist. It will easily tear. Continue working your way across and twisting until the whole piece is removed. Attack the second rib the same way.

The diagram in Figure 11-7 shows how everything fits together. The important thing is that you make all the right connections. You can connect the power wires from the relays and the RF module by crimping them in the small loops found on all the battery contacts. Simply strip a 1/8" piece of insulation from the wires, slip the exposed ends through the loop and crush the loop around the wire using pliers. Exactly how you manage to fit it all in there is difficult to describe, but one thing worth mentioning is that you can't drive your relay *and* the LED on the outer lock at the same time, so there's no need to connect the wire back to the harness leading to the outside bezel. This frees the inside harness to have its connector cut off and its wires pulled back through the lock's circuit board to the battery side.

> You may want to keep the connector on the LED harness to make it easier to change the batteries. If so, you'll have to carefully remove it to enable you to pull the harness through the board to the other side. You can accomplish this by using a hobby knife to press down the tiny ears that retain the contacts in the connector.

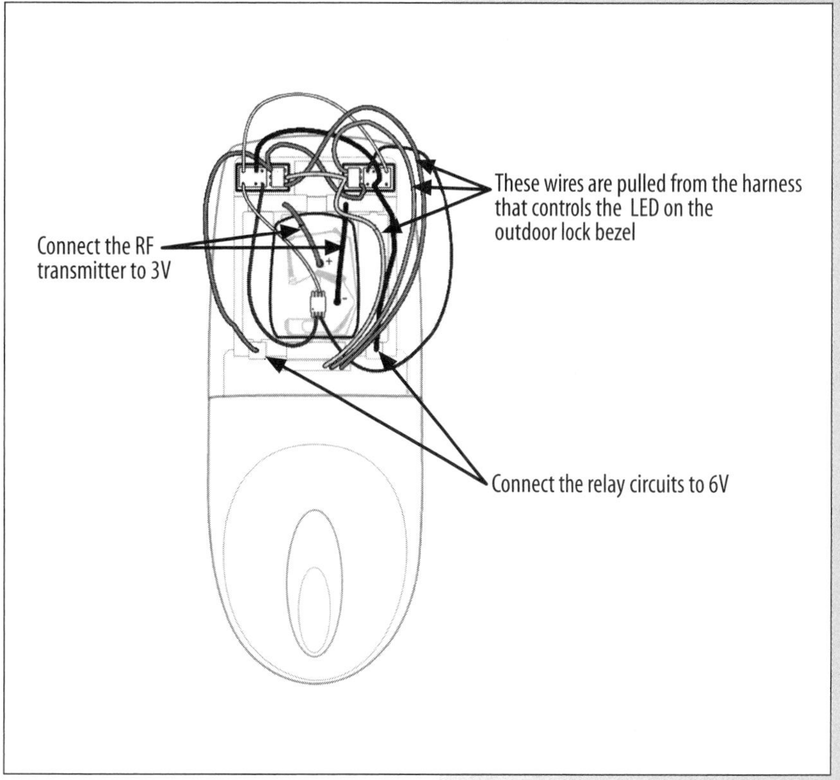

Connect the RF transmitter to 3V

These wires are pulled from the harness that controls the LED on the outdoor lock bezel

Connect the relay circuits to 6V

Figure 11-7. The connections between the lock and the remote assembly.

Figure 11-8. The hardware of the Control Medium: the CM11A and the RF base unit.

The Control Medium

Although there's nothing in the control medium component that you'll actually be building or modifying, it's still important to discuss here, especially if you aren't planning to implement the full system. The hardware that makes up the control medium can be implemented partially if you intend to omit the dispatcher for the sake of simplicity.

The control medium enables the transmission of control information to various endpoints, such as a lamp or your computer. It consists of an RR501 plug-in RF base, your home's power lines, and an optional CM11A computer interface (see Figure 11-8). The RR501 listens to the airwaves

for a radio signal that carries X10 commands and then retransmits the commands over the power lines.

You've already established that the lock will send A2 ON and A2 OFF signals when you lock or unlock the door. In the simplest system, you can plug a lamp directly into the RF base and set the base's address to A1. You can also configure any other devices you want to control to use the address A1. This allows the lock to communicate directly with the controlled devices via the RF base.

If you include the intelligent dispatcher, no device should be configured with the address A2. Instead, allow only the CM11A to pick up the commands so that they can be used to trigger scripted commands to be transmitted back to the power lines. Any devices addressed by the script will respond as requested.

The Controlled Devices

To control the lights, you need to install modules that will respond to X10 commands by switching the light on or off. Let's now turn our focus to the controlled devices component.

There are a number of chapters in this book that focus on X10-controlled lighting, so refer to Chapter 1, Automate a Light, for details of how to install the light switches. Instead, this section will discuss the planning involved in setting up the controlled devices component of your system.

As stated in the Project Overview, there are three major goals we'd like to accomplish by the end of this project. First, we'd like visual confirmation that the house is locked, and second, we want some sort of welcome-home event when we unlock the door. So let's start thinking about how to accomplish these two things.

When I come home late at night, I want a path of light that leads me all the way to my bedroom. I don't, however, need that path at lunchtime. I also want lights to flash when I lock the door, but only on the porch, not in the bedroom. So already I need at least two addresses assigned to the lights: one for the path to bed, and the other for just the entry. And to complicate things even more, I also want to turn on the kitchen lights if it's nighttime but too early for bed. That adds yet another address requirement.

So basically, you need a separate address for each light or group of lights that you want to have independent control over. In an ideal system, each device would be individually addressed; for our purposes, however, that is not necessary. X10 supports 256 unique addresses and, believe it or not, it's awfully easy to go through them quickly. Every individual macro you define needs its own address, which is assigned from the same pool of addresses that your devices use.

So here's the lighting situation in my house. I have two lights in my entry-way, one inside and one outside. Both are controlled by a single switch. I have three lights in my kitchen, one over each door, that are also on a single switch. In the downstairs hallway that connects the kitchen to the stairs leading to the bedrooms, I have two lights controlled by a single switch. Finally, the upstairs hallway has two lights, just outside the bedrooms, that are also controlled by a single switch. Since I intend to have these groupings play roles in other lighting scenes, not only those created for the entry system, it's best not to lump them all together. Table 11-1 shows the addresses I assigned to each lighting zone.

Table 11-1. Each device must be uniquely addressed

Address	Controlled devices
B4	Entryway
B5	Kitchen
B6	Downstairs hallway
B7	Upstairs hallway

Or, if you're happy just having one light or group of lights go on when you unlock the door and go off when you lock it, simply set the whole group to address A1 and forget about the intelligent dispatcher.

See Chapter 1 for detailed information about installing X10 switches.

The Intelligent Dispatcher

The final step of the project is to add intelligence to the system. This enables greater flexibility for device control. For that we need something that can function programmatically, like a PC with a CM11A computer interface.

Once again, Perl is the language of choice because it works on both Windows and Linux and is extremely capable. Your computer must have Perl installed with the appropriate X10 modules; a detailed guide to installing them can be found in Chapter 2, Automate Your Porch Light. Assuming that your system is all ready to go, let's dive right into the script.

The script in this project is similar to the others you've seen involving X10 control. However, keep in mind that this script is for my house—your house will likely require a different arrangement. Therefore, you'll need to understand what the script is doing in order to be able to customize it for your needs. There's a complete listing in Exhibit B but here we can take a look at it in detail.

The first section of the script sets up some variables that correspond to the devices I'm controlling. Table 11-2 explains the purpose of each variable.

```
# Configure user-modifiable codes. "hc" means "housecode"
my $lights_hc = "B";
my $entry_lights_unit = "4";
my $kitchen_door_lights_unit = "5";
my $downstairs_hallway_lights_unit = "6";
my $uptairs_hallway_lights_unit = "7";

# Events generated by door lock
my $events_hc = "A";
my $door_lock_event_unit = "2";

# Key hours of the day (24 hour time format)
my $daytime_hour = "8";
my $evening_hour = "18";
my $bedtime_hour = "22";

my $door_locked_event = $events_hc.$door_lock_event_unit.$events_
hc."K";
my $door_unlocked_event = $events_hc.$door_unlock_event_unit.$events_
hc."J";


my ($door_locked_state, $data)
my (@before, @now);
my ($OS_win, $serial_port);
```

Table 11-2. Variables used by this script

Variable	Description
`$lights_hc`	The house code for your lights.
`$entry_lights_unit` `$kitchen_door_lights_unit` `$downstairs_hallway_lights_unit` `$uptairs_hallway_lights_unit`	The unit codes for your lights.
`$events_hc`	The house code associated with sensor events.
`$door_lock_event_unit`	The unit code for the door lock events.
`$daytime_hour` `$evening_hour` `$bedtime_hour`	These variables store the hours when I wake up, when it gets dark, and when I go to bed. This script only marks time boundaries on the hour.
`$door_locked_event`	The four-byte command string that the motion detector sends when it hasn't detected motion for the time-out period. By default it is "A2AJ".
`$door_unlocked_event`	The four-byte command string that the lock sends when the door is unlocked. By default it is "A2AK".
`$door_locked_state`	Boolean variable (or as close as you can get in Perl) that keeps track of whether the door is locked or unlocked.
`$data`	Stores unprocessed X10 commands. When the script starts, it may find several commands stored in the X10 receiver's memory. This isn't a bad thing—it may give the script a clue that dusk has recently fallen, or that someone has manually turned on a light before the script started.
`@before`	Not used.
`@now`	Stores the current time.
`$OS_win`	Determines whether the script is running on a Windows or Linux system. Windows systems load the Win32::SerialPort module, while Linux systems need device:: SerialPort.
`$serial_port`	A reference to the serial port device that must be provided to the ControlX10 module when communicating with the X10 computer interface.

The next section initializes the X10 PC interface.

```perl
# Load the proper SerialPort module based on platform
BEGIN { $| = 1;
    $OS_win = ($^O eq "MSWin32") ? 1 : 0;
    if ($OS_win) {
        eval "use Win32::SerialPort";
        die "$@\n" if ($@);
        $serial_port = Win32::SerialPort->new ("COM1",1);
    }
    else {
        eval "use Device::SerialPort";
        die "$@\n" if ($@);
        $serial_port = Device::SerialPort->new ("/dev/ttyS0",1);
    }
}
die "Can't open serial port: $^E\n" unless ($serial_port);
$serial_port->error_msg(1);
$serial_port->user_msg(0);
$serial_port->databits(8);
$serial_port->baudrate(4800);
$serial_port->parity("none");
$serial_port->stopbits(1);
$serial_port->dtr_active(1);
$serial_port->handshake("none");
$serial_port->write_settings || die "Could not set up port\n";

use ControlX10::CM11;
```

Now the script enters a loop. Notice that the test condition for the loop is always true, creating an infinite loop that can only be exited by killing the process. This causes the script to continually check to see if there's anything to do. The script saves a copy of the time during each iteration of the loop for use in time-based variations in behavior, such as turning on the light only after dark.

```perl
while () {
    @now = localtime;
```

Next, the script checks the serial port for any waiting commands.

```perl
    # Grab the data from the X10 controller
    $data = $data.ControlX10::CM11::receive_buffer($serial_port);
```

If it finds a command, it processes it. A locking event causes the entry lights to blink.

```perl
    # Door lock event detected.
    # Locking...
    if ($data =~ $door_lock_event) {
        print "Door locking event detected.  Received: $data.\n";
        $door_locked = "1";
        $data = "";

        # Flash the entry lights
        light_on($entry_lights_unit);
        sleep 1;
        light_off($entry_lights_unit);
    }
```

An unlocking event causes various responses, depending on the time of day. If the door is unlocked during full daylight hours, the lights will blink just as a visual cue; after dark, the kitchen and entryway lights will go on; and at bedtime, a path to the bedroom will be illuminated.

```
# Unlocking...
If ($data =~ $door_lock_event) {
    print "Door unlocking event detected.  Received: $data.\n";
    $door_locked = "0";
    $data = "";

    # If it's during the day, flash the entry lights
    if (($now[2] >= $daytime_hour) && ($now[2] < $evening_hour)) {
        light_on($entry_lights_unit);
        sleep 1;
        light_off($entry_lights_unit);
    }
    # If it's evening, turn on the kitchen and entry lights
if (($now[2] >= $evening_hour) && ($now[2] < $bedtime_hour)) {
        light_on($entry_lights_unit);
        sleep 1;
        light_on($kitchen_door_lights_unit);
    }
    # If it's after bedtime, light a path to my bed
    if (($now[2] >= $bedtime_hour) && ($now[2] < $daytime_hour)) {
        light_on($entry_lights_unit);
        sleep 1;
        light_on($kitchen_door_lights_unit);
        sleep 1;
        light_on($downstairs_hallway_lights_unit);
        sleep 1;
        light_on($upstairs_hallway_lights_unit);
    }
}

}
```

Now the script goes back for another run through the loop. Most of the time nothing will be happening inside the loop (aside from storing the time and reading from the interface). It's only when a command—specifically, A1 ON or A1 OFF—is read from the interface that anything will occur.

For example, if you've just unlocked the door at 6:30 P.M. (18:30), the script will do the following:

1. A2AK is read from the interface.

2. A2AK is a door locking event.

3. Lock state is noted.

4. The time is after the evening key time but before the bedtime key time.

5. Entry lights turn on.

6. Kitchen lights turn on.

You can configure your script to run whenever Windows starts by placing a shortcut to it in your Start Up folder in Windows, or adding it to your */etc/rc.local* file in Linux.

Wrapping Up

In this project we tackled some extreme hardware hacking by inserting new circuitry into an off-the-shelf keyless remote entry door. In my house, this project garnered some funny looks from my family when I was first working on it—they found it to be a bit frivolous. Now that it's installed, though, it has become essential to all who live here.

In fact, we used the lock for about a month before I tried adding X10. While hacking the lock I managed to break it, which meant that we had to go back to using keys. We really felt its absence during the time we waited for its replacement.

Remember to periodically change the batteries. About once every three months is probably good, or more often if you find your batteries are dying quickly. If the batteries completely die while you're out of the house, you'll need to use the old-fashioned key to get back in—so don't throw your keys away just yet!

Extensions

My originally planned version of this project was vetoed by my family on account of being too elaborate. I'll describe the things that I would have done, though, just in case your family is a bit more adventurous!

By combining this project with Chapter 4, Make Your House Talk, you could have your house make some greeting announcement when you unlock your door. It could simply say "Hello," or you could get really crazy and have it provide status information like the current indoor temperature, the number of emails waiting, or the number of missed calls with name resolution using caller ID.

By combining this project with the whole-house audio system found in Chapter 9, Create Time-Shifted FM Radio, you can have the music of your choice start playing for you when you arrive home.

You could also create a log of each event that gets detected. You may discover some interesting things about your family's behavior!

Exhibit A: Bill of Materials

Item	Quantity	Part number
KwikSet TitanOne keyless remote deadbolt lock	1	Model 886
X10 keychain remote	1	Smarthome #4004
X10 plug-in RF base	1	Smarthome #4005X
X10 CM11A PC interface	1	Smarthome #1140
X10 lamp modules	Optional, as needed	Smarthome #2000
X10 wall switches	Optional, as needed	Smarthome #2031

Exhibit B: Script Source Code

```perl
#!/usr/bin/perl
use lib './blib/lib','./lib';

# Configure user-modifiable codes. "hc" means "housecode"
my $lights_hc = "B";
my $entry_lights_unit = "4";
my $kitchen_door_lights_unit = "5";
my $downstairs_hallway_lights_unit = "6";
my $uptairs_hallway_lights_unit = "7";

# Events generated by door lock
my $events_hc = "A";
my $door_lock_event_unit = "2";

# Key hours of the day (24 hour time format)
my $daytime_hour = "8";
my $evening_hour = "18";
my $bedtime_hour = "22";

# Door lock events
my $door_locked_event = $events_hc.$door_lock_event_unit.$events_
hc."K";
my $door_unlocked_event = $events_hc.$door_unlock_event_unit.$events_
hc."J";


my ($door_locked, $data)
my (@before, @now);
my ($OS_win, $serial_port);

# Load the proper SerialPort module based on platform
BEGIN { $| = 1;
    $OS_win = ($^O eq "MSWin32") ? 1 : 0;
    if ($OS_win) {
        eval "use Win32::SerialPort";
        die "$@\n" if ($@);
        $serial_port = Win32::SerialPort->new ("COM1",1);
    }
```

```
    else {
        eval "use Device::SerialPort";
        die "$@\n" if ($@);
        $serial_port = Device::SerialPort->new ("/dev/ttyS0",1);
    }
}
die "Can't open serial port: $^E\n" unless ($serial_port);
$serial_port->error_msg(1);
$serial_port->user_msg(0);
$serial_port->databits(8);
$serial_port->baudrate(4800);
$serial_port->parity("none");
$serial_port->stopbits(1);
$serial_port->dtr_active(1);
$serial_port->handshake("none");
$serial_port->write_settings || die "Could not set up port\n";

use ControlX10::CM11;

while () {
    # Store the current time
    @now = localtime;

    # Grab the data from the X10 controller
    $data = $data.ControlX10::CM11::receive_buffer($serial_port);

    # Door lock event detected.
    # Locking...
    if ($data =~ $door_lock_event) {
        print "Door locking event detected.  Received: $data.\n";
        $door_locked = "1";
        $data = "";

        # Flash the entry lights
        light_on($entry_lights_unit);
        sleep 1;
        light_off($entry_lights_unit);
    }
    # Unlocking...
    If ($data =~ $door_lock_event) {
        print "Door unlocking event detected.  Received: $data.\n";
        $door_locked = "0";
        $data = "";

        # If it's during the day, flash the entry lights
        if (($now[2] >= $daytime_hour) && ($now[2] < $evening_hour)) {
            light_on($entry_lights_unit);
            sleep 1;
            light_off($entry_lights_unit);
        }
        # If it's evening, turn on the kitchen and entry lights
if (($now[2] >= $evening_hour) && ($now[2] < $bedtime_hour)) {
            light_on($entry_lights_unit);
            sleep 1;
            light_on($kitchen_door_lights_unit);
        }
```

```perl
        # If it's after bedtime, light a path to my bed
        if (($now[2] >= $bedtime_hour) && ($now[2] < $daytime_hour)) {
            light_on($entry_lights_unit);
            sleep 1;
            light_on($kitchen_door_lights_unit);
            sleep 1;
            light_on($downstairs_hallway_lights_unit);
            sleep 1;
            light_on($upstairs_hallway_lights_unit);
        }
    }

}

# Release   the serial port
$serial_port->close || die "\nProblem closing serial port\n";
undef $serial_port;

sub light_on {
    print "Turning on: ".$lights_hc.$_[0]."\n";
    sleep 1;
    ControlX10::CM11::send($serial_port, $lights_hc.$_[0]);
    ControlX10::CM11::send($serial_port, $lights_hc."J");
}

sub light_off {
    print "Turning off: ".$lights_hc.$_[0]."\n";
    sleep 1;
    ControlX10::CM11::send($serial_port, $lights_hc.$_[0]);
    ControlX10::CM11::send($serial_port, $lights_hc."K");
}
```

Watch Your House Across the Network

12

Cost
$300 or less

Time
three to four hours

Difficulty
3 out of 5

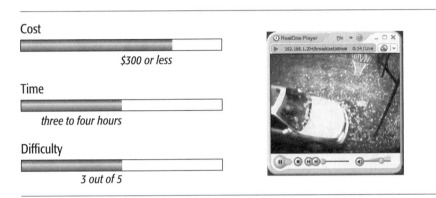

Chapter 13, Build a Security System, builds a real-time alerting system for your home. But what do you do when you actually receive an alarm? If you're at work and you get a message from your security system that a window was opened, it would be very nice if you could just take a look at that window before you rushed out to your car and drove home, especially since you'll probably discover that your cat knocked the alarm out of place.

This project provides you with a way to visually inspect your house from across the network using real-time video. Sure, everyone has a webcam, but this project is a bit different. We'll be monitoring several places around your home, so we'll need multiple cameras as well as the ability to switch between them. Since the cameras will be spread around the home, we can't rely on directly connecting the cameras to the computer. We'll need to find a way to get the video from the camera back to the computer that will stream it across the Internet.

If you're a webcam geek, you'll find this project interesting. The end result is a multi-camera system, where a user can click links on a web page to switch between the cameras. You can add as many as eight different cameras, so you could probably have one in each room of your home.

What You Need

- Three or more wireless cameras

- Wireless video receiver (compatible with wireless cameras)

- The X10 Firecracker Computer Interface (CM17A) and an X10 wireless transceiver, or the X10 Powerlinc Serial Controller (CM11A)

- Eight AAA batteries

- A stable, broadband Internet connection that allows inbound connections

- A computer running Windows (though you can do this project with Linux, too, with a bit of modification)

- A video capture card with composite video input

- Sticky poster adhesive

For a list of specific parts used in this project, refer to Exhibit A at the end of this chapter.

Figure 12-1 shows the conceptual architecture of this project. You visit a web page, and relay commands to your computer by clicking on links. Your computer controls multiple cameras, and determines which camera is currently active. The computer feeds the live video across the Internet to the your video player, which is embedded in a web page.

Figure 12-1. This project's conceptual design is basically the same one used by any closed-circuit camera system.

Project Overview

This project has five phases, which correspond to the layers in our conceptual design:

- Video Cameras
- Video Capture
- Video Transfer
- Video Playback
- Playback Control

Each of these components is modular, so you can complete them in a different order if you're waiting for a part to arrive or if you're particularly interested in a certain aspect of the project. You can even pick and choose the components you want to use. If you only want a single camera system, you can completely skip the Playback Control phase. If you want to monitor video on a computer that is connected directly to the video capture mechanism, you can skip the Video Transfer phase.

Shortcut: Buy a video camera with a built-in server that connects to your home's local area network, and watch it from anywhere. The "Video Cameras" phase describes these cameras in more detail.

Video Cameras

In this phase, you will plan your camera layout, select cameras that suit the locations you chose, and then physically install the cameras.

1. Plan your camera layout

The areas of your home that you need to capture on video and the locations where you install your cameras will determine the type of camera you need to purchase. For example, if you need to monitor your driveway to verify that the snowplow service is doing its job, you will need to position a camera overlooking your driveway. When monitoring outdoor locations, try to find a window where you can permanently position the camera. If there is not a window overlooking the location, find a spot on the outside of the house where you can fasten a camera, and drill a hole to the interior of the house through which to run power and video cables.

When planning the camera layout, think about the areas where you need to view the most detail, and position the camera near those areas. For example, if you want to see who is currently standing at your door, you will need a camera positioned near the doorway. Such a camera should not be too high up, though, or you end up with a view of the top of the person's head. If the camera were 100 feet away from your doorway, the person would be too small to recognize.

Inexpensive cameras have a built-in, moderate wide-angle lens. For example, the XCam2 cameras that I'm using have a 60-degree diagonal angle-of-view. A 60-degree diagonal angle-of-view is roughly equivalent to a 48-degree horizontal angle-of-view, given the 4:3 perspective of most video cameras. Figure 12-2 shows how this angle-of-view covers a typical room. If you're familiar with 35mm camera lenses, that's equivalent to a 38mm lens—a common focal length for inexpensive 35mm and digital cameras. While this is a good all-around choice in focal lengths, you'll find that it doesn't suit video monitoring applications particularly well.

If you wanted to film the entire room from a corner, you would need at least a 90-degree horizontal angle-of-view. Actually, it would need to be a bit wider than 90 degrees, because the camera would not be flush against the wall. A camera with a 120-degree diagonal angle-of-view would have about a 96-degree horizontal angle-of-view, as shown in Figure 12-3. This is perfect for viewing an entire room from one corner. Unfortunately, a wider angle-of-view means that objects will appear

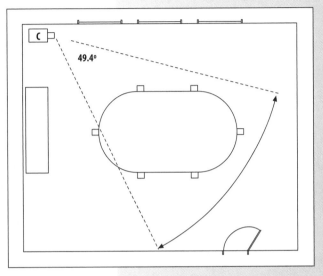

Figure 12-2. The lens attached to most inexpensive video cameras, with a 48-degree angle-of-view, can't cover an entire room.

Figure 12-3. Camera vendors tell you the diagonal angle-of-view, but that's much wider than the horizontal angle-of-view that you'll be using.

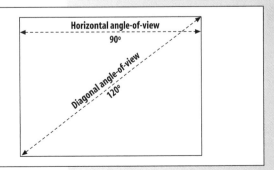

smaller and less detailed. Someone standing in the far corner of the room will be *very* small, in fact, and the image may not give you the detail you need to recognize the person. You will be able to tell that a person is there, though, and that may be enough information for you to call the police. It will probably not, however, be enough information for the police to identify the suspect.

If you want to view details of an object positioned far away from a camera, choose a camera with a telephoto lens. Telephoto lenses have a smaller angle-of-view, which means that objects positioned within the field of view take up a larger portion of the image. Using a telephoto lens is similar to zooming in on the subject with a zoom lens. Choose a telephoto lens when you can't position the camera close to the subject, and you are interested in filming a relatively small space.

Real security cameras support C-mount lenses. This is a standardized lens mount that enables you to change the focal length, angle-of-view, and iris of a lens by unscrewing the existing lens and screwing on a new lens. You can even find C-mount varifocal, or zoom, lenses. Unfortunately, cameras with C-mounts are much more expensive than those with fixed lenses, starting at about $100.

2. Select the cameras

There are hundreds of different types of video cameras that you can use for this project. Of course, you can use a video camera that connects directly to your computer, such as a webcam. Webcams, by definition, connect to your computer through the USB port. Both Windows and Linux have the means to pull the video from the webcam and make it available to applications that allow you to view it on a monitor, output it to another video source, or stream it across a network.

Even if you plan to use a computer as your video capture mechanism, as I did, you are not limited to cameras that connect to your computer. Most security cameras output composite video with a standard RCA jack. You can make this video available to your applications by installing a video capture card and drivers designed for your operating system. Video capture cards are discussed in more detail in the "Video Capture" phase of this project.

You can even mix-and-match cameras. You can use a webcam to monitor the room with the computer in it, and a wireless camera to watch the kitchen. We'll be creating our own playback control mechanism, which means we can use it to switch between completely different video formats without affecting the way video is transferred or played back.

For this project, I needed to semi-permanently install cameras in several different locations around my house. The most common solution is to install a hardwired closed-circuit camera system. However, this involves running video cable from each of the different cameras to a central location in the house. While I'm not afraid to cut open drywall, I have a finished basement and an almost inaccessible attic. So running video cable would be extremely difficult, and would probably require me to replace parts of my ceiling.

I therefore decided to investigate wireless camera systems. I have an 802.11g network at my home, so I was immediately drawn to the handful of 802.11b/g cameras that stream video directly from the camera. However, the prices seemed high: $110–$1000 per camera. Baby monitors are another appealing solution. They're produced in large quantities and targeted toward the consumer market, so they're cheap. A baby monitor camera will cost you about $75.

> If wireless cameras with built-in servers are your preference, check out the D-Link DCS-900W ($110), DCS-2100+ ($250), and DCS-3220G ($325), and the Panasonic BL-C30A ($300), KX-HCM250 ($750), and KX-HCM270 ($1000).

If you're using more than one camera, you'll need to think about how you're going to control which camera is active. Most likely, multiple cameras will not be able to run simultaneously because the bandwidth they're using to transfer the video to the receiver will be full. The simplest way to control which camera is active is to plug each camera into an X10 control module, and send signals to turn the cameras on and off from the playback control mechanism.

It's a little expensive to buy a personal video camera just to use as a webcam, but if you happen to have an old one lying around, you can make it a wireless camera using a wireless video transmitter/receiver pair (about $80). Personal video cameras make excellent video cameras to use with your computer because they have much better optics than a typical webcam, usually have an optical zoom, and can accept add-on lenses.

If you need to position a camera outdoors, you obviously need one that can tolerate the weather. You'll also have to think about where you're going to fasten it. You will need to screw it onto something, but you don't want to ruin the weather-proofing on your home. For example, if you screw the camera directly into aluminum siding, you may allow moisture inside the wall.

If you choose an outdoor wireless camera, there are still challenges. Wireless cameras aren't really wireless, of course, because they still need electricity. Outdoor cameras have a small power cord intended to run through a hole in the wall, and that connects to a power supply inside the house. It's still a wire, but at least you only have to run it to an electrical outlet, and not to your video capture mechanism.

If you want to monitor an outdoor area, such as your front doorstep, make every effort to place the camera in a window looking out. Keeping the camera indoors avoids the risk of weather-related damage, and it's much easier to connect it to an electrical outlet while it's indoors.

Figure 12-4. They're low quality and cheap, but they actually don't look so bad.

I hate to admit where I finally found an inexpensive wireless video camera (pictured in Figure 12-4): X10 pop-up ads. When you take advantage of one of X10's package deals (available at *http://www.x10.com*), the cameras are less than $60 each. Also, because they can be turned on and off using X10 signals, they are easy to control with a computer, and you don't need a separate component to switch between cameras. The package deal includes a wireless receiver that, like any other composite video output, you can connect to a video capture card in your computer. They capture color video, lack audio, and have miserable picture quality. If the room is anything but bright, the video quality drops even lower, and you can't see anything at all after dark. However, you can purchase more expensive black-and-white cameras from X10 that have improved low-light performance.

I use Firefox now, which blocks pop-ups, so I don't even know if X10 still uses them. If your current browser allows pop-ups and you're sick of them, you can get the Firefox browser at *http://www.getfirefox.com/*. If you're an IE die-hard, upgrade to Windows XP Service Pack 2, or head to *http://www.google.com/* and install the Google toolbar, which also stops most pop-ups.

The camera I'm using is called XCam2 Classic at *http://www.x10.com*. They have a variety of cameras that will work with this project, however, including wide-angle cameras, instant-on cameras, and cameras that work in low-light situations.

3. Install the cameras

You're now ready to install the cameras around your house. When positioning the cameras, follow these guidelines:

- Position the cameras as high as possible and pointed downward. This will increase the video coverage of the room.

- People don't feel comfortable knowing a camera is pointed at them. It's good if you can make a thief feel uncomfortable, but bad if your family feels that way. Make sure your family and guests know there are cameras, but make the cameras unobtrusive by placing them in bookcases and on top of furniture. Hiding the cameras will also decrease the chance of a thief stealing them, too.

- Though the cameras include screws to be permanently mounted, first attach them with sticky stuff, such as poster adhesive, until you determine the optimal location.

- Point the antennae toward the computer where the wireless video receiver will be.

For information on how to configure the X10 wireless cameras can be found in Chapter 3, Remotely Monitor a Pet.

Video Capture

The video capture component receives input from the playback control mechanism, controls the cameras, and sends the output to the video transfer mechanism. The method of video capture you choose will be entirely dependent on the type of video cameras you use and your choice of video transfer mechanisms. I'm using X10 cameras and I plan to transfer the video across the Internet, so my video capture mechanism needs to accept the composite video feed from the wireless video receiver and connect to my computer. The answer was obvious: a video capture card.

If you chose a camera with a built-in server that connects to the network, then this project is very easy—your capture and transport mechanisms are already built into the camera! All you need to do is configure your router to forward traffic to your camera and connect directly to the camera across the Internet. You can skip the other steps in this project.

1. Install the video capture card

Unlike traditional webcams, these wireless video cameras do not connect to your computer's USB port—they're actually intended to connect to a TV or VCR. You therefore need to add an old-timey analog video input interface into your computer. Fortunately, these are cheap and well supported by both Linux and Windows. After all, lots of people use video capture cards to record TV shows, so quite a bit of energy has gone into making sure the software works well.

The wireless receiver that we'll install next has a composite connection, so make sure the card you choose supports that. I used the Hauppauge WinTV-GO-FM card (part #00191) because I happened to have it lying around. These cards use the BT878 chipset, which is well supported by Linux (and, of course, Windows). Any card you choose with that chipset should work equally well. There's no need to get an expensive video capture card because it's not going to improve the performance or quality of your cheap cameras. You don't need any kind of sound support because the wireless cameras don't have microphones. As a rule, don't spend more than $50 on your video capture card.

After you purchase the card, install it according to the manufacturer's instructions. Generally, this is as simple as turning off your computer, opening the case, and inserting the card into an empty PCI slot. After restarting your operating system, install the drivers for the card. For more detailed instructions, refer to the "Install the TV tuner card" section of Chapter 7.

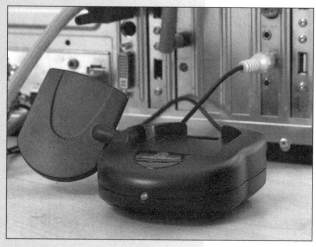

Figure 12-5. The wireless receiver connects to the computer's composite input.

2. Install the wireless video receiver

The wireless video receiver is a bridge from your computer to the wireless cameras using your video input card. You need to use the piece of hardware that came with the wireless camera—if there's another receiver that works, I'm not aware of it. My receiver is shown in Figure 12-5.

Use the following guidelines when positioning the video receiver:

- Take advantage of the length of the composite cord and position the receiver away from your computer.

- Point the antennas toward the cameras.

- If you have cameras positioned all around the house, try pointing the antennas straight up.

Of course, there's only so much tweaking of the placement you can do before you get the software configured. After the drivers are installed, you can use Movie Maker in Windows or XawTV in Linux to fine-tune the antennae placement.

Video Transfer

In this phase, you will encode and transfer the video feed from your video capture device to your chosen video playback mechanism. If you just want to view the video on the computer that hosts the video capture mechanism itself, then you have almost no work to do. On Linux, you can just launch XawTV. Video transfer is still occurring within the confines of your computer, but your operating system is taking care of it automatically. Video for Linux (v4l) makes the video feed available to applications such as XawTV. Windows XP doesn't really have a built-in tool to view live video, but Windows Movie Maker works with Video for Windows (VfW), and will do in a pinch.

However, you will probably end up implementing the video transfer mechanism across a network. Video can't travel natively over IP; it needs to be encoded. In the Linux world, most people use Camserv, which you can find at *http://sourceforge.net/projects/cserv/*.

In the Windows world, your options for free network video transfer are pretty limited. However, there are dozens of shareware webcam software packages available. I've used webcam32 successfully; it costs about $40, and can be downloaded from *http://www.webcam32.com/*.

> Watch out for the many different companies who advertise free webcam software, but require you to host the webcam on their web site.

However, I really want to keep the cost of these projects minimal, so I hunted down a free (though not open source) solution. Much like my choice of X10 wireless cameras, I ended up choosing a company that once was quite annoying to me: Real.

> I was annoyed with Real because they used to use a bit of trickery to get people to install optional, but very irritating, software along with their free client. They presented the user with a list of optional components, and all the visible checkboxes were deselected. If you scrolled down the list, you would see several software packages that were selected, but most people didn't notice this, which I'm sure was the point. No, it's not illegal, but it was shady. They've since stopped doing this, at least as far as I can tell. And I really like this product, so all is forgiven.

Real offers very powerful software for encoding and streaming video. After all, their target clients aren't webcam users, but enterprises. It's actually a bit of overkill for the average webcam, but it's great for security cameras because it supports higher resolutions, qualities, and frame rates than most webcam software. Plus, it's fun to play with. The "free" encoding package is Helix Producer Basic. The "free" streaming package is Helix Universal Server Basic.

1. Install Helix Universal Server

Helix Universal Server Basic is free software from Real that transfers encoded video across IP networks using several different formats. First, download the software from Real by visiting *http://www.realnetworks.com/products/server/* and clicking the "No Fee & Eval Servers" link. You'll have to provide your name to download the software, and a valid email address to retrieve the license key.

> I'm grateful to Real for making this software available for free. It's a great product, and if you enjoy working with it, you might consider lobbying your employer to purchase it for business use.

Double-click the file to launch the setup wizard. The setup routine is straightforward, until you reach the series of wizard pages that prompt you for port numbers for the following protocols:

Protocol	Default port number	URL prefix	Description
PNA	7070	pnm://	Protocol used by RealPlayer Version 5 and earlier.
RTSP	554	rtsp://	Protocol used by recent versions of RealPlayer.
HTTP	80	http://	Hypertext Transfer Protocol, the standard protocol used between web browsers and web servers. Used for streaming, primarily to allow clients to connect when they are behind Application layer proxy servers.
MMS	1755	mms://	Protocol used by Windows Media Player.
Helix Server	Random	http://	The browser-based administration tool.

Figure 12-6. You can change the port numbers later from the Ports page within Server Setup.

During the install, be sure to accept the default setting of installing Helix Server as a service.

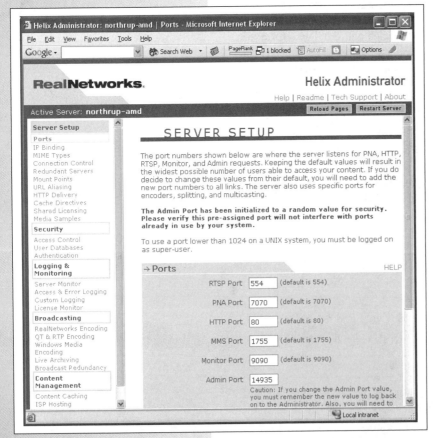

Helix Server doesn't have a graphical tool for administering it; instead, you'll administer it using a web browser to connect to the */admin/index.html* page using the random port number that Setup selected. Don't worry about typing the administrative URL into your browser manually; the setup procedure created a link to the Helix Server Administrator page under the Helix Server program group.

When you launch the Helix Server Administrator, provide the username and password you typed during setup, not your Windows username and password. Take some time to browse through the many configuration options, as illustrated in Figure 12-6, although you don't actually have to change any of the options for this project.

One of the nicest things about Helix is that you can monitor it using the

Performance snap-in, as illustrated in Figure 12-7. (After all, it is designed to be used by enterprises.) You can use this to monitor the current bandwidth being consumed, the number of users connected, and the types of connections users are making.

2. Install Helix Producer Basic

Helix Producer Basic is free software that encodes video. You have a great deal of control over how the video is encoded, including being able to choose different, and multiple, encoding rates. You can encode directly to a file, or you can transfer the encoded video to a server, as we will be doing here.

First, download the software from *http://www.realnetworks.com/ products/producer/basic.html.* You'll have to provide your name to download the software. Double-click the file to launch the setup wizard. The setup routine is extremely straightforward, as shown in Figure 12-8, so I won't describe it step-by-step.

After the install is completed, launch the Helix Producer graphical administration tool. You can find an icon for it directly under the All Programs group on your Start menu. Let's start by configuring the Input device so we can watch the live video feed:

1. Click the Devices radio button.

2. Click the Video drop-down list and select the video capture device you're using.

3. Click the Settings button. You'll see a list of available options for configuring your video capture device. These configuration options are native to Windows, not Helix.

4. Click each of the configuration options to configure your video capture device. I'm using a Hauppauge WinTV card, with the video input

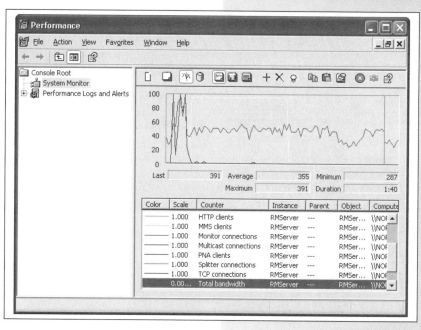

Figure 12-7. Unlike most webcam software, Helix adds counters that you can view with the Performance console.

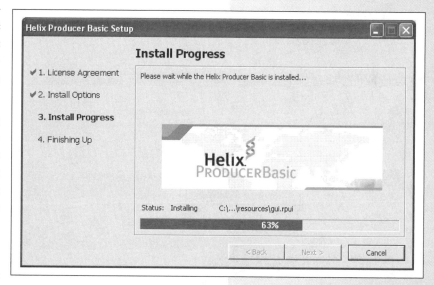

Figure 12-8. Helix Producer Basic encodes, but doesn't transfer, the video.

connected to the composite connector. All I had to do to configure it was click DirectShow Filter Hauppauge WinTV Crossbar and specify Video Composite In. You'll know you've configured it correctly when the Input window shows live video.

5. If you don't have an audio feed or don't care about audio, click the Audio drop-down list and select None.

Next, you need to configure the output device so that it pipes the video to Helix Universal Server, which will handle processing user connections. You'll also need to choose the quality and bandwidth of the video feeds that you want to make available.

1. Click the Audiences button. The Audiences dialog box appears.

2. If, like me, you don't have audio for your cameras, select No Audio from the Audio Mode list.

3. The "Audiences in Job" list displays bit rates and qualities of the video feeds that will be available (Figure 12-9). By default, very low bit rate audiences are selected. These settings will result in minimal bandwidth usage, but low quality and a slow frame rate. To add new audiences, you will need to remove one of the three default audiences, since the Basic version of Helix Producer is limited to three. Click the audience you wish to remove, and then press Delete (or click the trash can button below the list). Then, select the desired audience from the Templates list on the left, and click the arrow to move it to the "Audiences in Job" list.

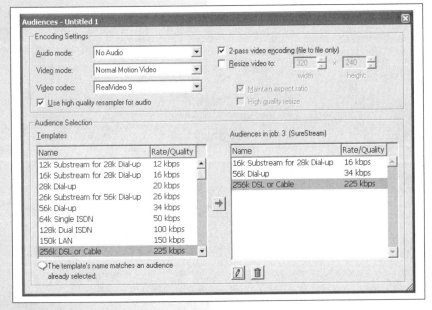

Figure 12-9. My audience configuration allows me to take advantage of my 800kbps upstream bandwidth.

4. Close the Audiences dialog.

5. Open the File menu and then click Add Server Destination. The Server Destination dialog appears.

6. Click the Templates button, and then click Edit Templates.

7. In the Template Name field, provide a creative name...like **Server Template**.

8. From the Broadcast Method list, choose "Push, Account-Based Login (Helix Server)".

9. In the Server address field, type **127.0.0.1**. That's a special IP address that represents the local computer.

10. In the Username and Password fields, provide the username and password you created during the setup of the Helix Universal Server (not your Windows username and password).

11. Select the Remember Password checkbox, as shown in Figure 12-10.

12. Click OK to return to the Server Destination dialog. The information you provided for the template should have been automatically filled in (that is the point of the template, after all).

13. Provide a name in the "Stream name" field, as shown in Figure 12-11. Something clever, like **stream.rm**. I added the .rm extension because we'll be using the Real Media player to play the video across the network.

14. Click OK to return to Helix Producer.

15. Finally, click the Encode button. You're on the air (Figure 12-12)! Now, you just need a client to connect to the video stream.

To view the output at different bandwidths, click the Output list and select a different setting.

If you're so inclined, you can configure both the Producer and Universal Server components of the Helix server to be redundant. That way, if a computer, camera, or connection fails, you can still receive your video stream.

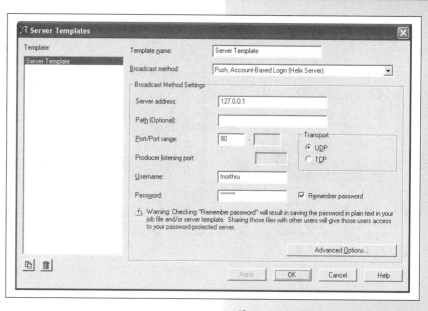

Figure 12-10. Create a server template to make it simpler to configure video feeds.

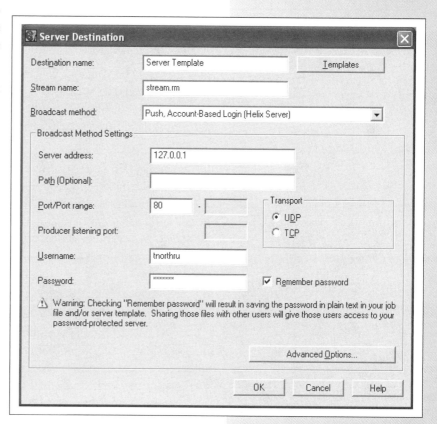

Figure 12-11. Helix Producer should be configured to send the video stream to the Helix Universal Server.

Figure 12-12. The Producer user interface shows video as both input and output.

3. Configure the network

Making your computer run as a server on the Internet definitely increases the number of attacks you'll be subjected to. Of course, it's not like your computer is safe if it's *not* a server, either—worms and viruses infect client-only PCs all the time. Nonetheless, before you set your system up as a server, you should mentally acknowledge that you're increasing your vulnerability. With that said, I'll do my best to make sure you connect your system to the Internet safely.

> In fact, chances are good that when you've completed this project, your computer will be more secure than it is right now.

Secure your system

The first step in securing your system is to go to *http://windowsupdate. microsoft.com* and let Windows Update scan your system. Apply all the critical updates. If it has been a while since you visited this site, you might need to visit multiple times after rebooting your computer to get all the patches installed.

Windows Update is a pain, and it's easy to forget to visit it, so set up Automatic Updates if you're using Windows 2000, Windows XP, or Windows Server 2003. It may be a bit scary to consent to letting Microsoft install updates on your computer, but it's for the best. Microsoft has done a good job of writing the instructions for setting this up, so I will not duplicate it here. For detailed instructions, visit *http://support.microsoft. com/?kbid=327838*.

If you don't have a router with packet filtering capabilities yet, set one up between your internal network and the public Internet, as shown in Figure 12-13. By default, routers with firewall capabilities block all incoming traffic and allow all outbound connections. Even if you've secured your PC's software, a filtering router is important because it protects your computer while you're in the process of setting it up. The simplest of these devices cost less than $100, and they're well worth the investment. Not only do they filter traffic without relying on your software's security, but they often include a switch to network multiple computers, and can even act as a print server.

I use a Linksys Cable/DSL Router, but several other vendors offer similar products. Here are some links to vendors of hardware firewalls:

- Linksys Routers: *http://www.linksys.com/Products/*
- Netgear Routers: *http://www.netgear.com/products/ details/FR114P.php*
- SMC Routers: *http://www.smc.com/index.cfm?sec=Pro ducts&pg=Product-List&cat=4&site=c*

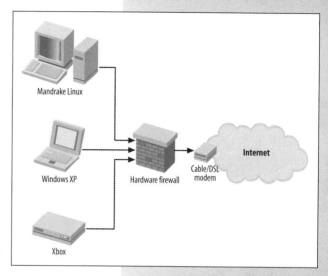

Figure 12-13. Hardware firewalls, or even a router with filtering capabilities, can do a lot to improve your security.

You should also install a software firewall. While having two firewalls may seem redundant, it's really not. Relying on firewalls only at the perimeter doesn't protect you from dangers that lie inside your own network. Many, many networks have been infected by worms that snuck past the firewall on a single computer. If you have a laptop, software firewalls are even more important, because you can't be sure your system won't be attacked when you're traveling.

Windows XP and Windows Server 2003 include Internet Connection Firewall (ICF). I wish this were running by default, but it's not. You can also get third-party firewalls that have additional features, such as protecting you from Trojan software and notifying you when you're being attacked. Follow Microsoft's instructions on setting ICF up: *http://www.microsoft. com/windowsxp/pro/using/howto/networking/icf.asp*.

If you use Windows XP and have installed Service Pack 2, ICF is updated to Windows Firewall, and is set to automatically start (a good thing!). Windows Firewall should automatically prompt you to allow traffic to the applications when you start them. If you have problems, read *http://support.microsoft. com/?kbid=875356* and *http://support.microsoft.com/?kbid=875357.*

Here are some links to vendors of software firewalls. (Some of these firewalls you need to pay for.)

- Kerio Personal Firewall: *http://www.kerio.com/us/kpf_home.html*
- Outpost Firewall: *http://www.agnitum.com/products/outpost/*
- Tiny Personal Firewall: *http://www.tinysoftware.com/*
- ZoneAlarm: *http://www.zonealarm.com/*

Configure a static IP address

Most people who use a router to access the Internet allow their router to assign private IP addresses using DHCP. In order to reliably use your computer as a server, though, it needs to have the same IP address each time it starts. In this step, we'll configure a manually assigned IP address. If your computer's IP address is assigned directly by your ISP, you don't need to change it.

First, make note of your computer's configuration. Open a command prompt and type the command ipconfig /all. You'll see output that resembles the following:

```
C:\Documents and Settings\tnorthru>ipconfig /all

Windows IP Configuration

        Host Name . . . . . . . . . . . . : northrup
        Primary Dns Suffix  . . . . . . . :
        Node Type . . . . . . . . . . . . : Hybrid
        IP Routing Enabled. . . . . . . . : No
        WINS Proxy Enabled. . . . . . . . : No

Ethernet adapter Local Area Connection:

        Connection-specific DNS Suffix  . :
        Description . . . . . . . . . . . : Intel-Based PCI Fast
Ethernet
Adapter (Generic)
        Physical Address. . . . . . . . . : 00-03-FF-B4-3B-46
        Dhcp Enabled. . . . . . . . . . . : Yes
        Autoconfiguration Enabled . . . . : Yes
        IP Address. . . . . . . . . . . . : 192.168.1.102
        Subnet Mask . . . . . . . . . . . : 255.255.255.0
        Default Gateway . . . . . . . . . : 192.168.1.1
        DHCP Server . . . . . . . . . . . : 192.168.1.1
        DNS Servers . . . . . . . . . . . : 10.127.202.19
                                            10.148.227.79
        Lease Obtained. . . . . . . . . . : Tuesday, August 19, 2003
2:23:39 PM
        Lease Expires . . . . . . . . . . : Sunday, August 23, 2020
9:12:10 AM
```

If you don't see Dhcp Enabled...: Yes, then you already have a static IP address. You don't need to make any changes, but do read through this section and identify whether your IP address is public or private.

Keep the command prompt open so that you can refer to this information later. You need to determine an IP address on the same network that your router won't try to assign to a different computer. Unfortunately, different routers handle this differently. My Linksys router assigns the IP addresses 192.168.1.100 through 192.168.1.150, and uses the IP address 192.168.1.1. So anything between 192.168.1.2 through 192.168.1.99, or 192.168.1.151 through 192.168.1.254 will work. I'll choose 192.168.1.203, but that may not be available on your network if you have different equipment.

If your IP address is in one of the following ranges, then you have a private IP address. If not, then you probably have a public IP address and don't need to change it. Contact your ISP if you're not sure.

- 10.0.0.0 – 10.255.255.255

- 172.16.0.0 – 172.31.255.255

- 192.168.0.0 – 192.168.255.255

If you do have a private IP address, update your configuration by following these steps:

1. Click Start, and then Control Panel.

2. Within Control Panel, click Network and Internet Connections, and then click Network Connections.

3. Right-click the network interface that connects you to the Internet, and then select Properties.

4. Select Internet Protocol (TCP/IP), and then click Properties.

5. Select "Use the following IP address." Fill in the IP Address, Subnet Mask, and Default Gateway fields using the new IP address, and the existing subnet mask and default gateway from the `ipconfig /all` output.

6. Fill in the "Preferred DNS server" field with the first DNS server listed in the `ipconfig /all` output. If more than one DNS server is listed, fill in the second DNS server in the "Alternate DNS server" field. Figure 12-14 shows a sample configuration.

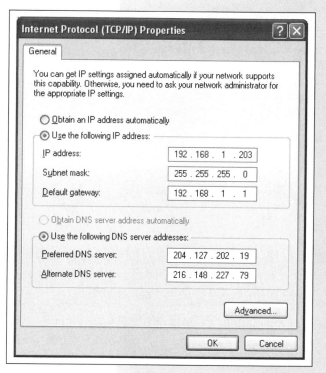

Figure 12-14. You need to configure a manual IP address for the computer you will remotely access.

Configure your firewall

After you get all the latest patches installed, you need to open the TCP port you specified on both your software firewall and your filtering router. Start with your software firewall. If you're using ICF and Windows XP, follow these steps:

1. Click Start, and then Control Panel.

2. Within Control Panel, click Network and Internet Connections, and then click Network Connections.

3. Right-click the network interface that connects you to the Internet, and then select Properties.

4. Click the Advanced tab, and then click Settings. The Advanced Settings dialog appears.

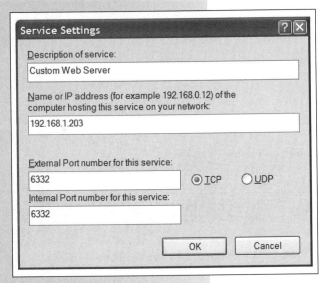

Figure 12-15. You need to open a port in your firewall for your web server.

5. Click the Services tab.

Notice that there's a service called Web Server (HTTP). If you were setting up a web server on the default TCP port 80, you could just select that and click OK. We're using a custom port, though.

6. Click Add. The Service Settings dialog appears.

7. Type a friendly name for the web server in the "Description of service" field. In the "Name or IP address" field, type the manually configured IP address your computer uses to connect to the Internet. Select the TCP radio button. In the External Port and Internet Port fields, type the custom TCP port number you configured IIS with. Figure 12-15 shows a sample configuration. Finally, click OK.

8. Click OK twice more to finalize the settings.

There's a lot more you can do to secure IIS. For more complete information, read the documentation available at *http://www.microsoft.com/*.

If everything worked properly, you should now be able to enter the URL *http://localhost:TCP_Port/* in your browser and see a web page served directly from your computer. Of course, there's no useful content on the web site yet, but we'll take care of that in other projects. You're using a custom port number (not TCP port 80), so you need to specify the port number as part of the URL. Specify the port number by adding a colon and the port number to the server IP address or hostname. For example, if you are using TCP port 6332 and your IP address is 192.168.1.203, you would type the URL *http://192.168.1.203:6332/* into your browser's address field.

While you can access the web server from your LAN, you can't access it from the outside world until you configure your router to forward packets with your custom TCP port to your computer's IP address. These instructions are different for every router, so consult your manufacturer's instructions. The following instructions are for my Linksys router.

If you determined that you were not behind a router earlier, you probably don't have a personal router protecting you from the Internet and you can skip this step.

---

1. Enter the URL *http://192.168.1.1/* into a web browser, and provide the administrative username and password when prompted.

2. Click the Advanced tab.

3. Click the Port Forwarding tab.

4. Type the custom TCP port number in both of the External Port fields of a new row in the Customized Applications table. Select the TCP Protocol checkbox. Type the private IP address of the computer running IIS in the IP Address field. Select the Enabled checkbox. Figure 12-16 shows my configuration.

5. Click Apply.

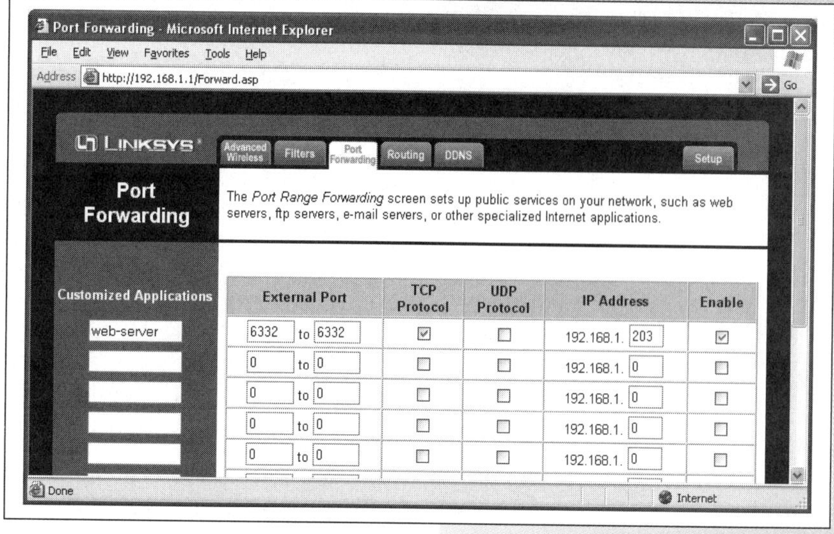

Video Playback

In this phase, you will set up a method for viewing the video feed you created in earlier phases. As always, it's entirely up to you how you implement this. If you want to view the cameras from a television, this phase could be as simple as installing video playback software and connecting your computer to your television using a video card.

If you're like me, however, you want to view the video across a network. This will allow you to see what's happening around your house from your desktop computer, a laptop with a wireless connection, or an Internet café. In the Video Transfer phase, we configured Helix Universal Server to make a video feed from Helix Producer available to Real clients. In this phase, we'll install the Free RealOne Player on a computer and get the video feed up and running. Real is a nice video format to use because the client is available for Windows, Linux, and the Mac.

1. Install Free RealOne Player

First, download the Free RealOne Player from *http://www.real.com*. This isn't as easy as it sounds, because Real really, really wants you to pay them for their software. They *do* have a free player, but they usually do a good job of hiding it and pushing the $20 RealOne Player Plus. So hunt around their web page and follow the trail of links for the "Free RealOne Player." Avoid the links that read "Free Download."

If you download the Free RealOne Player using Internet Explorer, the setup should launch automatically. If you're using another browser, you'll need to manually launch setup. The install wizard is easy. Be sure to do the custom install, deselect all of the Desktop Settings options, and deselect all of the Make RealOne Player My Default Player For options.

After you finish the install wizard, you'll want to disable the RealOne toolbar and opt out of receiving "important news, upgrades, and offers."

Figure 12-16. Each router is different, but this page configures my Linksys router.

When prompted, select the Basic Setup, rather than the Premium Setup. The RealOne Player is much less annoying than it used to be, but it can still be a little bit annoying.

> Once again, thanks to Real for making both the streaming client and server available for free, and for making them available on such a wide variety of platforms. As much as I complain about the various ads and pitches, I'm thrilled that it's available at all. I evaluated many different video streaming solutions for this project, and the Real solution was clearly superior.

After you finish the install, you'll still have to manually turn off the Message Center before you're done with Real's annoyances. (Maybe it would just be easier to buy the software!)

2. Establish the connection

Now that the RealOne Player is up and running, you're ready to connect to your video feed. From the File menu, click Open. In the Open field, type **rtsp://*server_ip*/broadcast/*stream_name***. My server's private IP address is 192.168.1.204, and I named the stream *stream.rm*, so I typed the URL *rtsp://192.168.1.204/broadcast/stream.rm*. Click OK. After a few seconds, RealOne will display the live video feed, as shown in Figure 12-17. Easy!

Playback Control

At this point, you have a live video feed that you can view from anywhere on the Internet. The final component of this project is a tool that will allow you to switch between the cameras. It would make sense to use the same computer to switch between cameras, since you've already established a connection to it. However, the way you implement the control mechanism will vary depending on choices you made in earlier phases.

There are several different ways you can connect across the Internet to control your home computer. You could SSH into your home computer and issue commands. You could export your X session on a Linux system or use Remote Desktop on a Windows system. In my opinion, though, the simplest way to enable control is to set up a web server, and create a web page that makes it easy to view the video feed and that provides buttons to switch between cameras.

1. Install the Firecracker

We need to send signals from our computer to our camera using X10. In other projects, we've used the CM11A serial X10 computer interface, which allows for two-way communications. However, this project does not require two-way X10 communications, so we're going to use the CM17A

Figure 12-17. The RealOne Player showing my car and basketball hoop (which I've hardly had the chance to use since I started this book!).

Firecracker X10 computer interface (Figure 12-18), which is included free with the camera packages. The CM17A Firecracker can only transmit X10 signals, so while it can be used to turn cameras on and off, it cannot receive signals from motion detectors.

The Firecracker is a small device that connects to the serial port of your computer and provides a serial pass-through. Unlike the CM11A, it does not connect directly to a power outlet. Instead, when it receives a command from your computer, it sends an X10 wireless signal. Because the Firecracker uses wireless communications, you must also have a wireless transceiver set to the same house code as your cameras. For detailed instructions on configuring the wireless transceiver, refer to the "Connect the wireless transceiver" section of Chapter 1.

Figure 12-18. The CM17A Firecracker enables your computer to send wireless signals.

If you have more than one serial port on your computer, connect the Firecracker to the first serial port. (You can actually connect it to whatever serial port you want, but you'll need to modify the Perl script in Step 4 to communicate with the correct serial port.)

You can also use the CM11A, but you'll need to modify the Perl script in this case as well. Refer to the scripts in other X10 projects in this book for examples of installing the correct Perl module and the command used to send X10 signals.

2. Install Perl

The simplest way to create custom logic to control your X10 devices from your computer is to use Perl. As you may already know, Perl is a scripting language that is commonly used for managing systems. Perl's key advantages are that it is free, available for just about every commonly used platform, and extremely flexible.

Perl is particularly useful for controlling X10 devices because of the availability of the ControlX10 package. ControlX10 lets you command your X10 devices with a single line of code. Additionally, the code you write to control your X10 devices can run on both Windows and Linux with minimal, if any, adjustment.

The open source MisterHouse home automation project, located at *http://www. misterhouse.net/*, uses Perl and is the biggest reason Perl is an excellent language for controlling X10 devices.

To install Perl:

1. Visit *http://www.activestate.com* and download the latest version of ActivePerl. The scripts in this project are based on ActivePerl 5.8.0, build 806, but will almost certainly run on other versions.

---

2. Install ActivePerl and the Perl Package Manager (PPM). You do not need to install the Perl ISAPI, PerlScript, or Examples components. Accept the other default selections and complete the setup procedure.

3. Restart your system to ensure that the changes made to your user profile take effect.

3. Install the X10 modules

Perl doesn't include modules for communicating with the serial port or X10 devices. So before you can create the script, you need to download and install modules for those two tasks.

1. Download the Win32::SerialPort module to any directory on your local computer. The module is available at *http://www.cpan.org/authors/id/B/BB/BBIRTH/*, and will be named *Win32-SerialPort-*.tar.gz*. If you're using Linux, you could grab the *Device-SerialPort-*.tar.gz* file instead.

You can find newer versions of these modules by digging through *http://www.misterhouse.net/*; however, the versions at the given URL work fine.

2. Download the ControlX10::CM11 (if you're using CM11A) or the ControlX10::CM17 (if you're using the Firecracker) module from the same location. The module is named *ControlX10-CM1*.tar.gz*.

3. Both the serial port and X10 modules have a *.tar.gz* file extension, and must be extracted before they can be installed. Use WinZip or WinRAR to extract these files. You'll have to extract it twice, because the *.tar* and *.gz* extensions represent separate functions that collect and compress the files.

4. Install the Win32::API module. This module can be installed using the Perl Package Manager. From a command prompt, issue the following command while connected to the Internet:

```
ppm install win32-api
```

5. Install the Win32::SerialPort module. From the command prompt, switch to the directory to which you extracted the Win32::SerialPort module. Execute the following commands.

If you have more than one serial port and have connected your X10 controller to a port other than COM1, change the first line to `perl makefile.pl <port_number>`.

```
perl Makefile.pl 1
perl install.pl
```

6. Install the Win32::ControlX10 module. From the command prompt, switch to the directory to which you extracted the module (either

ControlX10::CM11 or ControlX10::CM17). Execute the following commands:

```
perl Makefile.pl
perl test.pl
perl install.pl
```

4. Create the script

We need to be able to switch between our X10 controlled cameras, which requires sending an X10 signal. Perl will tell the CM11A or CM17A to send the signal, but first we need to create a script. Save the following script as *C:\homehacking\switchCamera.pl*. You can also download the script, along with any updates I've made, from *http://www.homehacking.com*.

There are many applications out there that make it easy to edit Perl scripts. Notepad works, too.

```perl
#!/usr/bin/perl
use lib './blib/lib','./lib';

my $camera_hc = "N"; #Set to house code of cameras

my ($OS_win, $serial_port);

# Load the proper SerialPort module based on platform
BEGIN { $| = 1;
    $OS_win = ($^O eq "MSWin32") ? 1 : 0;
    if ($OS_win) {
        eval "use Win32::SerialPort";
        die "$@\n" if ($@);
        $serial_port = Win32::SerialPort->new ("COM1",1);

    }
    else {
        eval "use Device::SerialPort";
        die "$@\n" if ($@);
        $serial_port = Device::SerialPort->new ("/dev/ttyS0",1);
    }
}
die "Can't open serial port: $^E\n" unless ($serial_port);
$serial_port->error_msg(1);
$serial_port->user_msg(0);
$serial_port->databits(8);
$serial_port->baudrate(4800);
$serial_port->parity("none");
$serial_port->stopbits(1);
$serial_port->dtr_active(1);
$serial_port->handshake("none");
$serial_port->write_settings || die "Could not set up port\n";

use ControlX10::CM17;

# Send on signal to camera
&ControlX10::CM17::send($serial_port, $camera_hc . $ARGV[0] . 'J');

# Release  the serial port
```

```
$serial_port->close || die "\nProblem closing serial port\n";
undef $serial_port;
```

This script can run under either Windows or Linux. The only interesting lines in this script are pretty self-explanatory:

```
my $camera_hc = "N"; #Set to house code of cameras
...
# Send on signal to camera
&ControlX10::CM17::send($serial_port, $camera_hc . $ARGV[0] . 'J');
```

Well, maybe it's not completely self-explanatory. The send command passes the house code, the unit code, and the letter "J" to the Firecracker. The unit code is represented by $ARGV[0], which inserts the first, and only, parameter that you pass to the script. The letter "J" just means to turn on; if we wanted to send an off signal, we would use "K". You don't need to turn the cameras off, though, because they automatically turn off when they detect another camera turning on.

5. Run the script from the command line

To run the script, open a command prompt and switch to the directory you saved it in (I suggested *C:\homehacks*). Then, simply type the name of the script and the camera number to switch to:

```
switchCamera.pl 1
switchCamera.pl 2
switchCamera.pl 3
```

Assuming that Perl and the required modules have been installed correctly, the script will run, send the signal to cause the video camera to switch, and then exit. If things don't work as expected, try moving your X10 computer interface and the wireless transceiver to different electrical outlets. You might even try connecting them, and the camera, to outlets right next to each other.

If you need to address cameras with unit codes greater than 9, you must use an uppercase letter. So, for example, to address a camera unit of 10, use switchCamera.pl A. Use B to address unit 11, C for 12, D for 13, E for 14, F for 15, and G for 16. It's almost hexadecimal, but not quite, because the numbering starts at one instead of zero.

Now, watch the video feed to see if the cameras switch correctly. If they do, congrats! If not, use another wireless remote to control the cameras. If that works but the Firecracker doesn't, make sure the house code is set correctly on the wireless transceiver, and consider moving the transceiver closer to the Firecracker.

6. Install a web server

Many of the projects in this book rely on being able to remotely connect to your computer. For example, in order to monitor your home security system while on vacation, you'll need to be able to pull up a web browser at an Internet café and connect to your home computer. Connecting your home to the Internet has a lot of potential. If you're coming home early from work and want to fire up the air conditioning so that it's cool when you arrive, remotely accessing your home systems across the Internet would allow that. You could listen to your home music collection across the Internet, or even schedule a show to record from your desk at work.

> You don't even need a broadband connection to do this; dial-up can work too. It'll be slower, but connecting to your home server won't be any slower than it is to browse the web from home.

To enable remote connection through a web server, you need to secure your system and then install and configure the web server software. If you're an Internet geek, you probably already know how to do this. If you're any other type of geek, you could probably use some guidance. This section will teach you the concepts of self-hosting a web server, including understanding DNS, dynamic IP addressing, and security. All the software and services suggested in this step are free, so you won't have to spend a dime.

You'll need to set up IIS to use a web browser as the frontend interface for your camera. This is a popular way to create a user interface, because the system can be remotely accessed from just about any type of computer (and many palm computers and cell phones). It's an especially convenient way to access your home computer while traveling, because there are Internet cafés in every town. Internet cafés probably won't allow you to install a remote desktop client, but they'll definitely have a web browser available.

Installing IIS

Now that you've locked your system down and have a manually configured IP address, it's time to install the frequently exploited IIS. You may already be running a web server without even knowing it. To find out, follow these steps:

1. Launch Task Manager by right-clicking the task bar and selecting Task Manager.

2. Click the Processes tab and look for a process named *inetinfo.exe* (Figure 12-19). If you see it, IIS is already up and running. If not, you need to install IIS.

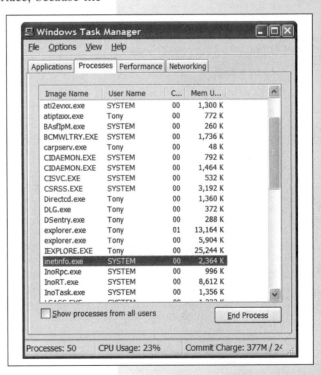

Figure 12-19. The inetinfo.exe process shows that IIS is already running.

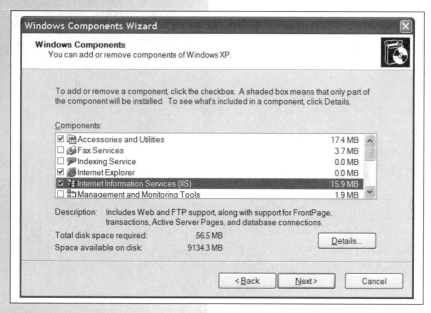

Figure 12-20. It's almost a little too easy to install a web server in Windows.

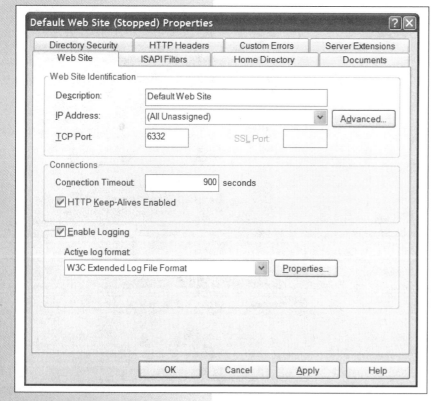

Figure 12-21. Administering your personal web server is done through an intuitive, graphical interface.

Some version of IIS comes with just about every recent version of Windows. The procedure to install IIS varies slightly between different operating system versions, but most are very similar to this procedure for Windows XP Professional:

1. In Control Panel, click Add or Remove Programs.

2. Select Add/Remove Windows Components. The Windows Components Wizard will open, as shown in Figure 12-20.

3. Select Internet Information Services (IIS).

4. Click Next to continue, and follow the rest of the instructions to complete the setup.

Now that IIS is installed, you need to visit *http://windowsupdate.microsoft. com* again. There's a pretty steady flow of critical updates for IIS, and you need to install them all. You might have to reboot your computer and return to Windows Update to install more updates.

Administer the web server software using Internet Information Services, which is found under the Administrative Tools program group in Control Panel. To view your web server's properties, expand the tree beneath your computer name until you find Default Web Site. Right-click on Default Web Site and select Properties. You'll see the Default Web Site Properties dialog box. As shown in Figure 12-21, you should change the default TCP Port setting to something other than 80. I suggest a number between 1024 and 10000 that you can easily remember.

WARNING

Keep in mind that changing the default port will protect you from most automated attacks such as worms, but it won't stop someone who does a complete port scan of your system.

Windows 2000 Professional and Windows XP Professional limit the number of people browsing your site to ten simultaneous users. This number is more than enough for the projects in this book. If you plan on getting slashdotted, you can either upgrade to Windows 2000 Server/Windows Server 2003, or find different web server software by searching for "HTTP server" on download sites such as *http://www.download.com*.

Determining your IP address

Now that your computer and router have been configured to allow remote access to your web server, all that's left is to determine your public IP address and optionally configure a domain name.

Earlier, you used the `ipconfig /all` command to examine your IP address configuration. If you determined that you did not have a private IP address, then you can skip this step—you already know your IP. If you do have a private IP address, you'll have to figure out what your public IP address is to connect to your computer from the Internet.

To learn your IP address, visit one of these sites from your home computer: *http://www.whatismyip.org/*, *http://www.whatismyip.com*, or *http://www.whatismyip.net/*. Unfortunately, there's a catch—the IP address that you have now may not be your permanent address. Most ISPs offer dynamic IP addressing, which means that your IP address may change from time to time. My personal experience with ISPs is that cable modem and DSL IP addresses rarely, if ever, change. However, it's important to understand this possibility when configuring DNS for your site. If you are using dial-up, your IP address will almost certainly change each time you connect to the Internet.

Getting a domain name (optional)

You are now successfully hosting a web site on your PC. However, it's accessible only by the IP address—not exactly a name that's easy to remember. Most people prefer to identify their site on the Web using a DNS name. If you don't already own a domain name, it's time to get one. There are many different organizations that can sell you a *.com*, *.net*, or *.org* domain name. For a complete listing, visit *http://www.internic.net/regist.html*.

Owning a domain name is good for many reasons. Most importantly, you can use the same email address for as long as you own the domain name. I use *tony@northrup.org* as my permanent email address, and forward it to whatever mailbox my ISP has given me this month.

Simply owning a domain name isn't enough, though; you need someone to provide ongoing DNS services. Providing DNS services is a little like an active telephone directory service: a DNS service provider on the Internet needs to take responsibility for your domain name, and provide your home IP address to anyone who enters your domain name into their browser. If your ISP uses dynamic IP addresses, you will need a way to automatically notify your DNS service provider of the changed IP address.

Many companies offer dynamic DNS management service for a small fee, and many others provide the service completely free of charge. Often, these providers offer software that runs on your computer to notify them if your IP address changes. For a listing of these organizations, visit *http://www.technopagan.org/dynamic/* or *http://www.geocities.com/kiore_nz/dynamicdns.htm*. You can also try searching the Web for "dynamic DNS management".

Once you identify a company to manage your DNS address, they will provide you with IP addresses for their primary and secondary nameservers. These nameservers are the actual computers on the Internet that will perform your address-book lookups for people surfing your site. Your domain name registrar will have a form available online to allow you to provide them with those two IP addresses. A few minutes after you've told your registrar the IP addresses of your DNS service provider, your computer will be accessible using your domain name.

Forwarding traffic from your router

You won't be able to access your web page from the outside world until you configure your router to forward packets with your custom TCP port to your computer's IP address. The procedure for configuring this is different for every router, so consult your manufacturer's instructions. On my Linksys router, I do the following:

If you do not have a router on your LAN, you can skip this step.

1. Enter the URL *http://192.168.1.1/* into a web browser, and provide the administrative username and password when prompted.

2. Click the Advanced tab.

3. Click the Port Forwarding tab.

4. Type the custom TCP port number in both of the External Port fields of a new row in the Customized Applications table. Select the TCP Protocol checkbox. Type the private IP address of the computer running IIS in the IP Address field, and select the Enabled checkbox (as shown in Chapter 3, Figure 3-15).

5. Click Apply.

Now, your computer and router have been configured to allow remote access to your web server, and all that's left to do is connect to it.

Connecting to your web server

To connect to your home web server from a remote location, simply open a browser window and enter a URL in the following format:

    http://domain-name-or-ip:TCP_Port/

So, if you used the TCP port 6332, purchased the domain name *northrup.org*, and assigned the hostname *www* to your home network's public IP address, you would enter the following URL:

    http://www.northrup.org:6332/

If you did not purchase a domain name, simply use the IP address instead:

    http://208.201.239.37:6332/

Your web server won't have a default page at this point, but that's okay. In fact, it's probably for the best. You don't ever need to set up a default page. Instead, just type the path to the application you've installed.

7. Configure a web page

First, let me warn you that I'm *not* a web designer. I have absolutely no artistic sense for colors or the layout of a web page; the web pages I create are functional, but hardly pretty. Feel free to use FrontPage, or something similar, if you want something nicer than the default fonts.

First, create the *C:\inetpub\wwwroot\camera* directory. Then, save the following as *cam.asp* in your *C:\inetpub\wwwroot\camera* directory. (Replace *ip_address* with the IP address or hostname of the server running Helix Universal Server.)

```
<html>
<head>
<title>Home Video Monitoring System</title>
</head>
<body>
<a href="rtsp://ip_address/ramgen/broadcast/stream.rm">
Open RealOne Player window with live video</a></p>
Switch cameras: <a href="cam.asp?camera=1">Camera 1</a>,
<a href="cam.asp?camera=2">Camera 2</a>,
<a href="cam.asp?camera=3">Camera 3</a></p>
```

```
<%
    whatCamera = Request("camera")
    If ( (whatCamera > 0) AND (whatcamera < 9) ) Then
        Response.Write ("Camera selected: " & whatCamera)

        Set WShShell = Server.CreateObject("WScript.Shell")
        WShShell.Run("c:\homehacking\switchCamera.pl " & whatCamera)
    End If
%>

</body>
</html>
```

You may also need to change the If statement. Ideally, you should verify that the input is a valid choice, keeping in mind that valid choices may be A–G if your cameras are numbered 10–16. For example, if your cameras are numbered 9, 10, and 11, you could replace the If statement with the following:

```
    If ( (whatCamera = "9") OR (whatCamera = "A") OR (whatCamera = "B")
Then
```

If your cameras aren't numbered 1, 2, and 3, you'll need to change the HTML to pass the correct arguments back to the recursive ASP script. Basically, this page passes the camera parameter back to itself when the user clicks the link. Issuing a GET request for cam.asp?camera=2 therefore calls the *cam.asp* file you created, and passes the parameter camera with the value of 2. The value passed in the camera parameter is passed straight through to the *switchCamera.pl* script in this line:

```
        WShShell.Run("c:\homehacking\switchCamera.pl " &
    whatCamera)
```

I chose ASP 3.0 and VBScript for this page because they're included with Windows 2000 and Windows XP. There's not much to like about ASP 3.0—it's inefficient and unreliable. ASP.NET is much nicer, and is what I use for my own personal web site, but using ASP.NET requires you to install the .NET Framework. I also could have called a Perl script directly from IIS, but I wanted to separate the web interface from the X10 script to make it easier to dissect and customize.

8. Run the script from the web page

It's showtime. Open a web browser on another computer that has the RealOne Player installed. Point the browser at *http://ip_address:port_number/camera/cam.asp*. Click the link to open the RealOne Player, and then resize both the browser window and the RealOne Player window so that you can see both on the screen simultaneously. Click the links in the browser window to switch between cameras. If everything is set up correctly, the video feed should switch within about a second of you clicking the link.

Wrapping Up

Even though this project used many different applications, setup was reasonably straightforward, and the project itself has proved reliable over time. This project shouldn't require any maintenance other than the constant patching required by IIS, which you can automate with Automatic Updates. There are a few things, however, that might cause problems:

- Unwelcome visitors discover your cameras.

- Someone figures out how to hack your Perl script.

- Interference from other 2.4GHz devices causes video quality to degrade.

- Bandwidth consumed by your video feed causes other services on your network to slow down.

But overall, the risk from this project is fairly low, and the problems are not severe.

Be sure to back up your computer so you don't have to start over from scratch if you have a hard disk failure. When backing up your system, be sure to include the *C:\Inetpub\wwwroot* directory and subdirectories, and the contents of *C:\homehacking*.

Extensions

I have several ideas about different ways this project could be used:

- A videoconferencing system could be built into a conference room, allowing the viewer to switch between multiple camera angles.

- You could implement the ultimate webcam, where two cameras are pointed at you from different angles, and the third camera is pointed at your screen.

- Motion detectors could be installed that cause the cameras to switch automatically. By setting up the motion detectors correctly, the cameras could automatically follow someone as the person walked through your house.

Exhibit A: Bill of Materials

Most parts are available from home automation web sites such as *http://www.smarthome.com*. X10 wireless cameras are available only from *http://www.x10.com*.

Item	Quantity	Approximate cost	Part number
Firecracker computer interface	1	$20 and up	CM17A
X10 wireless cameras	3	$170 for all of these items	XCam2 Classic
X10 wireless transceiver	1		4005X or 400s
Wireless video receiver	1		VR36A
Composite video input card	1	About $40	WinTV-GO-FM, 00191
Kwik-Fix Stick-E-Tak poster adhesive	1	$3	QSA2-01

Exhibit B: Software Versions

This list shows the versions of software components originally used to create this project. However, you can, and should, use updated versions whenever possible.

Description	Version
Operating system	Windows XP SP1
Helix Producer Basic	9.0.1
Helix Universal Server	9.0.2.802
IIS	5.1
RealOne Player	2.0
Perl	5.8.0
ControlX10::CM17	0.07
Win32::SerialPort	0.19

Build a Security System

## 13

Cost

$200 - $1000

Time

twelve hours

Difficulty

4 out of 5

What You Need

- X10 Powerlinc serial controller
- Eight AAA batteries
- 100 feet of 18–24 gauge wire (preferably white)
- Wire strippers/cutters
- Double-sided foam tape
- Two to ten X10 Powerflash Interfaces
- An X10 Powerhorn alarm
- Door and window sensors, as required by your home
- A stable broadband Internet connection
- A friend with a stable broadband Internet connection that allows inbound connections
- A computer running Windows
- Sticky poster adhesive
- A screwdriver

For a list of specific parts used in this project, refer to Exhibit A at the end of this chapter.

The first thing I did when I moved into my new home was to change the locks and install deadbolts. I needed to change the locks anyway, but I was shocked that deadbolts weren't already installed. After all, the house was built in the 1950s and had gone through several owners. You'd think at least one of those owners would have been willing to spend a few bucks to prevent any teenager from breaking in with a credit card.

Installing deadbolts on the three doors of my house took me about three hours and cost about $60. However, that minor improvement dramatically increased the security of my home. Sure, a few deadbolts won't turn my house into an impenetrable fortress. But it was cheap and easy to do, and definitely worth the effort.

Since then, I've been looking at other ways to improve my home's security. Naturally, I researched several businesses that install and monitor security systems. I have a great deal of confidence in these companies—they are, after all, security professionals. However, none of the standard solutions met my needs. While the up-front costs were relatively low, the ongoing cost of monitoring services was very high. Also, the systems were very inflexible, and integrating them with my software-based home automation system would be difficult or impossible.

> If you still want third-party monitoring, Smarthome offers a cheap service, and it sounds like they might even be willing to monitor a hacked-together system. Check out *http://www.smarthome.com/ALARM.HTML*.

I decided that the best way for me to improve the security of my home while staying within a tight budget was to build my own security system using off-the-shelf parts. Such a system can provide most of the features of standard security systems, as well as a few features found only in high-end security systems:

- Door and window sensors
- Motion detection
- Local audible alarms
- Video monitoring
- Off-site archiving of video feed
- Remote alerting using my existing mobile phone

The system should be designed to resemble Figure 13-1. Intrusion detection mechanisms will provide input to a script running on your computer. The script will use logic you provide to determine the appropriate response: take pictures or video through remote cameras, send you an alert, or do nothing if the system isn't armed. You can arm and disarm the system using anything that you can use to communicate with your computer, including a wireless remote.

Project Overview

In this project, you will design and implement an X10-based wireless security system using door and window sensors, motion detectors, video cameras, an Internet connection, and a whole bunch of software. This project has five phases, corresponding to each of the five components in the design: intrusion detection, intrusion deterrence, gathering evidence, arming, and monitoring and alerting. Each of these components is modular. For example, although this project as written uses Windows, you can very easily implement it using a Linux computer by replacing the monitoring/alerting component.

> Shortcut: You can buy home security kits from large hardware stores and many different sites on the Internet. However, they are not nearly as hackable as home-built systems, and you don't have as much control over the behavior.

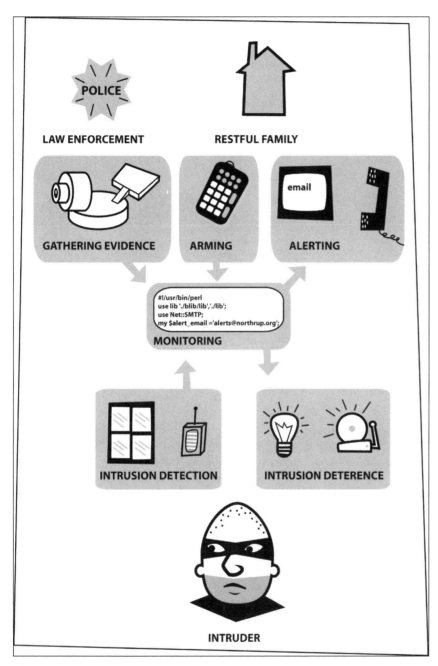

Figure 13-1. The components of a security system.

Intrusion Detection

You can't protect every inch of your home, but fortunately, intruders are pretty predictable in the methods they use to gain access. They don't like to make a lot of noise, so they probably won't cut through one of your walls. Instead, they'll try to enter through a door or window.

So we've narrowed down the possible points of entry, but most homes have several doors and windows. Protecting all of them could get expensive, so it's important to prioritize these potential entrances. First, focus your energy on doors and ground-floor windows that are concealed from the street. For me, I'm most concerned about the door at the back of my house that is completely concealed below a deck and a bulkhead. It's the door an intruder would most likely attempt to gain entry through, so it's the first one I need to protect.

You'll also want to protect the front door. Even if it's visible from the street, an intruder may boldly approach it and be able to quickly bypass your locks without looking suspicious. If he can pick or break your lock quickly, nobody may notice him breaking in. Certainly, he would look less suspicious than if he were climbing through a window.

For the remaining doors and windows, spend some time thinking about which ones an intruder may use to enter your home. Depending on the layout of your house, several of them may not need to be protected at all. For example, windows on upper floors probably won't be used by an intruder, unless they're accessible in some way other than by scaling the wall.

You can make a window less appealing to an intruder by planting a thorny bush below it.

After you've identified which doors and windows are most important to protect with intrusion detection mechanisms, you'll need to decide which tools you want to use to protect them. This will form your perimeter security. As a second line of defense against intruders that manage to bypass your perimeter security, you can add motion detectors to trigger an alarm if an intruder makes it inside your house.

1. Protect the windows

There are two ways an intruder can enter through your locked windows: by bypassing the lock and sliding the window open, or by breaking the glass. An intruder would certainly prefer to simply open the window, since breaking it would create a loud noise that could attract attention. Fortunately, you can use a very simple magnetic contact switch, as shown in Figure 13-2, to detect if a window has been opened.

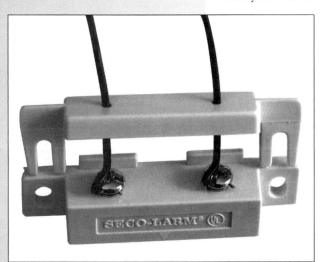

Figure 13-2. Use a magnetic contact switch to detect an opened window.

Like any electrical switch, a magnetic contact switch opens or closes a circuit. Depending on whether the switch is an open-circuit or closed-circuit switch, the circuit will be either opened or closed when the two halves of the switch are together. Only one half of the switch will be connected by wires, though; the other half is a magnet that controls the wired portion. Basically, in a closed-circuit switch, the magnet in the passive portion of the switch pulls a flexible wire in the active portion into contact with another wire to close the circuit, as shown in Figure 13-3.

Open-circuit switches are more secure than closed-circuit switches, because a closed-circuit switch can be disabled by simply snipping one of the wires. In contrast, snipping a wire in an open-circuit switch has the same effect as opening the door or window it's protecting—it triggers the alarm. Open-circuit switches are somewhat more complex and tend to be a bit more expensive. The cost of the switches themselves is pretty minimal, though—usually just $2–$5 per switch in small quantities.

If you're building a new house, you can just build these switches into the window frames, and run the wires through the walls so that they're completely concealed. My house was built in the 1950s, though, and my wife would kill me if I ripped the walls down. So, I need a cleaner way to send signals from the switches through the house.

I hate to do it, but I have to go back to X10. As shown in Figure 13-4, there are X10 transmitters that have two terminals you can connect to contact switches. When the switch is opened (or closed, depending on the switch and the settings), the Powerflash interface will send an X10 signal that can turn on a light, sound an alarm, or be intercepted by your computer.

Some switches have short wires built-in that you can connect directly to the Powerflash terminals, but usually you have to provide your own wires. You'll probably want to use your own wires anyway, because the wires included with the switches are typically too short to reach from your window to an electrical outlet. So head down to Radio Shack and buy about 100 feet of 18–24 gauge white wire. If you can find a cable with two suitable wires, grab that. If you don't have one yet, buy a wire stripper, too.

Position your contact switches on the window and plug your Powerflash interface into the nearest electrical outlet. Run wire from the contact to the Powerflash, doing your best to conceal the wire by forcing it into crevices and corners. You can run the wire through the wall later, but first you should make sure that it works properly and that you're happy with the location. For now, just determine how long the wire needs to be.

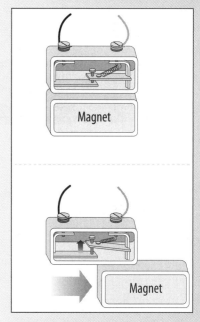

Figure 13-3. A closed-circuit security switch uses magnets to close the circuit when the two halves of the switch are together whenever the door or window is closed.

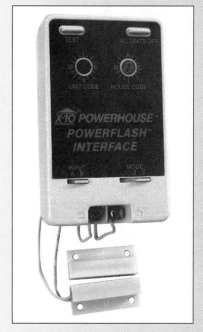

Figure 13-4. The Powerflash interface can convert signals from contact switches into X10 signals.

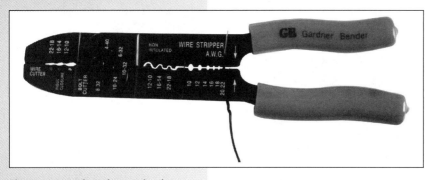

Figure 13-5. A wire stripper strips the insulation to expose the conductive core of wires.

Add an extra 6–12 inches to the length you identified, and cut off two pieces of wire that length. Use your wire stripper, shown in Figure 13-5, to pull the insulation off the ends of each wire. You'll want to leave about half an inch of exposed copper so that you can wrap it around the terminals.

Connect the wires to the terminals by wrapping the copper around the stem of the screw and tightening it down. If there are positive or negative markings on the switch (though there probably won't be), match them up to the markings on the Powerflash interface. Set the house and unit codes on the Powerflash. For now, connect a lamp to an X10 lamp switch, and set the lamp, house, and unit codes to the same settings.

If you're using the same Powerflash interface that I am, set the Mode switch to 3. This causes the Powerflash to send an On signal to the house, and unit codes when the sensor is tripped. When the sensor is returned to its normal state, the Powerflash sends an Off signal. Mode 1 sends an All Lights On signal to lights with the house code that the Powerflash is set to. Mode 2 sends repeated All Lights On and All Lights Off signals to flash the lights with that house code.

> Obviously, you need to have a security system processing the signals from the Powerflash. Otherwise, your lights would simply turn off after the intruder closes the door or window.

Set the Input switch to B. Press the Test button on the Powerflash, and the light should turn on. Now, hold the two halves of the window switch together, and the light should turn off. If it doesn't work, try setting the Input switch to A.

> You can use whichever house code you want, though you should use different codes for the wired and wireless X10 security devices. The standard X10 wireless devices are less secure, because an intruder familiar with your X10 system could send X10 signals from outside your house.

Now that you know that the switch and X10 interface are working properly, you can connect the switch semipermanently to the window itself. All switches will have holes that you can run screws through; when you permanently mount the switch, you should use these to ensure the switches don't fall out of place and cause a false alarm. For now, though, just use double-sided foam tape to stick the switch to the window. You may end up moving it later, because the wires get in the way, or you find the switch unattractive, or it blocks the window from opening and closing.

Exactly how you mount the switches will depend on your window and window frame. The two halves of the switches do not need to be flush against each other—the magnets just need to be within half an inch or so for the switch to report itself as closed. Place the sensor as low and close to an electrical outlet as possible. As Figure 13-6 shows, I placed my sensor at the junction of the two panes of my window, because I wanted the sensor to be triggered if either the top or the bottom windowpane was moved. Additionally, the structure of my window frame did not allow me to fasten the sensor to the side of the window.

Earlier I mentioned that there are two ways an intruder could break in through a window—by opening the window, or by breaking it. The contact switch could be quickly bypassed with a brick, assuming the intruder was willing to risk someone hearing the crashing sound. Fortunately, there are a couple of different types of sensors that can be used to detect broken glass; they physically attach to a window and detect the vibrations resulting from a broken pane. Alternately, acoustic glassbreak sensors are positioned inside a room and listen for the sound of breaking glass. This type of sensor is pricey—anywhere from $40–$130—but they can protect multiple windows simultaneously, and might be a good bet if you have a lot of windows in one room. Also, if you're using a regular glassbreak sensor that detects vibrations and a single window has multiple windowpanes, you'll have to protect each one, because the vibrations of breaking may not transfer from one pane to another.

However, my windows have only one pane, so I chose to use a glassbreak sensor on the windows I was most concerned about. Clean the window carefully, and position the sensor at least an inch away from the window frame. The model I chose, shown in Figure 13-7, included a sticker reading "Warning—Window is electronically protected against breakage," which would probably be enough to scare off the casual intruder.

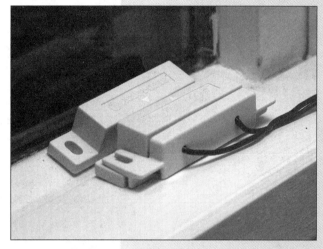

Figure 13-6. Attaching a switch to a window sends a signal when the window is forced open.

Figure 13-7. Position the glassbreak sensor one inch from the window frame to allow it to detect vibrations.

If you want to break into someone's house and they have a glassbreak sensor, just use a diamond ring to cut the glass pane. I think I saw that on *Mission Impossible*. Or *Mel's Diner*.

Some professional security systems offer custom-fit screens that trigger an alarm when the screen is cut or removed. This is a great option because it allows you to keep your window open without sacrificing security. I couldn't find the parts to add this to my custom system, though.

2. Install door contact switches

Your doors are the most important point of entry to protect. Before you begin with the intrusion detection, make sure you have the basics covered: install deadbolts, and choose metal doors that have small windows, if any. However, even with these precautions, intruders can still get in.

WARNING

If you install deadbolts on metal doors, don't buy a kit with drill bits included. Instead, buy the parts separately, and purchase drill bits designed to cut through metal doors. I made the mistake of using the drill bit included with a kit, and ended up ruining it.

Some intruders will have a key to get in your home. In fact, you might even have given them a key because they're a neighbor or a friend. Or, they may have grabbed a key when you invited them into your home. Someone working on your house may have spied a spare key lying around and grabbed it.

WARNING

Hanging your door keys on a nail next to the door is begging for trouble.

In college, I used to break into my friends' dorm rooms using a credit card so I could toy with them. It's easy, because door latches move freely and are angled so that you can close the door without turning the knob. Try it on your own door—just slide the credit card into the door jamb, and angle it up so that the corner of the credit card pushes into the angled side of the door latch. If the door fits loosely enough that you can get the credit card in there, you can push the door latch in and simply pull the door open. Of course, this trick won't work with a deadbolt, or most modern door latches. An intruder will need a lock-pick for those, or just take the path of brute force and use a crowbar or a sledgehammer.

There are two main types of sensors that you can use to monitor a door opening: those that attach externally, and those that are built into the door and doorframe. If you're building a new house, you should definitely build contact switches into the door and doorframe, because they're practically invisible. They won't detract from the appearance of the door, and they won't get broken or fall off.

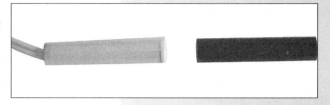

Figure 13-8. Small magnetic sensors are perfect for built-in door security.

Installing built-in door sensors is simple if you don't have drywall up, but will require you to remove your door trim if your house is finished. The sensors I have are cylindrical, as shown in Figure 13-8, and the two halves should be embedded lengthwise into the door and doorframe. To install them, I marked locations on the door and doorframe that match up when the door is closed. Then, I used a 1/4-inch drill bit to drill a hole into both the door and doorframe.

If you are installing the switch into a solid wood door, be sure to measure the depth of the hole you drill. It needs to be deep enough so that the switch is flush with the edge of the door, but not so deep that it is too far from the other half of the switch to close the circuit. If you have a hollow door, you'll only need to pierce the outside of the door. Hopefully, the door is thick enough to hold the magnet in place.

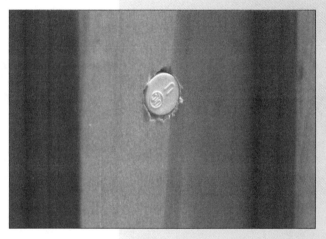

Figure 13-9. The cylindrical sensor fits into a quarter-inch hole and can be painted over.

Use a rubber mallet to push the unwired portion of the contact switch into the hole in the door. After installation, it'll look exactly like the head of a nail, as shown in Figure 13-9. To install the switch in the doorframe, start by feeding the wires into the frame, and then pull them through into the wall opening. You will need to run these wires to a Powerflash interface or directly to your security system. Gently push or hammer the switch into the doorframe until it is flush. When you close the door, the two halves of the switch should match up exactly.

If you already have drywall up, you'll either have to remove your door trim to run a wire behind the drywall, or use an external switch. External switches aren't so bad, and can be positioned at the bottom of the door so that they are hardly noticeable (Figure 13-10). The switch will have screwholes for when you want to fasten it permanently to the door, but wait until you've determined that it works and that you're happy with the location.

Figure 13-10. External door sensors are ideal when you cannot run wires through the walls.

As you did with the window switches, measure the length of wire required by running the wire from the switch to the nearest power outlet along the floor. Then, add about six inches to each length of wire, strip the ends of the wire, and connect the switch to a Powerflash interface attached to a nearby power outlet.

3. Install motion detectors

Motion detectors are a tremendously useful component of a security system. While door and window contact switches protect the perimeter of your house, a motion detector will detect an intruder if he somehow manages to get into your home. Ideally, you would have a motion detector in each room that could potentially be broken into.

Motion detectors do have drawbacks, though. You can't have motion detectors armed while you're active in the house, so, they're useless if someone breaks into your house while you're there and awake. You can arm them at night, but you'll have to disarm them if you get up.

Pets can make using a motion detector next to impossible. If you have a dog, you may be able to position the motion detector so that it only detects motion above two or three feet in the air. Theoretically, this would allow a dog to walk through the room, but would detect an upright intruder. I have a cat, though, and I've been completely unsuccessful at keeping the cat off of furniture, counters, tables, the fireplace mantel, and anything else with more than a couple of inches of surface area. The cat even has a habit of vertically jumping several feet in the air when chasing after moths, which would cause a motion detector to generate a false alarm.

You can, and should, use motion detectors with perimeter security. When you're at home, but up and about, arm the door and window switches to detect an intruder. If you're away from home, or staying in a single room such as your bedroom, arm the motion detectors to provide an additional layer of intrusion detection.

I've used motion detectors in several other projects, so I won't discuss them in detail here. Refer to Chapter 1, Automate a Light, for more information on installing motion detectors.

4. Install environmental sensors

Environmental sensors can detect a variety of different situations in and around your home that don't threaten your security but might make you unhappy, such as freezing temperatures, water on the floor, or high humidity. They're not exactly "intrusion detection," but environmental sensors are a common feature of commercial security systems, and can save you a huge headache and a big pile of money.

In the course of writing this book, my co-author Eric had his computer spread out on the floor of the basement of his new house. There was quite a rainstorm at the time, and Eric was unaware that the new house had a leaky basement until the water started pouring in. He discovered the leak after about an inch of water had covered the floor. Fortunately, the basement floor wasn't perfectly flat, and the computer parts happened to be on the highest point of the floor. If he'd had a water sensor and a security system set up, he would have known about the leak within a few seconds of the water accumulating.

If you're building an X10-based security system, you can connect the environmental sensors to a Powerflash interface exactly as you would a window or door contact switch. For example, the temperature sensor shown in Figure 13-11 could be configured to trigger an alert when the ambient temperature falls below 40 degrees Fahrenheit—giving you time to turn on a heater before the temperature hit freezing.

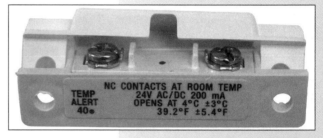

Figure 13-11. Environmental sensors can be connected to a Powerflash interface to send X10 signals based on the room temperature, the presence of water, or other factors.

You probably won't want the environmental sensor to start blaring an alarm through your house, but you will definitely want to be notified in some way. So you need to make sure that the monitoring and alerting component of this project has the ability to distinguish between these non-emergency alerts and those alerts that could signify someone breaking into your home.

5. Add a panic button

You've fallen, and you can't get up. And it's no laughing matter! Fortunately, you have your X10 wireless remote in your pocket. Push the button, and your computer sends an email to the mobile phones or pagers of your family and friends.

> Most mobile phones that can do SMS messaging can also receive email. Check with your service provider.

Adding a panic button is remarkably simple, given the flexibility of the sample script provided in the "Monitoring and Alerting" section. Simply define a new kind of sensor that is always armed, and configure the $alert_email variable with one or more email addresses that should receive a message when an emergency occurs. You might also have the script turn the lights on for you—so your rescuers can find you if you're injured in the dark. Keep in mind, however, that there's a significant risk of false alarms, because the buttons on these keychain remotes often get pushed accidentally.

Intrusion Deterrence

Of course, intrusion detection is only useful if your security system takes action in response to events. Typically, security systems kick off several different types of responses: intrusion deterrence, alerting, and recording evidence. This section covers intrusion deterrence mechanisms that will hopefully scare away the potential intruder.

> Silent alarms are good for catching an intruder in the act, because they notify the authorities while making the intruder feel like they have successfully broken in without activating an alarm. I'm more interested in my own safety than getting a criminal off the streets, though, so I'd rather scare an intruder away than catch them. If you would prefer a silent alarm, you can skip this phase of the project.

1. Install light switches

Simply turning on lights is an effective mechanism of deterring an intruder, because it lets them know they've been detected. If all you do is turn your lights on, the intruder could theoretically continue to explore your home. However, he probably wouldn't, because he would think he had either tripped an alarm or that someone was home.

The simplest way to turn lights on from a software-based security system is to use X10 lamp switches and X10 wall switches. These can be triggered either by the intrusion detection mechanism directly, or by a security system that processes the signals from your intrusion detection system. This project relies on software to process signals and decide how to respond. However, you can skip the middleman by having the sensors trigger the lights directly. To have a light turn on automatically when a door or window is opened, set the unit and house codes on the lamp switch to the same unit and house codes specified on your Powerflash interface.

I've used lamp and light switches in several other projects, so I won't describe them in detail here. Refer to Chapter 2, Automate Your Porch Light, and Chapter 1, Automate a Light, for more information.

2. Install audible alarms

Audible alarms are a great way to deter the intruder, and to notify anyone within earshot that a break-in has occurred. You can buy alarms called Powerhorns (Figure 13-12) that are triggered by X10 signals. They can then be triggered either by an X10-compatible security system or by your computer. Then, simply set the house and unit codes of the Powerhorn to a unique setting. Powerhorns aren't triggered by a simple On signal, though; they are designed to work with security systems, and can be triggered only

Figure 13-12. Finally—your computer can make a screeching sound in any room of the house!

by several sequential On-Off-On-Off-On-Off signals. You can turn them off again (and trust me, you'll want to) by sending an Off signal. Otherwise, the alarm will shut itself off after 30 seconds.

Gathering Evidence

Obviously, your first priority is to get an intruder away from your house and to keep yourself, your family, and your belongings safe. However, after everyone is out of danger, you should notify the police so that they can take steps to identify the intruder. You can help the police out by gathering evidence for them. First, you should record the feedback from your sensors—simply knowing the exact time an intruder opened your window can be very useful. Second, you can record visual information about the intrusion. Captured video of the intruder can be useful for identifying the intruder, and may even be used as evidence if the case goes to trial.

Many security systems have a significant weakness when it comes to recording evidence because they store the video on-site. A skilled thief who has a few minutes to spare will follow the video cable from a camera to a VCR, and steal the VCR, too. This section will describe how to record evidence and automatically ship it off-site, so that you won't lose important evidence if your computer is stolen.

1. Install cameras

Several of the projects in this book use video cameras, so I won't discuss them in detail here. For information about the types of cameras available and how to install them, refer to Chapter 3, Remotely Monitor a Pet, and Chapter 12, Watch Your House Across the Network.

When positioning your cameras, think about where they could best capture a potential intruder's image. It would be great to have cameras pointed at all of the doors and windows that could be used for entry. It could also be useful to capture the intruder's approach. For example, if the layout of your property requires an intruder to walk up a specific path, point a camera at that path. Sure, most of the video will be of pizza delivery guys and college kids selling magazines, but you'll also capture video of a potential intruder.

Also put extra consideration into protecting your cameras. If you have a camera mounted externally, a potential intruder might spot it and take steps to disable it. You can make this more difficult by positioning the camera out of reach, and by having cameras with overlapping views so that one camera can capture an intruder breaking the other one.

2. Install video capture tools

Other projects in this book used wireless video cameras to record still photos and to transfer a live video stream. This project has different requirements—we need to record video when activity is detected. We also need to transfer this video off-site so that it can be used in the event that the computer storing the video is stolen.

Ideally, the computer would be capturing video constantly. When activity was detected, it would save video from several minutes before the activity until several minutes after the activity. This would allow you to view the action leading up to the action that triggered your alarm. It's particularly useful because there's a second or two of lag between when a sensor is triggered and when the camera is activated.

Buffering is hard, although it could certainly be done. But instead, I'm going to use a program called Virtual VCR to record about 30 seconds of video to a file after a sensor is triggered. Then, I can transfer that file across the Internet to a friend's computer.

Thanks to Robbie Harris and Shaun Faulds for putting together such a useful application!

First, download and install the latest version of Virtual VCR from *http://virtualvcr.sourceforge.net/*. Then, launch the program (the setup procedure adds a shortcut to your start menu) and follow this procedure to configure it:

1. Click the Settings toolbar button (the one with the hammer).

2. Click the Video tab and select the Use Compression checkbox, as shown in Figure 13-13. You might not have the same compression codecs I do, so experiment with different codecs to find the one that provides a good compromise between quality and file size. You'll want enough quality to be able to recognize the intruder's features, but the bigger the file is, the longer it will take to upload. I selected the Indeo® video 5.10 Compression Filter.

3. Click the Audio tab, and deselect Capture Audio.

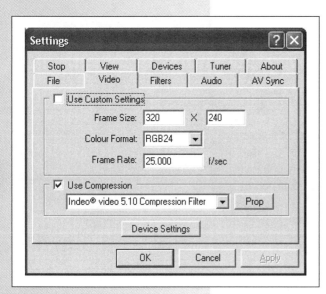

Figure 13-13. Picking the right compression algorithm is important, especially if you don't have much bandwidth to work with.

4. Click the Devices tab (Figure 13-14) and select your video device and video source. I'm using a WinTV capture card with the video feed connected to the composite connector.

5. Click OK.

6. Click the Save Current Settings button on the tool-bar—the one that looks like a floppy disk. Click OK.

7. Make sure that your video feed is configured correctly by clicking the Toggle Preview button on the toolbar (it's the button that looks like a blue box). Get the video working properly before you move on.

Now, you could use Virtual VCR (shown in Figure 13-15) to manually record video, but the reason I chose it is that it accepts command-line parameters for recording. For example, you can execute the command "C:\ Program Files\Virtual VCR\virtualvcr" -capture -runfor "10" -output "C:\homehacking\security\security.mpg" to save a video file. Unfortunately, Virtual VCR keeps running after the recording is finished, so you'll have to either close it manually or create a script to terminate the process. We can kill it from the Perl script after the recording is done, though.

If you want to be able to view the video your security system captures from a remote location, set up IIS on your computer as described in Chapter 12. Then, map a virtual directory in IIS to the directory you use to store the video clips, and enable directory browsing on that directory. If you get an alert from the security system, you'll be able to download and view the clips across the Internet. That should be enough to determine whether it's an intruder, or if your kid just forgot to disarm the alarm. For more information about IIS, refer to the Help and Support Center on your operating system.

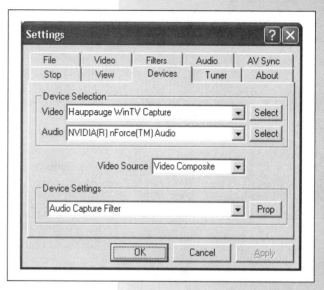

Figure 13-14. Specify the video capture device connected to your security cameras.

Figure 13-15. Virtual VCR isn't a true command-line program, but it'll do.

3. Configure off-site storage

Here's a feature not available in any standard home security system: off-site storage of video. Most inexpensive video security monitoring systems capture the video in analog. Specifically, they use old-fashioned VHS tapes, often slowed down to allow many hours of recording on a single tape. We're using digital, though, and there are some distinct advantages to that.

The first thing you need to do is find a friend with a computer and a broadband connection. It can't be just any friend, though. They have to meet these requirements:

- Their downstream bandwidth must be higher than your upstream bandwidth. In other words, if you have a cable modem with 1.5Mbps downstream bandwidth and 256Kbps upstream bandwidth, they should have at least 256Kbps downstream bandwidth.

- They must be constantly connected to the Internet.

- They must have a stable IP or DNS address to identify themselves.

- They must have a computer that stays online most of the time, and that has about 500MB of storage they're willing to give you.

Have your friend set up their computer as a File Transfer Protocol (FTP) server. If they're using Windows, they can follow these instructions to set up the FTP server in Windows XP:

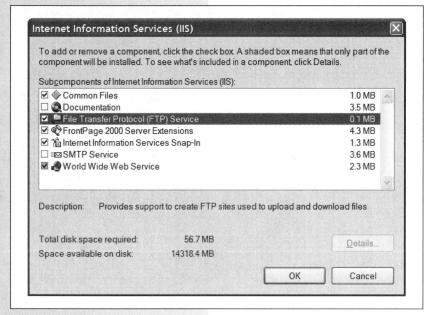

Figure 13-16. Enable FTP to transfer files between computers on the Internet.

1. Open the Control Panel and launch Add or Remove Programs.

2. Click Add/Remove Windows Components.

3. Click Internet Information Services (IIS), and then click Details.

4. Select the File Transfer Protocol (FTP) Service checkbox as shown in Figure 13-16, and then click OK.

5. Click Next. Windows XP will install the FTP service. It may prompt you to insert the Windows XP CD-ROM.

6. Open the Control Panel, open Administrative Tools, and then open the Internet Information Services console.

7. Expand the local computer node, then expand FTP Sites. Right-click Default FTP Site and click Properties.

8. Change the TCP Port field to something other than 21; I chose 2121.

9. Click the Security Accounts tab and deselect Allow Anonymous Connections. Click Yes when prompted about the dangers of clear-text passwords.

10. Click the Home Directory tab. Deselect the Read checkbox, and select the Write checkbox.

11. Click OK.

12. Click Start, right-click My Network Places, and then click Properties.

13. If your network interface card's status says Firewalled (and, for the sake of your computer's security, it should) and you are using Windows XP Service Pack 1, follow these steps:

    a) Right-click the connection and then click Properties.

    b) Click the Advanced tab, and then click Settings.

    c) Click Add. In the "Description of service" field, type **FTP server**. In the IP address field, type **127.0.0.1** (Figure 13-17). In both the External Port and Internal Port fields, type the TCP port you specified in Step 8.

    d) Click OK three times.

14. If your network interface card's status says Firewalled and you're using Service Pack 2, Windows Firewall should automatically open the custom port for you. If you have problems, read *http://support.microsoft.com/?kbid=875356* and *http://support.microsoft.com/?kbid=875357*.

You'll now create a user account so that your script can log in.

15. Open the Control Panel, open User Accounts, and then click "Create a new account."

16. In the "Type a name for the new account" field, make up something original and descriptive, like SecurityUpload. Click Next.

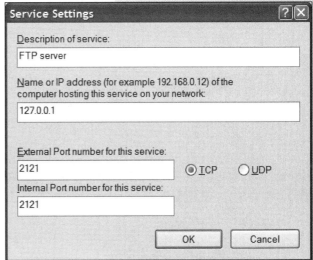

Figure 13-17. If you're using Internet Connection Firewall, you'll need to open a port to allow incoming connections.

17. At the "Pick an account type" page, click Limited. Click Next.

18. Now, click the SecurityUpload account, and then click "Create a password." Type the password in both fields, and then click Create Password.

Then, have the friend open a port in their router/firewall. If their firewall supports it and you have a stable IP address, they can filter incoming FTP requests so that they are allowed only from your IP address. For more information about opening ports in a firewall, refer to the "Video Transfer" phase of Chapter 12.

If you don't have any friends who can provide off-site storage, you can use an online storage provider. A quick Google for "online storage" turns up several options. For example, XDrive (*http://www.xdrive.com*) charges $10 a month for 500MB of storage, and comes with a better service level agreement (SLA) than most friends will be willing to provide to you.

Now you have a place where you can upload your video. Next, you need a script that will connect to your friend's FTP server, negotiate authentication, upload the file, and then disconnect. We could do this with a batch file, because every version of Windows that I can remember included the FTP command-line utility. This tool isn't terrible easy to script, though. It can be scripted, but only if you provide it a text file that includes all of the commands. So, what we need to do is create a batch file that creates a text file full of FTP commands and then calls the FTP command.

You could do this with Perl, too. However, I prefer to use batch files whenever possible, because they don't require any additional software to be installed on the Windows computer.

Following are the commands you would send to the FTP command to transfer a file named *C:\homehacking\security\filename.mpg*. Of course, you'll need to change the FTP server hostname, port number, username, and password.

```
open ftp.northrup.org
user SecurityUpload
pass MyP@55w0rd
binary
send C:\homehacking\security\filename.mpg
close
quit
```

Now, we'll write a batch file that uses the ECHO command to create a text file, and then calls the FTP command. It would be nice to create a log of the movies that we uploaded, so we'll echo the filename, date, and time to a text file. Save this file as *C:\homehacking\security\sendfile.bat*.

```
echo open ftp.northrup.org> upload-movie.txt
echo SecurityUpload>> upload-movie.txt
echo MyP@55wOrd>> upload-movie.txt
echo binary>> upload-movie.txt
echo send %1>> upload-movie.txt
echo close>> upload-movie.txt
echo quit>> upload-movie.txt
ftp -s:upload-movie.txt
echo File %1 sent at %date% %time%>>C:\homehacking\security\ftplog.txt
```

Again, replace the hostname, port number (2121 in the example), username, and password with the values you created earlier in this phase. Now, you can upload the file to your friend's computer with a single command, such as:

```
C:\homehacking\security\Sendfile.bat movie.mpg
```

Arming

The challenge of security is striking a balance between denying access to unauthorized users while minimizing the inconvenience imposed upon authorized users. In the context of home security, you need to allow your family to arm the alarm system when they leave the house or go to bed, and disarm it when they enter the house or wake up in the morning. Traditional alarm systems use a digital keypad, and when someone needs to arm or disarm the system, they enter a 4–10 digit code.

In Chapter 11, Keyless Entry Welcome Home, Eric provided a creative way to both unlock your home and disarm your system. A wireless transmitter sends an X10 signal that, when received by your computer, could disarm the alarm system. It's not the most secure thing, of course, because wireless X10 is a simple, unencrypted, unsigned protocol, and anybody with a wireless transmitter could disarm your system. However, they would have to know that you're using an X10-based alarm system and have talked to you about how your system is implemented. Hopefully, nobody that you know that well will attempt to break into your house!

Figure 13-18. You can use a lock switch to control your computer and home automation devices.

You can step up the security a level while still using X10 by purchasing a lock switch, as shown in Figure 13-18, and connecting it to a Powerflash device. The lock switch uses physical wires that are located inside your home, so the signals can't be easily faked. When you place a key in the lock switch and turn it on, it sends an X10 On signal. Similarly, turning the key to the Off position sends an X10 Off signal. Of course, it would still be possible for a clever, knowledgeable intruder to connect an X10 transmitter to a power receptacle on the outside of your house to disarm your system, but again, they would have to know how you implemented your security system, and I'm assuming that you're not babbling on about such things while standing in line at your local coffee shop.

To install a lock switch, you'll need to drill a hole from the outside of your house, and then run the wires through the wall to a Powerflash Interface inside your home. If you're just building your house, it's easiest to install a lock switch after the outside walls have gone up, but before the drywall inside your house has been installed. It's certainly possible to retrofit it to an existing house, but you'll have to drill through the drywall to pull the wires through.

If you have an old laptop or PDA lying around, you could place it near the entry (or perhaps even build it directly into the wall). Then, you could use the computer to arm and disarm the alarm system. If you have a touchscreen, you could even tap out a PIN with your fingertips. The computer could then send a signed, encrypted message to your alarm system across a wired or wireless network. Certainly, it's more secure than X10 messages.

Monitoring and Alerting

The monitoring component of a security system ties all the other components together. It receives signals from the different intrusion detection mechanisms, and determines whether it needs to take action based on whether the alarm system is armed. If it does need to take action, it starts up the intrusion deterrence mechanisms by turning on the lights and sounding an alarm. If available, it'll record video and ship it off-site. It will also notify you somehow, either audibly or by sending a message to your phone, email address, or pager.

1. Install remote speakers

Luckily, not every type of alarm calls for a blaring siren. For example, if a sensor has detected water in your basement, what you'd really like is a calm voice telling you that a leak has been detected. A voice response system would also be useful if an intruder was detected, because it could tell you exactly where the intrusion was detected—allowing you to go directly to the problem, rather than checking every door and window.

You can use the remote audio system described in Chapter 4, Make Your House Talk, to implement a sophisticated voice feedback system. To do this, add a set of remote speakers to each of the rooms in your home. Connect the speakers to an X10 interface, and set all of the unit and house codes to the same address. Then, your script can turn all of the speakers on at once, and read an announcement throughout the home.

2. Connect the X10 computer interface

If you haven't yet connected your X10 computer interface, connect it now. If you have more than one serial port on your computer, connect the X10 controller to the first one. Of course, you can connect it whichever serial port you like, but you'll need to modify the Perl script in this project to communicate with the correct port.

Plug the power cable of the computer interface directly into a wall socket. Do not plug it into a power strip or surge protector, and definitely don't plug it into a UPS. The more devices you have between your X10 computer interface and the power lines in your house, the more likely it is that the signals will be obscured.

3. Install the Perl modules

If you haven't already, install Perl, the Win32::SerialPort module, and the ControlX10::CM11 module as described in Chapter 2. You can download the modules from *http://www.cpan.org/authors/id/B/BB/BBIRTH/*.

4. Create the Perl script

It's time to place the last piece of the puzzle—the script that will handle the input from the intrusion detection and arming systems, and start the intrusion deterrence and evidence gathering mechanisms. We'll also perform alerting functions directly from this script.

As with most projects, Perl is my choice for gluing multiple components together. Save the following script as *C:\homehacking\SecurityMonitor.pl*. You can also download the script, along with any updates I've made, from *http://www.homehacking.com*.

```perl
#!/usr/bin/perl
use lib './blib/lib','./lib';
use Net::SMTP;

my $alert_email = 'alerts@northrup.org'; # REPLACE WITH OWN E-MAIL
my $smtp_server = "127.0.0.1"; # REPLACE WITH OWN SMTP SERVER
my $audible_unit = "9";
my $audible_hc = "D";
my $speaker_unit = "8";
my $speaker_hc = "D";
my $sensor_hc = "D";
my $light_hc = "E";
my $camera_hc = "F";
my $video_path = "C:\\homehacking\\security\\";
my $virtual_vcr_path = "C:\\Program Files\\Virtual VCR\\virtualvcr";
my $seconds_to_capture = 10;

# @units is a two-dimensional array containing the following columns in
each row:
# 0) A description of the tripped sensor
# 1) The code the sensor transmits when it is tripped
# 2) The code of the corresponding light ("0" for all lights, or zero
```

```
        for no lights)
# 3) the code of the corresponding camera (0 for no camera)
# 4) Whether to send an e-mail alert (1 or 0)
# 5) Whether to capture video (1 or 0)
# 6) Whether to sound an audible alarm (1 or 0)
# 7) Whether to sound a spoken alarm (1 or 0)
# 8) Armed or disarmed by default (1 or 0)
# 9) Minimum arm level (0-@#arm_levels)
# unit codes can be 1-9 or A-G for 10-16.
my @units = (
    ["Office windows",    "1", "0", "1", "1", "1", "1", "1", "0", 1],
    ["Kitchen window",    "2", "0", "0", "1", "0", "1", "1", "0", 1],
    ["Front door",        "3", "0", "3", "1", "1", "1", "1", "0", 1],
    ["Side door",         "4", "0", "4", "1", "1", "1", "1", "0", 1],
    ["Freeze alert",      "5", "0", "0", "1", "0", "0", "0", "1", 0],
    ["Water in basement", "6", "0", "0", "1", "0", "0", "1", "1", 0],
    ["Motion detectors",  "7", "0", "0", "1", "1", "1", "1", "0", 2],
    ["Panic: Call me!",   "8", "0", "0", "1", "0", "0", "1", "1", 0]
);

# @arm_levels contains a list of different levels that the
# security system is armed at, and the X10 code that sets that level
my @arm_levels = (
    ["Disarmed", "G1GK"],
    ["Night", "G1GJ"],
    ["Vacant", "G2GJ"],
);
$current_arm_level = 0;

my ($OS_win, $serial_port, $data);

# Load the proper SerialPort module based on platform
BEGIN { $| = 1;
    $OS_win = ($^O eq "MSWin32") ? 1 : 0;
    if ($OS_win) {
        eval "use Win32::SerialPort";
        die "$@\n" if ($@);
        $serial_port = Win32::SerialPort->new ("COM1",1);

    }
    else {
        eval "use Device::SerialPort";
        die "$@\n" if ($@);
        $serial_port = Device::SerialPort->new ("/dev/ttyS0",1);
    }
}
die "Can't open serial port: $^E\n" unless ($serial_port);
$serial_port->error_msg(1);
$serial_port->user_msg(0);
$serial_port->databits(8);
$serial_port->baudrate(4800);
$serial_port->parity("none");
$serial_port->stopbits(1);
$serial_port->dtr_active(1);
$serial_port->handshake("none");
$serial_port->write_settings || die "Could not set up port\n";

use ControlX10::CM11;
```

```
while ()
{
    $data = $data.ControlX10::CM11::receive_buffer($serial_port);
    $data = <>;

    if (!$data) {
          sleep 1; # Let the processor rest if nothing has been
detected
    }
    else {
        print "Processing: $data\n";
        # Check to see if any of the sensors transmitted a code
        foreach $s (0..$#units) {
            my $loop_code = $sensor_hc.$units[$s][1].$sensor_hc."J";
            if (($data =~ $loop_code) && ($units[$s][8] eq "1")) {
                light_on ($units[$s][2]) if ($units[$s][2] ne "0");
                audible_on () if ($units[$s][6] eq "1");
                send_email ($units[$s][0]) if ($units[$s][4] eq "1");
                capture_video ($units[$s][3]) if ($units[$s][5] eq
"1");
                speak_alert ("Alert: $units[$s][0]") if ($units[$s][7]
eq "1");

                $data = "";
            }
        }

        # Check to see if any of the arm codes were transmitted
        foreach $t (0..$#arm_levels) {
            if ($data =~ $arm_levels[$t][1]) {
                $current_arm_level = $t;
                speak_alert ("Security level set to $arm_
levels[$t][0]");

                foreach $u (0..$#units) {
                    # If the minimum arm level for a sensor is less
than the
                    # specified arm level, arm the sensor. Otherwise,
disarm it.
                    if ($units[$u][9] <= $t) {
                        $units[$u][8] = "1";
                    }
                    else {
                        $units[$u][8] = "0";
                    }
                }
                $data = "";
            }
        }
    }
}

$serial_port->close || die "\nclose problem with serial port\n";
undef $serial_port;

sub light_on {
    print "Turning on: ".$light_hc.$_[0]."\n";
```

```perl
    ControlX10::CM11::send($serial_port, $light_hc.$_[0]);
    ControlX10::CM11::send($serial_port, $light_hc."J") if ($_[0] ne
"O");
}

sub audible_on {
    print "Sounding alarm!!\n"; # Send on-off three times in a row
    foreach (1..3)
    {
        ControlX10::CM11::send($serial_port, $audible_hc.$audible_
unit);
        ControlX10::CM11::send($serial_port, $audible_hc."J");
        ControlX10::CM11::send($serial_port, $audible_hc.$audible_
unit);
        ControlX10::CM11::send($serial_port, $audible_hc."K");
    }
}

sub send_email {
    print "Sending email to $alert_email about $_[0]!!\n";
    my $smtp = Net::SMTP->new($smtp_server);

    $smtp->mail($alert_email);
    $smtp->to($alert_email);

    $smtp->data();
    $smtp->datasend("To: $alert_email\n");
    $smtp->datasend("From: $alert_email\n");
    $smtp->datasend("Subject: Alert: $_[0]\n");
    $smtp->dataend();

    $smtp->quit;
}

sub capture_video {
    print "Capturing video!!\n";
    ControlX10::CM11::send($serial_port, $camera_hc.$_[0]);
    ControlX10::CM11::send($serial_port, $camera_hc."J");
    @now = localtime;
    $videoname = sprintf "SecurityCam-%02u%02u%02u-%02u%02u%02u.mpg",
$now[5]-100, $now[4]+1, $now[3], $now[2], $now[1], $now[0];
    print `$virtual_vcr_path -capture -runfor \"$seconds_to_capture\"
-output \"$videopath$videoname\"\n`;
    sleep $seconds_to_capture;
    print `tskill virtualvcr\n`;
    print `C:\\homehacking\\security\\sendfile.bat
\"$videopath$videoname\"\n`;
}

sub speak_alert {
    # Send on signal to speakers, then speak
    ControlX10::CM11::send($serial_port, $speaker_hc.$speaker_unit);
    ControlX10::CM11::send($serial_port, $speaker_hc."J");
    print `C:\\homehacking\\security\\Say $_[0].\n`;
    ControlX10::CM11::send($serial_port, $speaker_hc.$speaker_unit);
    ControlX10::CM11::send($serial_port, $speaker_hc."K");
}
```

5. Understand and hack the script

A big chunk of this script is the configuration of about a dozen different variables. Modify the variables in Table 13-1 to specify the house and unit codes you used to implement the sensors and alarms in your house.

Table 13-1. SecurityMonitor.pl variables

Variable name	Description
$alert_email	The email address to send alert messages to. If you wish to send to multiple emails, separate the list with semicolons. For example, you would use: $alert_email='alerts@northrup.org; alerts@thefaulkners.org';
$smtp_server	The IP address of your SMTP server. This should exactly match the IP address you have configured as the SMTP server in your email client.
$audible_unit	The unit code of the audible alarm (the Powerhorn in this project).
$audible_hc	The house code of the audible alarm.
$speaker_unit	If you are using the voice alerting feature, the unit code of the X10 appliance interface controlling the power to the remote speakers and the wireless transmitter and receiver.
$speaker_hc	The house code of the remote speakers.
$sensor_hc	The house code of all the sensors.
$light_hc	The house code of all the lights
$camera_hc	The house code of all the cameras.
$video_path	The path in which to save the video files.
$virtual_vcr_path	The path to the Virtual VCR executable file.
$seconds_to_capture	The number of seconds to capture video when the alarm that specifies capturing video footage is triggered.
@units	A two-dimensional array with 10 columns per row. You should add a row for each sensor that you install in your house, and then configure the 10 columns for that row with settings specific to the sensor. The meanings of the columns are described in the comments immediately preceding the definition of this variable, so I won't describe them here. However, the last two parameters deserve a bit more discussion. The ninth parameter (labeled #8, since numbering starts at zero) contains either a "1" or a "0". If this is set to "1", then the sensor will be "armed" when the script first starts up. You probably don't want door and window sensors armed when the script starts, because if you restart your computer in the middle of the day, you'll set off a false alarm when the script restarts. However, you always want to hear alarms from environmental sensors, so they should have this value set to "1". The last parameter (#9) determines the minimum arm level. This corresponds to the rows in the @arm_levels array, with the first row starting at zero. In the default settings, the environmental sensors are armed even when the arm level is set to "Disarmed". At the "Night" arm level (row 1 in the @arm_levels array), all of the perimeter sensors are armed. At the "Vacant" arm level, I assume that nobody should be walking through the house, and the script should sound an alarm if the motion detectors are tripped.
@arm_levels	An array with two columns. The first column is a description of the arm level, and the second column is the X10 signal that, when received, sets the arm level. Note that the first two characters of the X10 signal are the X10 house and unit codes being transmitted. The second two characters are the X10 house code, and either the letter "J" for an On signal or the letter "K" for an Off signal.
$current_arm_level	The default arm level, corresponding to the rows in @arm_levels array (starting at zero). The script updates this variable when you change the arm level.

The infinite while loop continuously reads data from the serial port and takes action when required. Inside the while loop, the foreach $s (0..$#units) loop checks each of the sensors you have configured in the @units array to determine if the On signal was transmitted for that unit and house code. If it was transmitted, a series of if statements takes action by calling a set of subroutines.

The second foreach loop checks to see if you've sent an X10 signal to change the current arm level. If it finds the X10 signal, it changes the arm level. Then, the script executes another loop to parse each of the rows in the @units array. For each row, it arms or disarms the sensor if the current arm level is equal to or greater than the minimum arm level for that sensor.

The subroutines are mostly self-explanatory. light_on sends an X10 On signal to the specified house and unit code. audible_on sends three consecutive On-Off signals to turn on the Powerhorn or other similar X10 siren. send_email puts together a short message, with the entire contents of the message contained in the subject line.

The capture_video subroutine turns on the camera that you've specified in the @units array for that sensor, and begins recording video using the Virtual VCR program. The subroutine then assembles a string based on the current time that will be used as the filename for the captured video. The format of the filename is SecurityCam-*yymmdd-hhmmss*.mpg.

The following line calls the Virtual VCR executable. If you're using a different program to capture video, you will need to edit this line:

```
print `$virtual_vcr_path -capture -runfor \"$seconds_to_capture\" -
output \"$videopath$videoname\"\n`;
```

The subroutine then sleeps for several seconds, and issues a tskill command to end the Virtual VCR process. Then, the *sendfile.bat* batch file that you created in the "Gathering Evidence" phase is called to upload the video file off-site.

The last subroutine, speak_alert, turns on the remote speakers and calls the "Say" C# program created in Chapter 4 to generate a voice.

6. Schedule the script

You want this script to run every time you start your computer. The "right" way to do this is to implement the security system as a Windows service, and then configure that service to start automatically. The hack way to do this is to schedule the script to start automatically. Refer to Chapter 2 for detailed instructions on how to make the *C:\homehacking\SecurityMonitor.pl* script do this.

Wrapping Up

On the whole, I feel like this project increases the security of my home, and I enjoy having complete control over the logic behind the security system. It doesn't add value to my house like a conventional security system would, and my insurance company certainly isn't going to give me a break on my rates, but then again, I can take it with me when I move.

My wife seems comfortable arming and disarming the system. There was certainly a learning curve, but we haven't had too many false alarms so far. We haven't had any break-ins either, though, so I can't be completely confident that it would successfully thwart an intruder.

There are a couple of aspects of the system that need maintaining. Each time the cameras are triggered, they'll capture video and store it both on my hard disk and on my friend's hard disk. So, I end up regularly deleting video footage of me opening the front door without disarming the security system. This process could certainly be automated by writing a script that deleted video older than a week.

I also have to regularly check the sensors to make sure they're still working correctly. During the trial period, I've attached them with double-sided foam tape, but that doesn't hold up very well, and the sensors tend to fall out of place (and trigger an alarm, if the system is currently armed). After I permanently attach the sensors with screws, this issue should disappear.

Extensions

This project has already grown quite a bit from my original plan, but it could be taken even further. One of my biggest concerns is the relative lack of security associated with the arming/disarming mechanism. While I don't expect that a typical thief will be able to disarm my homemade X10-based security system, I don't like to rely on security by obscurity. A knowledgeable thief could bypass the entire system using an electrical outlet on the exterior of my house.

There are a few different ways I could improve the security of the arming mechanism. I could use a disarming method that communicated with my computer using a means other than X10, such as a device that connected to my wireless network. I could also build intrusion detection into the script to alert me if a potential intruder were randomly transmitting X10 signals to find the signal that disarmed my system. Of course, that does exist to some extent, since the intruder would probably stumble across an X10 signal that would cause an alarm to be thrown rather than disarming the system.

If I added just a couple of lines to the Perl script, it could keep track of the current state of doors and windows. This would enable the script to notify you if a door or window were in an unsafe state at the time of arming. The voice response mechanism could even speak to you: "Warning: The kitchen window is currently open." Currently, if you open a window when your alarm is disarmed, and then arm the system, you won't receive an alarm if an intruder enters through the open window—which, of course, would be the window the intruder would choose. Your motion detectors would still detect the intruder, of course.

Currently, the security system is configured by editing the Perl script directly. That's fine by me. In fact, that's the way I prefer it—I don't need a GUI. However, these tools would be accessible to a much wider audience if they could add sensors using a GUI. (Of course, such applications already exist.)

There's always the possibility that, at the crucial moment of the break-in, the remote FTP server won't be available to receive the video footage. So, it would be useful to build a fail-over mechanism into the script to check for several different FTP servers.

Right now, it takes a couple of seconds for the video camera to start recording. I could decrease that delay by immediately forking a process to start the video recording when a sensor is tripped. Forking the video recording to a different process would also allow the script to switch to a different camera if the intruder moved to a different area of the house. Currently, the script sleeps while video is recorded for 10 seconds.

Many security systems flash the lights on and off when an intruder is detected until the alarm system is disabled. The idea behind this is that it draws attention to your home and helps the police find you. My script doesn't do this, but it certainly could with a few more lines. I would simply add variables named $flash_lights and $flash_lights_state, both set to zero by default. When $flash_lights is set to 1, the script would check $flash_lights_state in each iteration, and turn the lights either on or off depending on whether $flash_lights_state was true or false. It would then switch the state of the $flash_lights_state variable as well.

Exhibit A: Bill of Materials

Most parts are available from home automation web sites such as *http://www.smarthome.com*. X10 wireless cameras are available only from *http://www.x10.com*.

Item	Quantity	Approximate cost	Part number
Serial Powerlinc computer interface	1	$35 and up	CM11A
X10 motion detector	3	$20 and up (each)	MS14A-C or MS13A
Door/window contact switch	5	$2–$10	Varies
Window glassbreak sensor	5	$10–$20	Varies
Water sensor	1	$20–$40	Varies
X10 Powerflash interface	11	$22	4060
X10 audible alarm	1	$25	7362
X10 lamp module	5	$10–$15	2000
X10 wireless cameras	3	$170 for all of these items	XCam2
X10 wireless transceiver	1		4005X or 400s
Wireless video receiver	1		VR36A
Composite video input card	1	$40	WinTV-GO-FM, 00191
Kwik-Fix Stick-E-Tak poster adhesive	1	$3	QSA2-01

Exhibit B: Software Versions

This list shows the versions of software components originally used to create this project. However, you can, and should, use updated versions whenever possible.

Description	Version
Operating system	Windows XP SP1
Perl	5.8.0
ControlX10::CM11	2.09
Win32::SerialPort	0.19
Virtual VCR	2.6.9

Index

About the Authors

Tony Northrup, a Boston-area network security consultant, developed his interest in home automation after renting an apartment where every light was controlled by pulling a string. Tony turned to home automation products to add light switches without needing to hire an electrician or cut into the drywall. Tony later bought a house and now uses computers to control and monitor virtually every system in his home: electrical, home theater, security, even plumbing. Tony's wife, Erica, ensures that his home hacking projects are user-friendly and reliable, while his cat, Sammy, mangles every project within paw's reach.

Eric Faulkner's love affair with technology began as a child with his first electronics project kits from Radio Shack. In his early teens, a friend's Texas Instruments TI99/4A introduced him to computers and programming, thus sealing his fate as a lifelong geek.

Professionally, Eric's experience is diverse. He worked for a voice messaging pioneer in the 1980s. He spent three years in the Army working with nerve agents. He designed fully automated manufacturing facilities for the precast concrete industry. Then he went to college.

These days Eric makes a living as a technology consultant and systems engineer. He also finds time for writing, teaching, and editing. He lives in Massachusetts with his wife, Alyssa, their daughters, Amanda and Lily, and the girls' grandparents, Will and Jean.

Colophon

Our look is the result of reader comments, our own experimentation, and feedback from distribution channels. Distinctive covers complement our distinctive approach to technical topics, breathing personality and life into potentially dry subjects.

Emily Quill was the production editor and copyeditor for *Home Hacking Projects for Geeks*. Sada Preisch was the proofreader. Rick Schlott and Emily Quill did the typesetting and page makeup. Marlowe Shaeffer, Sarah Sherman, and Claire Cloutier provided quality control. Mary Agner provided production assistance. Julie Hawks wrote the index.

Edie Freedman designed the cover of this book using Adobe Photoshop CS and Adobe InDesign CS. The cover image is an original photograph by Edie Freedman. Emma Colby produced the cover layout with Adobe InDesign CS using Linotype Birka and Adobe Formata Condensed fonts.

Melanie Wang designed the interior layout using Adobe InDesign CS, based on a series design by David Futato. This book was converted from Microsoft Word to InDesign CS by Julie Hawks. The text and heading fonts are Linotype Birka and Adobe Formata Condensed, and the code font is TheSans Mono Condensed from LucasFont. The illustrations and screenshots that appear in the book were produced by Robert Romano and Jessamyn Read using Macromedia FreeHand MX and Adobe Photoshop 7. The "geek" illustrations that appear at the beginning of each chapter were created by Mark Frauenfelder.